Seize Today
Making the Most of Your Last Years

By Elizabeth R. Wright

*Best of luck
Betty Wright*

Ice Cube Press
North Liberty, Iowa

SEIZE TODAY
MAKING THE MOST OF YOUR LAST YEARS

Copyright © 2002 Elizabeth R. Wright

First Edition
2 4 6 8 9 7 5 3 1

ISBN 1-888160-88-8

The Ice Cube Press
205 N Front Street
North Liberty, Iowa 52317-9302
icecube@inav.net
319.626.2055
http://soli.inav.net/~icecube

Library of Congress Control Number: 2002100085

Manufactured in the United States of America on acid-free, recycled paper meeting library standards.

No portion of this book may be reproduced or reprinted in any fashion without the consent of the publisher, or author, except for brief quotations in an article, or review, in which case the publisher and author shall be sent copies.

To Brooks, for his loving encouragement
and editorial help
and to Caye for her valiant fight.

ACKNOWLEDGEMENTS

My profound appreciation and respect to the following:

Reverend Linda Anderson; Nan Bissette, and all the staff and residents of Nan's Hacienda, Sahuarita, Arizona; Reverend Barbara Brecht; Aileen Cochran; Margo Cole; Nancy Dill of the Simeon Co-Housing Project; Deborah Fishman; Rea Getzels; Edna Hargrove, Mid-Hudson Memorial Society; Randy Johnson; Lorraine Kantor; Jean Kemble; Stephen and Ondrea Levine, Omega Institute, Rhinebeck, New York; Nina Lynch, Dutchess County (New York) Office of the Aging; Charlotte Menaker; Gordon McLean; Irene McLean; Hal Myers, Executive Director of Green Valley Assistance Services; Quartzsite, Arizona Chamber of Commerce; Sister Joyce Rowland, Our Lady of the Valley Church, Green Valley, Arizona; the Saturday Discussion Group, Green Valley; Stu Samovitz, Green Valley (Arizona) R.V. Resort; Mikel Shilling, First Vice President, Green Valley Coordinating Council, Green Valley, Arizona; Reverend Carl Scovel of King's Chapel, Boston; Ann Scharf and Dr. Paul Scharf, The Fellowship Community Chestnut Ridge, New York; James Schroeder; Vera Sievert; Alice Stark; Evan Stark; Tom Yohannan, June Wortman, Aldrich and Martha Wright for their encouragement and especially to Anne Wright for all her help in the process of getting this published.

And most especially my appreciation and respect to all of the many friends and others whom I interviewed, and who contributed so richly their own stories. For reasons of confidentiality, I cannot give their names. BUT WE HAVE MUCH TO LEARN FROM EACH OTHER.

CONTENTS

ACKNOWLEDGEMENTS

INTRODUCTION .... pg. 11

CHAPTER I .... pg. 17

THAT HAPPY AGE: Planning for Retirement
- When to Start Planning
- The Planning Process
- Financial Planning
- Wills
- Living Trust
- Insurance
- Living Wills
- Health Care Proxy
- Power of Attorney
- Preparing a Legal Packet
- Geriatric Care Managers
- Summary

CHAPTER II .... pg. 37

"WE'RE SPENDING OUR CHILDREN'S INHERITANCE": Travel and Recreation
- Recreational Vehicle Travel and Parks
    - Full-Time RV'ers
    - Meg's Odyssey
    - "And Then There Is Quartzsite!"
    - Is RV Travel for Everyone?
- Volunteering At a National Park
- Planning Your Own Travel
- Special Tour Groups for Senior Citizens
- Day Trips from Home
- Volunteerism and Paid Employment
- Education
- Recreation
- Summary

CHAPTER III .... pg. 65

ABIDE WITH ME?: Sex and Marriage
    Sex and Older Americans
    Viagra
    Depression, Alcoholism and Domestic Violence
    Marital Breakups
    Sex and the Nursing Home Patient
    Death of a Partner
    The Dating Game
    "Shacking Up"
    Late Life Marriages
    Older Lesbians
    Summary

CHAPTER IV .... pg. 81

"THERE'S NO PLACE LIKE HOME": Living Independently
    How to Remain Independent
    HUD Senior Housing
        Wells Manor
    Co-Housing
        Simeon Center
        Cantine Island Co-Housing
        Sonora Co-Housing
    Retirement Communities
    Leisure World
    Gays and Retirement Communities
    Mobile Home Communities
    Summary
    Appendix I

CHAPTER V .... pg. 121

"YOU BETTER GET IN WHILE YOU STILL CAN": Institutional Living
    Adult Homes and Assisted Living Facilities
        Sunset Hall
        Nan's Hacienda

    Continuing Care Retirement Communities
        Duncaster
        The Kendal Continuing Care Communities
    Nursing Homes
    The Fellowship Community
    Summary

CHAPTER VI .... pg. 151
"DOCTOR, PLEASE LISTEN!"
    Doctors and Nurses
    The Psychology of Illness
    Cancer
    Breast Cancer
    What You Can Do to Help Prevent Cancer
    How You Can Help in the Event of Cancer
    Heart Disease and Stroke
    Ways We Can Prevent Heart Disease and Stroke
    Alzheimer's Disease
    A Special Kind of Caretaker
    Alternative Medical Treatments
    Summary

CHAPTER VII .... pg. 193
A BETTER DEATH
    Withdrawal of Treatment
    Facing Life and Death with Courage and Grace
    Hospice
    The Role of Friends
    The Role of the Clergy
    Assisted Suicide
    Summary

CHAPTER VIII .... pg. 223
IN MEMORIAM
    Bereavement
    Practical Considerations
    Funerals and Mourning Practices

"The American Way of Death"
Memorial Societies
Anatomical Donations
Summary

CHAPTER IX .... pg. 247

THE MANAGED AND THE MANAGERS: How to Survive the Systems
    Health Maintenance Organizations and Medicare
    HMO's
        How Managed Care Now Affects Everyone
        Some of the Economics
        Patients' Rights and Managed Care
    National Health Care and Universal Health Care
        The Clinton Health Plan
        The Canada Health Plan
        The Health Plan for Ontario
        Some of the Practicalities
        The Swedish System of Social and Health
            Programs for the elderly
    Summary

CHAPTER X .... pg. 271

TAKE HOLD AND SEIZE TODAY
    Taking Hold Politically
    Politics Aside
    The Healing Tasks
    The Successful Elders
    The Final Responsibility
    Summary

REFERENCES .... pg. 285
RESOURCES .... pg. 299
INDEX .... pg. 307

Introduction

Only when you drink from the river of silence
Shall you indeed sing.
And when you have reached the mountain top,
Then you shall begin to climb.
And when the earth shall claim your limbs,
Then you shall truly dance
Kahlil Gibran, 1923, *The Prophet*

In most societies, the old have traditionally been esteemed as role models, advisors, spiritual leaders, repositories of stories, myths, knowledge and lore. They have been our link to the past. Now that I am in my seventies and am doing this writing I find that a number of my friends are also writing books about what they have seen and experienced in their lives. Before it is too late, we wish to share what we have learned.

This book is about the many options that seniors have in a variety of areas: housing, recreation, personal and intimate ties, health care and effective relationships with health care personnel, and how and what to look for in considering institutional care. It also includes various ways of facing death, and the roles that families, professionals, and friends can take to make the end of life easier, bereavement, funerals, and burial. I have also included information on various health plans here and abroad, and how to survive our complicated and often frustrating medical and social systems.

I have not intended to recommend any one life-style or locality. But, with information, and with a willingness to be flexible, we gain strength, so above all else this book is meant to be empowering so that we can make those choices that are best suited to our own individual needs and circumstances.

My husband and I divide our time between a village in upstate New York and a retirement community in southern Arizona, two very different communities-geographically, environmentally, economically, sociologically, politically, and obviously in the age range of their residents. The two states are also very different in the way they see their responsibility in solving or at least relieving social problems. New York has a long history of providing a range of public programs that relieve the myriad of problems that its aging population faces. Arizona, on the other hand, spends as little as possible on public programs. Individualization and keeping taxes at a minimum are of paramount importance in such a state, which means that much less public money goes into programs for the aged than does in New York. It is expected that families will assume more responsibility for their aged, and there is more reliance on volunteerism, both of which are commendable values, but it also means that there are fewer community services, lower standards in long term care facilities and less over-all professionalism. In the book, I have discussed services for the aged in both states just because I am familiar with them but also because they represent two very different views of how to provide for and care for their aging population.

In my last ten years before retirement I worked for the state agency in New York that licensed and regulated health care facilities, supervising social workers who went out as part of interdisciplinary teams to survey nursing homes and other health care facilities. After what I considered my official retirement, I was a consultant, and then director of a social service department in a nursing home. I had started to regulate nursing homes in New York in 1976 just after major nursing home abuse and neglect scandals there had resulted in much stricter laws, particularly ones that safeguarded patient rights and safety. During all those years when I interviewed many, many nursing home patients and their families, I became convinced that there needed to be a wider range of living arrangements available to seniors, as well as options around other issues of aging.

As life expectancy increases, what is old is being redefined. Myths about aging are being discarded. A group of medical researchers led by John W. Rowe, MD and Robert L. Kahn PhD of the MacArthur Foundation Study on Aging over some years interviewed thousands of older Americans about what it means, physically and mentally to be over 65. They found that one of the most prevalent myths is that it is inevitable to be sick if one is old. In fact, nearly 90% of people between the age of 65 and 74 are in very good health and three quarters of those between 75 and 84 have no disability that interferes with their enjoyment of life. Another myth is that old people no longer can change or have the capacity to learn; this too is nonsense. A third myth is that it is too late for old people to change their health habits; this just is not so. Also, it is felt that "it's all in the genes," whereas only about 30% of your physical aging at 65 can be attributed to the genes passed on by your parents. As we get even older, genetic factors are less significant than environmental ones, so each of us has the opportunity to shape our lives by our lifestyle and attitudes. A great many people, particularly the young, are convinced that old people don't have or cannot have a sex life, but chronological age alone is not the reason for such a failure, and many people have active sex lives well into their eighties.

Attitudes about oneself and life in general contribute a great deal to physical and mental health. Most people, I think, have their own internal view of how old they are; if happy, positive and busy, old people will either never think of their age, or will have a feeling that they are younger than they actually are. For instance, for years I felt at the top of my form as if I were still a thirty-five year old woman; then, at age 60, when I had lung cancer and was both physically ill and also depressed, I suddenly felt my age or older. These days I am again feeling vital, and therefore do not feel my age. So I'm often astonished if I very suddenly look in the mirror and see an overweight old woman of 75, and occasionally am surprised when younger people give me a helping hand or their seat.

Because of improving medical technology, drugs and services, people are living much longer than they were just twenty years ago, and living with better health and vigor than ever before. Many studies reveal surprising patterns of health. It has been shown that the rate at which people die rises steadily from middle age up to and through the eighties, and then declines. After the age of one hundred and ten the death rate returns to what it was for people in their eighties. My observation of many nursing homes confirms studies showing that many people who have reached their nineties are in robust health and do not have serious physical or mental incapacities until just before they die. In fact, they are often in better health than people ten or fifteen years younger. Those who reach one hundred usually have had no dementia or serious cognitive problems up through their mid-nineties. There are now fifty thousand centenarians in the United States, thirty percent of them absolutely alert and able to live in the community, some of them independently, and people like Willard Scott on NBC's *Today Show* are increasingly honoring people who are well over one hundred. Most of us say we absolutely would not want to live <u>that</u> long, but how attractive and happy many of these people are. Some researchers say that we should change our attitudes about old age. Instead of seeing it as a curse, we should see it as an opportunity.

Life expectancy has increased by thirty years since the beginning of the twentieth century. The average is now 76 and disability is decreasing, so that people can continue to lead active, meaningful lives. An article in the *New York Times* of June 25, 1998 reported that, whereas 25 years ago 65 was considered old, now gerontologists refer to those people between the age of 75 and 84 as the young-old and those over 85 as the oldest old. People now can survive with chronic illness, or recover from what would surely have been considered a terminal illness several decades ago. As an example, my husband is a well-controlled diabetic who has recovered at the age of 79 from two medical crises and I, at the age of 75, am leading a relatively active life after lung cancer surgery and many subsequent complications. We survived these events largely because we both had very good medical care, the support of friends and family and sensible living arrangements that have accommodated our personal needs.

So this book is about choices: choices for seniors through the various stages of the last years, which are referred to in the Ernst and Young <u>Retirement Planning Guide</u> as 1) the go-go years 2) the introspective years, and 3) the years when care is needed. This book is also about issues which cannot possibly be separated from the stages of aging, for what is appropriate at 60 may not be so ten years later, and something that never was an issue at 60 may become an enormous problem in five to ten years.

In addition to professional experience, I have drawn from my own personal experience, from that of family and friends, and from information secured in workshops and from reading. Also, believing that there is much wisdom to be gained from personal anecdotes, I have tried to interview as many people as possible, and each one I talked to led me to others. Along the way, I have met some fascinating, wise and courageous individuals who are leading rich lives. I have learned a great deal from them and hope that you will also. I have found that other people can teach us a great deal, and can also be a great source of comfort. To protect privacy, real names have not been used, and I have tried to eliminate all possible identifying data.

Over and over again, from my own personal and professional experience, from people I have interviewed and observed, and from readings and workshops, I have become absolutely convinced that once each of us has directly faced and accepted our inevitable death, we are then freed to make many more choices than otherwise, and to find precious each moment and each person within our scope.

As the French essayist, Montaigne noted, death is easiest for those who have thought about it the most, as if by doing so they were then always prepared for death to happen at any time. Thus, we are enabled to serenely die resigned and reconciled, having experienced life more fully because of the constant awareness that it may soon come to an end. The value of living consists not in the length of days but in the use of time, otherwise a man may have lived long, yet lived but a little.

Chapter I:
That Happy Age:
Planning For Retirement

For years, most of us have had dreams of retirement. We think of it as "that happy age when a man can be idle with impunity," to quote Washington Irving. As we fantasize, we consider retirement our reward for the many years of hard work we have given to careers and to raising families. Because people are living longer and enjoying a more healthy life in those retirement years, Americans are finding they have far more opportunities than their parents or grandparents had. In the 19th century people worked generally all their lives, or until they were no longer able to. The country was still largely agricultural; farmers worked along with their grown children until their children took over, and then the older generation remained where they were, with the children sharing the household or building a separate house on the same farm. When Social Security was enacted in 1935, a man had a life expectancy of 63 years; if he lived until 65 when he could collect social security he could expect to live another two years. When Social Security started in 1935, over 50% of the elderly lived in poverty; now the figure is around 10%.

In 1927, my grandfather was totally incapacitated by a stroke which for the remaining three years of his life left him unable to move or to speak, and therefore unable to work. He and my grandmother had few savings but did own a two-family house, which brought in some rental income. At that time, there was no disability insurance, no kind of social security or public welfare programs as we now know them. Until the institution of Old Age Assistance under the Roosevelt administration, my widowed grandmother was without any outside resource other than the rental income, and therefore for years she spent her spare time on the telephone trying to sell magazines, a discouraging and sometimes humiliating job. During the Depression, her children helped her financially as they could. In the mid 1930's, she became eligible for Old Age Assistance, on which she managed until the late fifties when she went into a nursing home. Then, before the enactment of Medicare and its standards for nursing home care, nursing homes were merely warehouses for the very sick old. Patients were often lined up in large dreary rooms, were seldom taken out of bed and were rarely provided with any stimulation. My grandparents were examples of elders who were trapped by circumstances without the financial benefits and care provided by Social Security, Medicare and the variety of other programs that are now available to senior citizens. They did not have the rich choices that we have.

When Social Security began, an American man could expect to live only another two or three years. Today, an American man turning 65 can expect to live another eighteen years, and women several years longer. Now, we are reaching the end of the period when the last of the post World War II generation that also became the first suburban generation is retiring. Even with pensions and social security, unless they have other savings, these people will not be able to live as well as they once did. Their children, the Baby Boomers, will have to save even more. In fact, without a major change in the social security system, it is expected that it will no longer exist in 2030 when those same Baby Boomers will have reached their *own* retirement. In addition, fewer and fewer companies are setting up clearly defined pension plans by which the company puts aside money for its workers for retirement. Instead, companies are resorting to contribution plans such as 401K by which an employee who chooses to participate has an individual account set up into which part of his pay is placed. (Some companies match a portion of the employee's contributions but most make no contributions to the 401K account.) The account grows without being taxed until it is closed out when the employee reaches the age of 59 ½ to 70 ½, at which time the money is taxed at the current rate. If the 401K is withdrawn before the age of 59 ½ there will be penalties, so check with your personnel director.

WHEN TO START PLANNING

Obviously, employees must think about pension benefits well before they retire. In fact, many people choose to remain on a job just because of benefits alone, especially if the company offers a pension. It is important to remember early to set aside savings for retirement purposes, whether the company offers the pension benefit or not, because, in general, the pension alone will not be enough. At the latest, one should start retirement planning in one's fifties, but ideally this is much too late as it gives you little time to accumulate savings and to choose the best financial course for your particular circumstances and future desires.

It can't be stressed enough that people should start very early to save for retirement, and increase the percentage of those savings annually. To put aside consistently each month a certain percentage of your salary involves a great deal of determined discipline. Every year that this saving for retirement is delayed, the amount that you must put away just gets that much larger. But, if you haven't been this prudent, it is never too late to start.

Planning for retirement of course involves much more than the pension and savings and investments. It is a lengthy process that considers many issues, as retirement means embarking on a new stage in life that may last twenty to thirty years.

THE PLANNING PROCESS

There are many options for retirement including choosing not to retire at all. Some people who are happily immersed in their careers and are still vigorous may choose not to retire. I was particularly impressed with this at my husband's fiftieth college reunion, where we met a surprising number of self-employed businessmen or professionals who had decided that they did not wish to leave work. Some figures show the percentage of those who choose not to retire to be as high as 12%. Some people decide at retirement to change to another line of work. And some people, who are not yet willing to give up the reins of work, choose to wind down by working only part-time. But the majority of seniors choose to retire at 62 or 65 in order to pursue long-sought leisure time that they expect will be free of cares, and many of these people also make major decisions to move to different locations.

Be sure that whatever plan you choose has been jointly arrived at with your partner, one that each of you will be contented with, even if it is only a compromise. Both retirement and moving are among the most stressful events of anyone's life. Once the plan has been decided on, and you are approaching the retirement date, if you notice sudden illness or mood swings or unusual behavior in your partner, take heed, as this may indicate ambivalence or unexpressed reluctance about the plan that has been made. Relationships always take precedence. Plans can usually be changed, or even can be reversed once in place. For example, against the advice of a close friend who had known us many years, my husband and I retired to a much beloved summer home that we had in a rural farming area. She felt we should try out the plan for a year without selling our home in the New York City suburb where we had lived for decades. Charlotte was right. Living permanently year round in a summer home is quite different than doing so over weekends or summers. We missed our old friends; we missed being close to the cultural life of New York; and the medical care was less than adequate. Later, we did move to a more suitable area, but at considerable financial, physical and emotional cost. By contrast, one of the people I interviewed for this book, who works for a hospice and is 54, is already making a major addition to her house in preparation for retirement ten years hence. She and her husband know that they will want to stay in the New York City suburbs, and are therefore adding on a downstairs bedroom and bathroom in preparation for those years when climbing stairs will be a burden. She says that working for a hospice has made her much more sensitive to the needs of older people.

If you are thinking of remaining in the home where you have lived for years, can you afford to do so on your retirement income? Are you still physically well enough to manage the many chores involved with house ownership? If you live in the northern half of the country are you and your partner still able to tolerate cold weather? Are you still willing and able to shovel snow? Do you still have the energy to mow the lawn and clean leaves out of the gutters? Be sure to examine your support systems: friends, family, and organizations. Are they so meaningful to you that moving a great distance would present a threat? If so, and you need to move for whatever reason, can you make the move within the same geographical area so that you can maintain these ties? If you hate cold weather, can you afford to spend the winter in a warmer climate? Choosing economical housing, such as winter rentals, condos or mobile homes, can make wintering in a warmer climate more affordable.

If you are moving to a totally different area, do you wish to live in a retirement community where residents are all over 55? Or is it important to have children and younger adults as neighbors? One man we know decided that he wanted children around him and so he and his wife moved to a neighborhood in Scottsdale, Arizona, where he could see the school bus picking up children in the morning, and teen age boys playing basketball in the afternoon. Have you checked out the quality of the medical care in the new area and how close the hospital is, what the cultural, educational and recreational opportunities are and whether, if this is a consideration, your spiritual needs can be met? How are you going to occupy yourself after retirement; do you already have hobbies; are there hobbies or interests you wish to develop, and can you do so if you move to a new community? If you have a partner, how much of your time will be shared, how much will be spent independently?

If you are a single person, will you fit in? Some communities happily integrate single people into the social life, others are rigidly bound to a social structure that revolves around married partners. Many retirement communities will offer support groups for widowed men and women, but often the person who has never married or has been divorced many years, or who is gay, is not provided for. Retirement communities are apt to be conservative about homosexuals and thus gays may lead hidden lives.

When making retirement plans, remember to take into account that you and your spouse or partner will be separated by death at some point. How is the other person going to manage financially? Discuss this eventuality openly, and write out information on assets and their location, and include the names of people who are important financial contacts. Frequently it is the husband who has taken total responsibility for the family's finances, who then dies first, leaving his wife to struggle to figure out his bookkeeping system, and where things are. One friend of mine related to me that this problem was so common in her retirement community that her husband took on the role of helping new widows straighten out financial matters. So, together, try to work out an estimate of the surviving partner's expected income and expenses. Give the same information to your children, or more particularly the person who will be the executor of the estate. Sudden illness can leave the surviving partner too incapacitated or confused to deal with financial responsibilities.

FINANCIAL PLANNING

If possible, do plan for pension benefits long before you are ready to retire. There are many financial planning computer programs, magazines, books, internet sites, and, of course, professional financial planners. (You can find such services in the yellow pages under "Financial Planning Consultants.") Meet with your personnel department or union representative to find out how long you must work for your employer in order to get the most income and accompanying benefits under your pension plan. When will you be fully vested and therefore eligible to draw the pension? What options do you have other than a straight pension that provides a fixed monthly sum: lump sum, annuities or a combination? In general there may be the following pension options: Single Life Annuity, Joint and Survivor Annuity, Life Annuity With a Term Certain, and Lump Sum. Single Life Annuity pays a monthly amount only for the life of the retiree. Joint and Survivor Annuity provides a monthly income to the retiree, and at his death, a percentage of that monthly amount to the beneficiary. A Life Annuity With a Term Certain, gives the retiree a monthly amount, but if he dies within a designated period of time, full payments are made to one or more beneficiaries for a fixed period of time. With the Lump Sum option, the retiree takes a lump sum and manages it himself, which the spouse must consent to. At the time my husband retired, his union was recommending that retirees choose to take part of the pension in a lump sum to be invested within a specified period of time in life insurance, the rest of the money taken as the pension itself. I would suggest that you consult a financial consultant before you choose any option that is not a straight pension since a large sum of money and complicated planning are involved.

Also, as an additional help in planning, find out from your local social security office what your social security check will probably be. This information can also be secured by calling 800-772-1213 or by visiting its Web site at http://www.ssa.gov to get the form *Request for Earning and Benefits Statement*. Nowadays, most women are also working. Each of the partners should develop his own retirement plan, and if possible not depend on the other spouse. It is generally safe to plan on needing 75% of your pre-retirement income for your retirement needs, with an allowance for taxes and inflation.

Unfortunately, about one third of employees who qualify for the 401K do not contribute, and many who have a 401K account borrow against it and do not repay the money. Then there are many people who leave a job, and receive a lump sum payment from their tax deferred accounts which they fail to roll over into other tax deferred accounts, that money then being subject to immediate taxation and a penalty.

Individual Retirement Plans (IRAs) are do-it-yourself pensions, in which anyone can invest. Only self-employed people, however, are eligible for a Keough Plan, about which your financial advisor can give you the particulars. The fees for managing all of these plans can be high; those sold to individuals have higher fees than those accounts managed for employers. The U.S. Labor Department has a booklet, "A Look at 401 (k) Plan Fees," which is part of a larger study of retirement plan fees. Get in touch with the Labor Department's Internet site (www.dol.gov/dol/pwba) or through a toll-free hot line (800 998-7542).

Since the 1980's, many large corporations have been switching to "cash balance" retirement plans, which are of benefit to younger workers who may not stay with the company, as these plans are portable. Separate from whatever 401K plans the company offers, the cash balance plan is a retirement program in which an annual uniform percentage of pay is placed in an account earning about five percent depending on short term interest rates. If the worker quits after vesting in the plan, usually after five years of service, he or she can remove the cash in a lump sum without penalty and then roll it over and invest it in a self-directed IRA. Because a uniform percentage of an employee's pay is taken out, no matter how long that person has been employed by the company, the plan is of less advantage to employees of long standing, but is certainly of advantage to younger workers who do move frequently from corporation to corporation. Older workers, however, should be wary when a company switches to a cash balance plan that is not designed to protect them. Traditional pensions always were weighted to favor the employee's final years of income as the pension was calculated on years of service and on an average of the last few years of earnings on the job which, of course, were the highest. However, with cash-balance pensions the percentage of pay set aside for pensions basically stays the same over many years of service. Workers who have been with a firm over many years can lose a great deal of money when the firm converts from a traditional pension plan to a cash balance plan. Some companies have offered employees who are within ten years of retirement the choice of the better of two plans.

Although the qualifying age will surely change in the future, at this point retirees who are eligible may draw social security at age 62. Under the age of 65, a social security recipient may earn additional income of no more than $10,080 without losing benefits; for additional earnings, $1 is lost for every $2 earned. As of January 2000, after the age of 65 there is no limit to what can be earned.

According to U.S. Bureau of Labor Statistics for 1992, the following is a suggested average budget for an urban household where the occupants are 65 or over:
      Housing—33.8%
      Food—16.2%
      Transportation—15.1%
      Medical Care—10.4%
      Clothing & Personal—6.1%
      Contributions—5.0%
      Entertainment, Reading, Education—5.3%
      Other—8.1%
Social Security accounts for only 40% of the income of people over 65.

Unless people have a large surplus of disposable income and a high level of financial knowledge and sophistication, it is inadvisable for them to handle their own investments, although many people these days are tempted to do so through the internet. It is also unwise to follow a ruinous pattern of placing a great deal of money in the stock market when the market is "hot." When the market experiences a downturn, as it invariably does, it is easy to become disillusioned, and sell your stock at a loss. This type of investing is risky and is not recommended for anyone, but particularly for those nearing retirement age, as they cannot afford to put their nest egg in jeopardy. Investing in mutual funds is usually safest, as they are balanced between stocks and bonds (company, municipal and treasury), and are handled by experts who know what they are doing. I'm sure that your public library has financial resources that would have reports giving past performances of various mutual funds, so that you would have more information in choosing one. You can also contact the various mutual fund companies directly and request a prospectus and performance history.

Those retirees who were not able to save enough under qualified plans (pensions, 401K, Keoughs etc.), can try to supplement their savings with investments through brokerage houses or mutual funds, they can plan to work longer on their job, or take another job after retirement or even reduce their retirement budget. Another option is a tax-deferred annuity sold by insurance companies, but fees for these are even higher than for mutual funds. When you are shopping for a mutual fund, be sure to inquire how the fees are charged: whether you pay for each transaction or whether the fees are front-loaded, that is charged at the start. As an alternative, you can create your own annuity by investing in an index fund, a mutual fund that follows an index such as Standard & Poor's 500 Stock Index where there is such little turnover in stock that there is little in capital gains taxes. When such holdings are sold after retirement, the capital gains are taxed at favorable rates, whereas money coming out of ordinary IRAs or other qualified plans is taxed as ordinary income.

WILLS

Every person of legal age who is mentally competent, and especially anyone who owns property, should prepare a will, no matter how much or how little money he or she has. Often people prepare their first wills shortly after they first marry, and both husband and wife should have wills. It is especially important after the birth of the first child to have a will. The documents should be reviewed periodically, changed as necessary with an amendment called a codicil, or initialed and dated if there are no changes to be made. All old wills should be destroyed, and wills should not be kept in safe deposit boxes as these are automatically sealed upon the death of the testator. If one has a lawyer, he should get the original copy that has been signed; other copies should be kept in a readily accessible place.

A will is a written document in which the person making it disposes of his estate consisting of property and assets, and designates how it will be administered on his death. The elements of the will take effect on the death of the testator, the person who signs the will. A simple will assumes that the husband, wife and children have good relationships.

Each state has its own distinct rules for the content of wills, and those of the state where the testator lives must be followed. The following information is from N.Y. state law. An executor, who will handle the settling of the estate, will be designated in the will, as well as a backup executor to take over in case the executor cannot carry out the role. The will should also take into account the possibility of the beneficiary dying before the testator, so a secondary beneficiary should be named; without this inclusion, the money will automatically go to the beneficiary's children. A Fiduciary Bond may be secured to cover benefits in case the executor does something wrong, but it is better to waive this if you trust the executor. If there are children in the will who are under eighteen, a trust must be set up with the trustee, a prudent person. The trust usually terminates when a child reaches the age of twenty-two. There should be a total disaster clause in case several potential beneficiaries die at the same time. There should be provision for an executor or trustee to manage the funds of minor grandchildren in the event that they are beneficiaries. Every will should include the identification and address of the testator and a clause revoking all previous wills.

At the end of the will, there must be two witnesses, neither of whom can be a beneficiary, as a beneficiary obviously cannot be a disinterested witness. Actually, it is better to have three witnesses, as you must produce two of the witnesses for probate court. Wills that are not witnessed are invalid.

If a person dies intestate (without a will), the state, by law, decides who will get the estate by what is called "per stirpes," by the natural succession in the family (wife, to children to grandchildren. Without these successors, the estate would go to brothers and sister and parents etc.) Settling an estate without a will can be very complicated, very time consuming, and many times very nasty, so it is advisable to prepare a will well ahead of retirement.

I personally do not think that either wills or trusts should be prepared without the help of an attorney who knows the applicable laws of the state, and will dot every "i" and cross every "t." If you feel that you can not afford an attorney, call your local legal aid society, or even a law school.

Living Trust

A living trust resembles a will, but the trust becomes the legal owner of all of your property. It bypasses probate, as do assets that are jointly owned or that have named beneficiaries such as pension or profit sharing plans, IRAs, other tax-deferred plans, and life insurance policies. Therefore setting up a living trust is done to bypass probate, which can be lengthy and expensive. It should be a revocable trust, which can be amended or even cancelled. Each partner should have his or her own trust.

Currently, the first $675,000 of an estate is exempted from federal estate taxes. This exempt amount will increase regularly until there is no federal estate tax by 2010; (according to the 2001 tax law, on January 1, 2011, the provisions must be reapproved.) All assets, including home or homes, life insurance, income, retirement benefits, securities, savings, business properties and interest, etc. are included in the trust. If the trust exceeds the $675,000 non-taxable limit, you may sign over part of your assets to your spouse to balance the two separate trusts. Joint ownership may complicate matters, so it is better to register some things to one spouse, some to the other. You can also reduce your assets by using annual gifts of not more than $10,000 to each beneficiary. It is usual to have a will as well as the trust.

Under the living trust, the estate is settled without a court proceeding. But even with a living trust, you should have a "spillover will" to take care of anything that comes up that is not covered by the living trust. On death, the successor trustee distributes the assets according to the trust's instructions. All transfers of title must be certified by a notary public. The whole process is cheaper and quicker, and because it avoids probate it is more private than a will alone and may save a good deal on estate taxes. As with the will, the living trust should be regularly reviewed with an attorney. As with other legal documents, I would strongly advise that you have an attorney draw up both the trust and the will for you.

INSURANCES

What is called Medicare Supplemental Insurance that is provided by most major insurance companies is absolutely necessary, since Medicare does not cover all of the costs of service; the supplemental insurance picks up the rest.

Studies have shown that 25% of seniors over the age of 85 are patients in nursing homes; a much smaller percentage are there between the ages of 75 and 85. Of course, there is no way of predicting which of us will end up in nursing homes. For this reason, long term care insurance is recommended to help protect savings and assets that we all would like to leave to our children, especially because Medicare covers only a very small part of the cost of nursing home care.

The limitations of Medicare coverage always surprise people who are faced with the need for nursing home care for themselves or a relative or friend. The cost of nursing home care, of course, depends on where you live. (Costs of care are such that even long term care insurance is only one source of payment.) In New York, in 1996, nursing homes in upstate New York were averaging $167 a day or $61,000 annually, while in the New York City metropolitan area the daily rate averaged $232 a day or $85,000 annually. This has meant that many patients have had to spend down their resources, and then depend on Medicaid for their care. Long term care insurance is not meant for everyone, as it is very expensive, generally costing more than one hundred dollars a month, and can be even higher depending on the age of the buyer and the benefits that are chosen. Of course, the younger you are, the cheaper the premium. Some people as young as 35 or 40 are applying for long term care insurance, anticipating that fees for care will certainly rise, increasing the need for insurance. People with certain diseases such as Multiple Sclerosis, Alzheimer's and

Parkinson's Disease, among others, or who are already bedridden may be turned down by an insurance company for long-term care coverage. I was turned down by one company because of a history of cancer, but was accepted by another, so shop around if you have a preexisting disease or a history of one. Most policies have a sixty-day deductible period after which there is a $100 daily benefit for nursing home, assisted living and home care for a specific period of time. Compare policies to see what features are offered. In addition to those types of services, ask about adult day care, informal care by family or friends, medical equipment, and home modification. Make sure you find out how long the benefit period is. It is also advisable to choose a company that has been in the business for five years or longer and to use an independent rating service such as Moody's Investors Service (212-553-0377) or Standard & Poor's (212-438-2400) and your state insurance department to check out the company's track record.

New York State has been authorized to establish what it calls a Partnership for Long Term Care program, sponsored and partly funded by the Robert Wood Johnson Foundation, to help residents of New York State who meet financial and medical qualifications. (I have been told that only four states, California, Connecticut, New York and Indiana, have been able to set up such a system under this foundation.) You buy Partnership Long Term Care Insurance and continue to pay to keep it in effect even for a limited period of time after admission to a long term care program. In New York, once you are in a program, as of 1997, the insurance was required to pay a minimum of $122 for nursing home care, $61 for home care, the daily benefits to increase by 5% each year. You are responsible for the remainder of the cost through other insurance and income sources. If you should exhaust the benefits allowed under the policy (three years of nursing home care, six years of home care) you may apply for Medicaid without having to spend down your assets. You must, however, continue to contribute your own income toward the cost of care.

Some retirees very fortunately have prescription plans under their retirement benefits. Under such a plan, the recipient pays a standard fee for each prescription, sometimes more for especially expensive drugs with a yearly maximum allowed. Under our plan, we pay $5 per prescription. New York State has instituted what it calls EPIC for seniors on limited incomes, $18,000 or less annually for single people, and $23,700 or less for a married couple. You are ineligible if you receive Medicaid benefits or some drug coverage that is better than EPIC. Under the plan, you spend full price for drugs until you spend the required annual deductible for your income, then you save more than one half on drugs for the rest of the year. See if your state has a similar plan for seniors with limited incomes.

LIVING WILLS

A Living Will is an advance written directive stating that you wish life sustaining treatment stopped should you become terminally ill (usually defined as having a disease that is incurable and irreversible, and that death is expected to occur within six months). The definition also includes patients who become permanently unconscious, or do not wish to be resuscitated should their heart stop When you make out your living will, be very specific in what you do not want, for instance, *no gastric or nasal tube feeding, no antibiotics, no mechanical resuscitation, no cardiac resuscitation, etc.*

There must be two witnesses to the signing of the document who are not directly involved in the care of the principal (the person making the living will.) In Arizona, one of the witnesses cannot be related by blood or marriage to the principal, or entitled to any portion of the estate under a will or codicil to the will, cannot be a claimant against any portion of the estate, or be financially responsible for the principal's medical care.

I'm sure that the living will is considered more persuasive if it has been made prior to any critical illness that might result in death, for if a person is in great pain and/or sedated, competency questions could be raised. Also, a living will prepared with the help of an attorney will probably be considered more seriously. It would be advisable to give a copy to your physician for your medical file, and to give copies to those who may later be responsible for your medical decisions, and even a copy to your clergyman. Keep the signed original at home; review, initial and date periodically, and be sure to take a copy with you when you travel, though it may not be honored in another country.

HEALTH CARE PROXY

A Health Care Proxy is a legal document that designates a person to make medical decisions for you in case you are unable to do so because of incapacity.

POWER OF ATTORNEY

A Power of Attorney enables another person to make financial decisions for you in the event that you are unable to do so. Be sure to prepare a Power of Attorney long before you ever need it.

PREPARING A LEGAL PACKET

Most of the above legal forms can be obtained in an office supply store. It is advisable to prepare a packet of legal documents for your own convenience, but also for your partner and others who may be responsible for you. This should include personal documents, such as birth certificates, passports, Social Security information, marriage certificate and divorce decree, military discharge papers, naturalization papers, your and your partner's wills, and adoption papers. It should include retirement and death benefit information such as any annual statement you might have and the address of the Retirement Systems. You will need Income Tax information in the form of the latest copies of state and federal income tax returns. Also include Property Tax bills, liens and other such information. Be sure to include insurance policies, health, auto, homeowner's, liability and life insurance, and information on bank accounts and credit cards. If you have made out a list of how you wish personal possessions such as household furnishings and jewelry distributed, that should be included. Lastly, include information on funeral and burial plans.

Geriatric Care Managers

Geriatric care managers are used once an elderly person has reached the point of no longer being able to cope with planning and finances. A geriatric care manager is a new occupation that has come into being with the surge of older Americans, the geographical separation of families and the complexity of the health and other systems that the elderly must deal with. The care managers perform a role that was once filled by a family member. They are usually social workers or psychologists who have geriatric experience or training and usually act as private practitioners who charge an hourly rate. They do not do hands on care, but they do evaluations, make recommendations, help manage health plans and financial affairs and a myriad of other problems that come up for the elderly person and will keep in close touch with the family. Often, the elderly will listen to the care manager before they will accept the advice of the children. The manager will continue to monitor the elderly person beyond the crisis period if this is what is needed and wanted. This is a convenient service for busy children who are physically separated from their parents. A good resource for the purpose of finding help is the national Eldercare Locator that can refer you to many local support services (800-677-1116 weekdays from 9 a.m. to 8 p.m. ET or www.aoa.gov/elderpage/locator.html.)

Summary

Above all else, plan early so that you can start early to save for retirement. Your personnel office should be able to give you information on company pension plans and specifically what you might expect to get in dollar terms. Make sure that your working spouse also has a plan so that you both can take maximum advantage of whatever is offered and whatever you can purchase in the way of retirement benefits. At the same time, be aware of the need to be flexible in your eventual plans, as needs change, and you will have a much more satisfactory retirement if you are ready to make changes when they are necessary or even before they are necessary.

There are certain legal documents that are absolutely necessary, such as wills, trusts, living wills, health care proxies or medical power of attorneys and general power of attorneys. It is advisable to consult an attorney on these matters, as laws vary from state to state.

Chapter II
"We're spending Our Children's inheritance!"
Travel and Recreation

During the first years after retirement many people who can afford to travel a great deal. Taking trips and pursuing a variety of recreational activities are seen as their reward for all the years of hard work and the raising of children, and those early years are when retirees are their healthiest and feel their most energetic. There are many ways to travel and to spend one's free time. The following information may help you decide what kind of travel and recreation would best suit you and your budget.

Recreational Vehicle Travel and Parks

For about five years my husband and I drove across the country each winter to spend several months in sunny Arizona. On most of the treks, we took great pleasure in making side trips to areas of the country which we had never seen in states such as Texas, Oklahoma and Arkansas, and in revisiting areas of the south which we had especially liked on previous visits. We took as little as five days and as many as ten to make the trip between upstate New York and southern Arizona, but always, the last leg of the trip would be picking up Interstate 10 in southern New Mexico for the last three hundred miles to Tucson. What with one trip or another, we have traveled the whole length of I-10, which runs east to west from Jacksonville, Florida to Los

Angeles. Because it is such a continuous route, it has a great deal of interstate trucking and tourist travel. In the winter months you see many recreational vehicles travelling west in November and December, and then back east at the end of April, lines and lines of them at those times, sometimes in caravan formation. (I'm sure that one would see the same sight on routes from the Northeast and Midwest to Florida.) Some of the larger and more elaborate vehicles have a rear bumper sticker that defiantly reads, "We're spending our children's inheritance!"

About 8.6 million American families own recreational vehicles, mostly for occasional family trips or annual flights to the Sunbelt. People who own recreational vehicles and do a lot of travel in them have great fun. Many keep moving from RV park to RV park and from state to state. Most of them are retirees who have the time to travel, and they are generally the youngest of the old who still have enough energy to withstand the rigors of travel. There are so many on the road because although the initial expense for the RV may be high, it is an inexpensive way to travel long distances. If the retirees remain in one park, it is an inexpensive living alternative. They have a minimum of space and a minimum of possessions. Living so simply, they enjoy a tremendous sense of freedom.

Some of the RVers have a destination in mind, such as a particular resort park where they stay every winter or summer, making reservations long in advance. Or they may buy what is called a park model, which remains in the park and for which they pay an annual rent. Some people choose to live year round in resort parks. One manager of such a park told me that although the initial expense of buying a recreational vehicle is high, seventy percent of full timers spend less than $2000 a month on expenses.

Life in the resort park is a world unto itself, especially in the larger parks where there are showers and laundries, elaborate recreational facilities, ballrooms, swimming pools, courts for all kinds of sports and even stores. Because the living spaces are necessarily restricted, there is much more outdoor activity and socializing than in many retirement communities where it is much easier to hide behind one's door. RV living and travel is such a way of life that there are special newspapers that give relevant information and tips.

I visited the Green Valley R.V. Resort in Green Valley, Arizona, where I talked with the manager. He also is responsible for a mobile home community across the street, which is under the same ownership. He sees a much livelier group of people in the R.V. Resort, describing them as outgoing, friendly, active, and constant doers.

The park has three hundred and four spaces, which are almost completely reserved for the winter months by August. Many people return year after year, and therefore leave their units in the park, or buy park models, which are standard four hundred square foot rectangular manufactured homes to which additions may be made. There are fifty full time residents. Those who have a lease pay an annual rent of about $2,100, which includes water, sewer, garbage pickup and full use of the park. Those people also pay an annual personal property tax to the county in the neighborhood of $200. A new park model costs between $25,000 to $30,000; resales of the park models range from $20,000 to $50,000 because of additions that have been made. People add sheds, awnings, and Arizona rooms (windowed sunrooms, that are called Florida rooms in Florida.) What is inside also adds to the value of the model. Rental of space at the Green Valley RV Resort is about $31.00 a day during high season, and about $20.00 a day during the summer months.

Recreation vehicles can range considerably in price depending on age and size and appointments. In 1999 in Tucson a "cab-over" 1984 model which was 24 feet long was listed at $25,000, a 1997 36 foot coach that had an extra slide-out space was selling for $89,000 and a similar one for $122,000. Thus, even the used vehicles were almost as expensive as a traditional home in less expensive areas of the country. Some new RVs sell for hundreds of thousands of dollars. According to a dealer, gas mileage amounts to no more than 8 to 10 miles a gallon, making the motor homes expensive to operate.

During the economic boom of the late 1990's, many spent their money instead of squirreling it away for possible hard times ahead. Some spent their extra money on large luxury items, including expensive motor homes, which they are using for vacations or year round travel. Some motor homes can cost up to a million dollars with washers, dryers, air-conditioning, three burner stoves, tiled baths, surround-sound stereos, and storage compartments under the wheels that are called "basements." Nowadays, there can be as much conspicuous consumption in motor homes as there is in suburban developments. The money now being invested in RVs far exceeds the gains in income that most Americans have made during the boom. As little as ten percent is needed as a down payment on some of the motor homes, and though some families probably really cannot afford this kind of luxury, they will scrimp to make the payments, as they enjoy the kind of life experienced at an RV resort.

My impression is that Green Valley RV Resort is pretty typical of the RV resort parks all over the country. Its large administration and recreational building includes a well-stocked library, game tables, a woodworking shop, a lapidary shop, arts and crafts shop and a room where stained glass work is done. Computer and stained glass classes are taught by residents, and there is a women's group called Crone Circle that meets weekly. A large hall with a stage is used for Wednesday potluck dinners, for plays, movies, and dinners and dances, at which bands and combos play. Outside, there is a heated pool with adjoining barbecue patio, a putting green and horseshoe courts.

Most of the residents come from the Midwest, two hundred and twenty with annual leases and about eighty renting on a monthly basis. It is an age-restricted community, meaning that at least one person in a household must be over fifty-five and no one under the age of eighteen. However, HUD, which regulates the parks, allows up to twenty percent of the park to be as young as forty-five if they buy a new park model home.

The Voyager R.V Resort in Tucson advertises that it was voted the "National R. V. Resort of the Year" by the National Association of RV Parks and Campgrounds in a 1992 survey. It is certainly a huge operation with a total of 1576 spaces, 350 of which are for year-round residents. Unlike the Green Valley RV Resort, which is age-restricted to seniors, Voyager is for adults only but adults who can be as young as nineteen years of age. As a matter of fact, I chose to look at this RV resort after I met in a bookstore a working woman in her late forties who was a full time resident at Voyager. She spoke enthusiastically of the caring kindness of her neighbors, and how much more of a community it was than her previous neighborhood.

There is a separate overnight area for winter space rentals for R.V's in January, February and March, and a separate area for seven hundred and fifty park models, most of which are owned. The resort provides a security guard twenty-four hours a day, a chapel with its own chaplain, a bank on the grounds, a store and restaurant, a beauty salon, nine hole golf course, and two outdoor and one indoor pool. There is also a thirty-six-room inn on the grounds for guests of residents and for prospective residents. According to the activities director I spoke to, during the winter season there are two hundred activities, including book discussion groups, bird watching, hiking groups, computer classes, genealogy and astronomy classes, Spanish classes and even vegetarian covered dish suppers. These activities are in addition to the usual arts and crafts and exercise classes. Most of the classes are taught free of charge by residents of the RV resort.

In 1998, the Voyager RV resort set aside a gated area with twenty-one park models to be used as assisted living suites. Eventually, they hope to have eighty-three units, with a clubhouse for every twenty-one units. The resort already had residents who needed assistance and support in order to bathe, dress or groom themselves. Those same people also needed monitoring of health and medications and help with shopping and preparation of meals. There will be a registered nurse available at certain hours of the day, a certified nursing aide will be on duty twenty-four hours a day, meals and activities will be provided, and the park model will be adapted to the needs of these residents. Residents will have use of resort facilities. This program is a joint project with Handmaker Jewish Services for the Aging in Tucson. It enables residents who need assistance to remain in the community, leading as independent a life as possible but with the support and protection that they may need.

Full Time Rv'ers

According to the Recreational Vehicle Industry Association, more than a million families are full-time nomads in their recreational vehicles. Almost all of them are retirees who have dreamed for years of becoming this free, and therefore upon retirement sold their homes and invested the proceeds in motor homes. They also are the youngest of the elderly who still have good enough health and energy to be able to do this. Some baby boomers are taking early retirement and are joining the ranks of the full timers.

There appears to be a cycle that full timers undergo. At first, they travel and sight-see full time in a motor home or pull a big trailer. As they age, driving the large vehicles becomes too much of a physical strain so they trade them in for smaller rigs that are easier to drive and spend more of their time in resort parks or camp-sites. Eventually, they stop altogether and settle into one of the camps or resorts or in a child's yard full time. There are others who manage the full time life for only a short time, perhaps only a few months and then give it up as not for them. There is too little privacy or too little space, or too little contact with children and grandchildren, or all of these reasons and many more. Many people find they cannot stand the rootlessness. Some marriages do not survive the enforced intimacy.

However, for those who are able to continue and who enjoy the nomadic life, there is a wonderful sense of freedom and a ready sociability among those who have chosen this life. The social life in the parks or campgrounds is much like that in a city neighborhood, where people in warm weather spend a good deal of time outdoors on the sidewalk or front stoop. In the RV parks, people spend a lot of time in front of their space from which they wave to neighbors or chat with them, or even share meals. Strolling in the RV park is another way of greeting friends and making new ones, and there are always groups around the pool or barbecue area. Friendships are made very quickly; the old life has been given up, and new communities and relationships are formed. Just the nomadic life alone is a tie that brings people together. Sometimes friends made in a campground or RV park will plan to travel together in caravans or to meet in another park further along the road.

The assisted living service offered by Voyager RV Resort is beginning to be offered elsewhere. One such program is called CARE, Continuing Assistance for Retired Escapees, offered at Rainbow's End, a camp in the woods of East Texas with space for 400 vehicles. Here, the twenty-eight people who need help remain in their own vehicles, where they receive housekeeping and laundry services. A nurse is on duty weekdays and on call on weekends and at nights, and exercise and craft classes and breakfast and lunch are served at extra cost at a center. Half of the participants in the program need only minimal services and therefore go their own way most of the time; the other half need pretty much full time services. The program enables people to maintain their independence in the community where they have settled.

MEG'S ODYSSEY

In the early 1970s a newly divorced friend of mine in her early fifties with grown children quit her administrative job, cashed in an insurance policy, bought a trailer, and became a solo traveler for ten years. She wanted to get out of the rut she felt she was in, and so for a while traveled along with a friend who also had her own trailer. She found there were a lot of other people out there also traveling alone. Gas then cost forty cents a gallon and people would almost always park in the desert, which would relieve them of the usual charges at a campground, making it a very inexpensive way to live. Beyond the cost for food, their only expenses were for gas and the upkeep of the trailer. At first, Meg owned an Airstream pulled by a car. The trailer could be disconnected from the car, which then was used for shopping and other small trips. (If you had a recreational vehicle set up in the desert and went off in your RV, you were apt to find your desert space taken when you returned.) During the ten years when she wandered, Meg had three different trailers, but by the end, when she had a thirty-two foot one, gas was getting too expensive.

People who lived this way followed the good weather. Generally in the cooler weather, the "boondockers" would camp in the deserts of the southwest or head down to Mexico. Meg occasionally picked up small jobs at Forest Service Camps. Early on, she and a Tucson friend met a photographer and his wife who became permanent friends. From them they learned photography and became nature lovers. This friendship soon grew to a nucleus of friends who were especially interested in nature and who spent their winters in Bly, California or Why, Arizona "dry camping" in the desert. (At that time, these were two places where they could park without a charge.) Trailers are cold in the winter and hot in the summer, and Why was especially hot in the summer, so they would take off for Canada or cooler parts of the U.S. in the warm weather.

Meg would have checks and mail sent in large batches to a particular spot where she knew she would be staying. Why, for instance, had a post office. She used the telephone a great deal to keep in touch with family and friends. As a help in making new friends, there were a number of network organizations for RV full-time travelers such as "Loners on Wheels," and there were groups of Airstream trailers that traveled in caravans, keeping in touch with each other with CB radios. But Meg found caravan travel not to her liking. Her first trip to Mexico was with a caravan, and she went on several more caravans but decided that too much time was spent on organizing everyone.

Obviously, Meg liked the freedom and spontaneity of this kind of travel and almost always found people friendly and helpful. Her first trip took her to Detroit, where a cousin lived, then east to Niagara Falls, over to Massachusetts and down the eastern seaboard to Florida and Key West. From there, she went west to Texas, and eventually south to Mexico and the Yucatan and finally turned north to Tucson, eventually ending up in Why, Arizona. On that first trip, she never had any concrete idea where she would be many days ahead, but she always met other travelers who would recommend sights to see and places to stay and she even found temporary jobs along the way. Every winter she managed to get back to Mexico for a bit, but spent most of her time in the desert around Why.

On her trips, she met all kinds of people, and as many men as there were women, all of them interesting and "doers." She felt safe until drug users took over parks, which forced one to be more wary. In the end it was finally personal responsibilities that drew her away from the life. But during the ten years she came to value nature and a more simple life and at times she still feels nostalgic for her days on the road.

And Then There is Quartzsite!

Quartzsite, Arizona is located in La Paz County in the northwest section of the state bordering California. The nearest town to it is Blythe, California; the closest settlement in Arizona is Parker, which is thirty-five miles to its north. Located in the desert, the singular feature to Quartzsite is that in the winter it is probably the biggest settlement of trailers and recreational vehicles in the whole country, and then clears out to almost nothing during the spring and summer and fall months.

Quartzsite is not incorporated, but has a Chamber of Commerce, and two medical clinics associated with hospitals in Blythe and Parker, the county seat. When I visited in the early 1990's and again in 2000, I did not see anything resembling a center to the settlement or any supermarket or gas station. As I remember, it was in March when there were still many people there and what appeared to be a lot of activity in yard sales, evening dances and potluck suppers. However, this was well after the peak season during the last of January and the first week of February. That is when Quartzsite holds its large gem and mineral show, just before the large gem and mineral shows in Tucson, which are reputed to be the largest in the world.

During the shows in Quartzsite, there are a million and a half people in the area of Quartzsite parked in its ninety-two commercial campgrounds, but mostly on Bureau of Land Management desert land surrounding Quartzite. I was told that in addition to privies built on the desert for people camping there, dump trucks for a fee deliver water and empty out RV tanks daily. The concentrated settlement now has its own sewerage facilities and is on town water. People come from all over the U.S. and Canada; it is obviously a popular place to stay if you do not feel uncomfortable in such crowds. There are now twenty-five hundred year-round residents. For information, call the Quartzite Chamber of Commerce at 520-927-5600.

Is RV travel for everyone?

Those people who like RV travel seem to like it very much. It offers an unparalleled sense of freedom like nothing else. Without a reservation or a lease at a RV resort, one can be spontaneous about where one stays and for how long and therefore lead quite a nomadic life. Living costs are low since except for the initial expense of the vehicle, and the high cost of gas, what one pays per night is far, far less than one pays for a motel, and often the surroundings are more attractive. If one has a lease, the monthly or yearly cost is by the same token much less than other housing and in addition there is considerable free recreation offered at the park. Several observers have found that those people who regularly stay in RV parks socialize more with neighbors than in other living situations, probably because space inside the RV is so limited that there is necessarily more outside living and therefore access to people. They also describe residents as particularly vital, youthful and as "doers." It is evident from RVers I talked to and literature I picked up at resorts that there is a whole culture built up around RV living.

However, if one is living year-round in an RV, there are many things that have to be sacrificed. In order to afford the RV, most people have to sell their homes, and if they are leading a nomadic life, they give up roots in an area and close contact with children, other relatives and friends. Furniture, books and other belongings have to be sold or given away. Arrangements have to made in advance for mail to be sent to certain post offices or resorts where one knows one is going to stay, but people have told me that the advent of ATM machines has made banking easier and safer. Because of the nature of the nomadic life, friendships are made easily but can never be of great depth because one is always moving on. Thus, people who have strong roots in a particular piece of property or region or feel bound to possessions, and those who have strong ties to relatives and friends would not be happy at all with the nomadic life. Sometimes it takes a few months of such travel to test out this way of life, so that perhaps it is best not to give up the old property and ties and instead rent an RV during that test period. Remember, flexibility is a key to success in retired living.

Volunteering At A National Park

There are hundreds of volunteers, many of them retirees, who give their time as hosts at national, state, county and local parks all over the country for weeks or months at a time. Some people have been doing this for many years. Their duties as hosts involve registering people, checking camping site availability, and answering questions. If there is a problem that they cannot handle, such as a medical emergency or a nuisance bear, they can contact a park ranger by radio. It is expected that the hosts will work a minimum of four hours a day, five days a week but of course, most people put in more hours than this. Volunteers must have their own RVs or trailers. In exchange for their work, they get free sites and free hookups for water and electricity. In addition, the volunteers learn a great deal about the park, and from rangers and their own experiences they learn a great deal about the animals and plants there. Some full time RVers travel from one national park to another to volunteer. Some hosts do this as an affordable way of traveling, others wish to make a contribution to our country.

If this is something you wish to do, write to a national park in the region of your choice to ask if there are any openings as volunteer hosts, and ask for an application. Plan to spend at least a month; some parks may want hosts for the whole summer. Remember that not all parks have laundry facilities, and doctors and grocery stores will be some distance from the park. If you need to be close to a doctor, choose one close to a sizable town that would have a doctor or emergency clinic.

In 1997, almost ninety-nine thousand people volunteered for the national parks; another thirty thousand worked 1.4 million hours for the Fish and Wildlife Service, and the numbers increase every year. People are increasingly conscious and appreciative of the environment; the more people who are involved in preserving our parks by volunteering in them, the greater assurance we will have that the parks will be preserved. No special skills are needed.

The Fish and Wildlife Service can use you to feed fish, band birds, pick up litter, or even help out in the office. Volunteers are especially needed in the U.S. Forest Service's Northern Region. If applicants have a special talent, the Forest Service will try to fit them where they can be used, but they should not be too specific about what they will do, as what is needed may not fit their specifications. Generally, people volunteering for the U.S. Forest Service are used to maintain trails, build up streambeds, clean up trash, plant trees, monitor wildlife, staff information booths, and even for computer and library work or photography. If people go with a general background and a willingness to work, usually work can be found for them.

Because of the isolation of the parks and forests, people should be in good health. There is a limit to the number of cabins available, so people who own RVs or bring camping equipment are especially welcome. The park will provide a campsite and hookups. It also will provide uniforms, identification badges, supervision and sometimes training and coverage for workmen's compensation and liability insurance. If you would like to volunteer, you should contact the regional office for the chosen park.

For a list of national parks, write to: National Parks Listing, The National Park Service Office of Information, 1849 C St., N.W., Washington, D.C.20240.

For a list of national forests, write to: U.S. Department of Agriculture, Forest Service, Washington, D.C. 20250.

For a list of national wildlife refuges, write to: Division of Refuges, U. S. Fish and Wildlife Service, 441 North Fairfax Drive, Arlington, Va. 22203, Attn. Nancy Marx, Phone (703) 358-1744.

If you know a specific state park where you wish to volunteer write to the following regional offices:

—Intermountain Regional Office IMDE, National Park Service, P.O. Box 25287, Denver, CO 80225-0287; phone: 303/969-2630 (Colorado, Montana, Utah, North Dakota, Nebraska).
—Dr. William Kirk, c/o The U.S. Fish and Wildlife Service, Alaska Regional Office, 1011 East Tudor Road, Anchorage, AK. 99503, Phone: 907/786-3391.
—Human Resources Programs; USDA Forest Service, Northern Region, P.O. Box 7669, Missoula, MT 59807 (Montana, Idaho, the Dakotas).
—U.S. Fish & Wildlife Service, P.O. Box 25486, Denver Federal Center, Denver, CO 80225; Attn: Volunteer Coordinator; (Colorado, Kansas, Montana, Nebraska, North Dakota, South Dakota, Utah, Wyoming).
—Paula Stevens, Sequoia National Forest, 900 West Grand, Porterville, CA.93257, Phone: 209/784-1500.
—Kathy Tevyaw, National Park Service, North Atlantic Regional Office, 15 State St., Boston, MA 02109, Phone: 617/223-5072 (New England, New York, New Jersey).
—Marc Koenigs, Superintendent, Assateague Island National Seashore, Route 611, 7206 National Seashore Lane, Berlin, MD 21811, Phone: 410/641-1411.
—Volunteer Coordinator, "Trash Tracker" Program, Glen Canyon National Recreation Area, P.O. Box 1507, Page, AZ 86040, Phone: 520/645-2471 (14).

PLANNING YOUR OWN TRAVEL

If you need to save money and if you have your own computer or access to one, the Internet increasingly has on-line sites for travel information and reservations. One can read reviews of hotels and restaurants, confirm air fares and room rates, make reservations, and if you are considering visiting a foreign country you can even get a State Department report on the area of the country you are intending to visit. This is especially helpful if the country is undergoing turmoil, as the report will address that problem and advise you whether an area is safe or not. Travel books and guidebooks, of course, are a good source of information, as are the travel section of newspapers, travel agents, travel programs on radio and television and word of mouth. There are also tour groups that specialize in travel for senior citizens.

The American Association of Retired Persons has its own Web site, http://www.aarp.org. One section of the site, Trips n' Travel, which you can reach by clicking on What's New, lists hotels, cruise lines and such that offer discounts to A.A.R.P. members. If you dip into the hotel section, you will get a long list of hotels and motels that give discounts of at least 10% to AARP members. The site also includes road trips with suggested itineraries, Web resources, and an interactive bulletin board where you can share travel tales. Membership in A.A.R.P. costs only $10 a year, for which there are many benefits, including the aforementioned discounts, and also the magazine <u>Modern Maturity</u> and the newsletter, <u>A.A.R.P. Bulletin</u>, both of which are excellent sources of information of interest and significance to people over fifty, but particularly to seniors.

For low airfares to forty major U.S. cities with daily updates, and reservations, use http://www.air-fare.com. Another Web site for bargain fares, weekly specials, and links to hotel, car rental, airplane and Cruise Web sites, can be reached through http://www.bestfares.com. Or use http://www.cheaptickets.com, which issues discounted airfares, car rentals, and reservations at Hawaiian hotels. Other Web sites for bargain travel are http://www.expedia.com, described as an entertaining site to explore, and http://www.frommers.com, for many bargains and tips from Arthur Frommer's travel organization. For vacation packages, reservations, a fare finder and a travel newsletter, use http://www.previewtravel.com. The general site for senior citizen concerns, http://www.senior-center.com can be used for links to travel bargains and information on health, money, and retirement information. For discount on foreign travel, use http://www.etn.nl/discount.htm.

Through AOL one can get a great deal of information by clicking on Travel, then on Senior Travel. As an example, when one goes through AOL to Senior Travel and then to Discounts, one can get information on the following: travel discounts, AARP, Continental's Freedom Passports, Senior Airline Coupons, other airfare discounts, car rental discounts, Elderhostel, train discounts, Greyhound Bus discounts, National Parks, etc. Through Altavista one can also get much information by clicking on Travel & Vacations, then click Types of Travelers, and then click Senior Travelers, under which there are several dozen topics, including home exchange, companions, and tour companies. With some computer programs, you can plan driving trips with maps.

Arthur Frommer has a quarterly travel magazine specializing in inexpensive travel: Arthur Frommer's Budget Travel. For a subscription of $16 a year, write to PO Box 420772, Palm Coast, Florida 32142-8518 or call 800-829-9121. Consumer Report's Best Travel Deals (Consumer Report's Books, 1998, $9.95) reports on everything you need to know. Another newsletter, The Mature Traveler, is a newsletter that reports on discount travel for people over fifty. For a free sample of the monthly newsletter, which is $29.95 a year, call 800-460-6676 or send a postcard to TMT, PO Box 50400, Reno, NV 89513 (AARP members who order a new subscription and mention Modern Maturity get a free book.) For tips on travel for singles, Travel Companions has an excellent bi-monthly newsletter for $48.00 a year. Write to Travel Companions

Exchange, Inc., PO Box 833, Amityville, NY 117010833 or call 800-392-1256.

Any good bookstore will have a large section of travel guidebooks for trips within the United States and abroad. In addition there are television programs that feature travel, in particular the National Geographic programs, and Rick Steves' programs over PBS. Steves has specialized in bargain travel for individuals and families. Though his books and TV programs are not specifically geared to senior citizens, they are very interesting and give helpful information on ways of saving money.

The American Automobile Association has travel agencies in major cities over the country, which will help members of AAA free of charge to plan travel in the U.S.A. and abroad. They have very good guidebooks and employ travel agents who will assist you in mapping out a trip and making reservations. They will advise you of roads and areas to avoid in a foreign country. They even sponsor cruises such as ones to Alaska. During certain times of the year, AAA members can save 5 to 20 percent on fares on airlines, Amtrak, and Hertz car rentals in various parts of the world.

SPECIAL TOUR GROUPS FOR SENIOR CITIZENS

There are a few tour groups that specialize in trips for seniors. The following are two groups we have used that are specifically geared to the physical needs of seniors, but that also offer interesting and well-directed trips and workshops.

Elderhostel is a non-profit organization that provides high quality and affordable educational opportunities for older adults, age fifty-five and above. It began its program in 1975 on five New England campuses; there are now two thousand participating institutions in the United States and

Canada and in seventy foreign countries. Elderhostel strongly believes that learning is a lifelong process. In both the United States and abroad, programs are often located at colleges or universities and offer courses that may last two or three weeks on a variety of subjects, but usually ones related to the particular geographical area or particular institution. There are even intergenerational programs. Generally, the international programs are physically more strenuous, involving extensive walking on a variety of terrain and intensive schedules. Many programs will include day trips to sites in the area, or may even include several places to stay during an itinerary. Usually the description of the program will include information on how much free time is allowed and how strenuous the trip is, which is important to know in deciding whether it is an appropriate trip for you. In addition to the U.S., Canadian, and foreign programs, there are also Elderhostel Service Programs in poor neighborhoods or third world countries, where physical labor or teaching or other kinds of work is done. There are three different catalogs offered by Elderhostel to describe these three different kinds of programs. Examples of programs in the U.S. and Canada are: in April, <u>Birds of Vancouver</u>, at a Lifeline Learning Canada center twenty-two miles from Vancouver; <u>Minerals to Generals: Galena's Unique History</u>, in Galena, Illinois, an attractively restored town in northwest Illinois; or Islamic Art and Architecture at the University of Chicago. Examples of foreign programs are: <u>Oaxaca: Spanish Language and Hispanic Culture</u>, in Oaxaca, Mexico; <u>The Many Faces of Scandinavia</u>, nineteen days of travel and study in Denmark, Norway, and Sweden; or <u>Art and History: Treasures of Italy and Austria</u>, twenty days in Lower Austria, South Tyrol and Venice. I know a couple who have taken three service programs: teaching Navaho children on the Navaho Reservation in northern Arizona; monitoring seabirds on Midway Island; and teaching

English to university students in Xi'an. Each of their work experiences was different, but gratifying .

The other group I am familiar with that is especially designed for people fifty years and older is *Saga Holidays,* the world's largest tour operator for "mature adults," which originated I believe as a British tour group that expanded to build retirement communities in England. (It has a U.S. office in Boston. See Reference Section under Travel.) For years, my husband and I traveled with Saga and were very satisfied, as the pace was slower and the tour leaders knowledgeable. On many tours, you would settle down in one place for the entire time period and then take day trips out. Saga also has added Road Scholar tours that combine learning with travel; reading is expected, and lectures are given by top experts in their field. Popular Road Scholar tours among many others are entitled <u>French Impressionism, Color and Light</u>; <u>Turkey, Crossroads of Civilization;</u> and <u>Navajo Country and the Mysteries of Tony Hillerman.</u> Saga's Smithsonian Odyssey Tours are a partnership between the Smithsonian Institute and Saga to provide travel to diverse destinations at affordable prices with scholars and experts from various institutions. Examples of such trips are <u>Paradors of Andalusia</u>, <u>Sojourn On The French Riviera</u> and <u>Cruise: Australia And The Java Sea.</u>

A third group is Grand Circle Travel, which offers an extensive list of tours and cruises to all parts of the world as well as to Canada and the U.S. Grand Circle was founded in 1958 by a retired school principal who wished to help retired Americans lead more "vital, challenging and politically active lives." So she established the American Association of Retired Persons (AARP) and Grand Circle Travel. Grand Circle offers flexibility in planning your trip with chances to combine trips or add on short visits to other destinations. (See notes on how to reach them.).

Occasionally you can read in newspapers or magazines about unusual trips for seniors. For example, the travel section of our local Arizona paper featured fall of 1998 trips to the Himalayas with a group called Eldertreks, one two week trip to Tibet, and a seventeen day trip to Bhutan, with a limit of 15 people to each group. For future trips, the tour group can be reached through their web-site at http:// www.eldertreks.com or by calling Gary Murtagh at 1-800-741-7956.

Another adventurous trip that I found written up in the *N.Y. Times* was an elderhostel group of fourteen Seniors who spent a mid-August week in Alaska twenty-six miles above the Arctic Circle meeting Inuit elders and experiencing their way of living. These were two very different cultures that have very different views toward the aging: our society that worships youth, and the Inuit, where the elderly are highly respected.

Foreign Travel

The following information contains helpful tips on travel to foreign countries.

You can always learn about the current safety of a country by checking into the State Department web page, which will frankly urge people not to visit a country where the politics may be unstable.

Especially with travel to third world countries, immunizations may be necessary. Often, your family physician can tell you what is needed for the country or countries you are travelling to, and where to get the shots. (In some states there are special clinics for the purpose.) If you cannot get specific information from your doctor, either call your county health department or use the following web page: www.cdc.gov. If a country requires certain immunizations, you will need proof that you have taken them, or have medicine for such diseases as malaria.

Medicare does not cover medical care overseas, so that you will need to get travel insurance for that purpose. If you should need a doctor in a foreign country, often hotels have a list of qualified physicians who speak English or clinics that cater to English-speaking foreigners. You can also get referrals to doctors and hospitals from the local U. S. consulate. It is also helpful to carry information on your medical condition and a list of your medications in your wallet, and if you have serious heart problems, travel with a wallet-size form of your cardiogram. On airplanes, it is always advisable to carry your medicines in your carry-on, so they are available should you need them and not in possible lost luggage.

When you are travelling by air, wear loose comfortable clothing that does not bind in any way and cause circulation problems. Years ago, I flew to Italy with a tour group and violated three rules that everyone knows today. It was when women were wearing elasticized panty girdles that were tight enough to easily cut off circulation and on the plane I did not move around. When I arrived at the hotel in Rome, instead of resting, I was so excited that I immediately took off to walk for hours, which only added to the stress on the circulation in my legs. When I arrived back at the hotel one of my legs was crimson from what was diagnosed as phlebitis. Even something as serious as blood clots can follow a plane flight if a passenger does not move around and stretch. So, on the flight move and stretch, don't drink alcohol and after a long trip, once you have arrived, take the time to rest from your trip and to acclimate yourself to the time change.

If you have limited energy and medical problems that limit your mobility, you may decide that it is in your best interests not to travel with a tour group. By travelling on your own, you have the freedom to set your own pace and to go sightseeing or not. My husband and I did this six years ago with a trip to London, where we slept late if we wished, took day trips to localities outside of the city, and if one was sick and the other not, the ill one stayed in the hotel while the other went out. We did not have to keep up with a group schedule or to socialize when we were tired.

Day Trips From Home

For those people who do not wish to make overnight or longer trips, or who cannot afford to do so, there are still many interesting day trips that can be taken by car or by public transportation with or without a group. Now that you have retired and have the time, explore your city, town or county, sight-see while driving, take hikes in scenic places, or visit museums or parks that you never had time to see. Make a list of those places you have missed and go by yourself or with family or friends. Remember that most museums and parks have lower entrance fees for seniors. Also, buses, subways and trains have reduced rates for people over sixty-five in most localities. Many senior citizen groups take trips to near or far distant museums, which saves you the hassle of driving in more congested traffic. For those visiting national parks, there is the Golden Age Passport costing ten dollars, which allows the holder of the card who must be at least sixty-two years old to enter any national park system free of charge for the remainder of his life. The card can be purchased at the entrance of any national park.

Volunteerism and Paid Employment

I have included the subject of volunteerism in this chapter, as it is an important activity for so many senior citizens. As well as filling spare time, it is a way of giving to our community, or even returning to our community for some service we may have received from it. Many senior citizens, who have worked all of their adult lives, feel a great gap after retirement, and volunteering can to a certain extent fill that sense of loss. The United Way in our county in New York publishes a guide to volunteer opportunities in the county, which I picked up in the Office of the Aging. Often there are articles in local newspapers specifying the need for volunteers in a certain organization, and many hospitals and social service organizations will have an employed person in charge of volunteers. Some people choose to continue to hold a paid job, or wish to return to paid employment for financial or other reasons.

However, I find that, particularly in communities with large numbers of senior citizens, there may be such an overload of people who want volunteer jobs that insufficient use is made of people's working experience or specific talents. Instead, volunteers are often given "make work" tasks that can be totally unrelated to their experience or talents. I am saying this without denigrating volunteer work such as office work or visiting lonely people or feeding nursing home patients, for these are very necessary and meaningful tasks, but it does seem like such a waste not to use specific skills.

It is my impression that although many seniors are anxious to fill their time with some kind of work they are too timid to present themselves as assertively as they might have done in seeking a paid job during their working years. People who can forthrightly but civilly offer their talents sometimes can end up with satisfying work situations. For example, a well, alert seventy-five year old person I know who had had a career as a legal secretary found a young attorney just starting out who desperately needed a secretary, but could not afford to hire one at that point. She and the lawyer came to an agreement that she would work for him at her own choice of hours, delaying payment of her salary until his practice was stable enough to pay her for work already done. This understanding worked out for both parties, and she was able to continue working at her own pace without undue stress. A year later she still had not been paid, but, without resentment, she said that she would be lost without meaningful work.

Recently, I read the obituary for an eighty-seven year-old woman who worked full time until the day she died! Another eighty-seven year old woman, a former biology teacher, has been instrumental with the help of neighbors in turning fifty-eight acres of bog, which she and her late husband bought in 1955, into a state park. Some of the land, which is under the flight path of the Tacoma-Seattle International Airport, was bought by the state, the remainder was donated to it. Since the early 1970's, she has dedicated her life to leading tours of the land and educating adults and children about the importance of wetlands. In Las Cruces, New Mexico, there is an eighty-four year-old woman who is chief chef in a Mexican restaurant that is so popular that it serves one thousand meals a day on weekends. She has no plans to retire. A well-known folklorist in Tucson after his retirement continued to work on his ongoing studies almost as many hours as he had when he was employed. He averred that he just didn't have a "job," for a job paid money.

Work for many people is an expression of their individual identity, so for them retirement may represent a cutting off of their sense of self. This may be why many men seem to deteriorate both physically and emotionally shortly after retirement. Perhaps more people who feel they have a special talent or experience that could valuably be used should go with resume in hand to a prospective place of employment for either a paid or volunteer position, even if the employer has not advertised for either volunteer or paid help.

Education

Retirement is a wonderful time to fill in gaps in your education, or to extend your knowledge in a particular field. In almost every community, two-year colleges and four-year colleges and universities are offering courses that would interest senior citizens and that are affordable to them. These courses may last from one day to six or eight weeks, and may be arts and crafts, computer courses, literature courses or discussion classes on contemporary issues. Many teachers find teaching senior citizens an enjoyable experience as seniors have more confidence than the ordinary college student and draw from many life experiences in contributing to discussions. In a Greek Mythology course which I took, that used books by Mary Renault, our class got into a discussion on contemporary U.S. politics and concluded that what we really needed was a fearless leader such as Theseus to bring together our country. I have one friend who has just retired as a nurse and is now getting her Bachelor's degree in fine arts, having done a great deal of painting over the years. Fordham University, where she is studying, has given her two years' worth of credits for her previous work and life experience. In Tucson, the University of Arizona has an "extended university" for seniors called SAGE, (Seniors' Achievement and Growth through Education) now ten years old, which offers courses, largely taught by retired teachers and professors. The program is so popular that a lottery system has to be used to enroll registrants in the classes. I'm sure that if you call your local public school system or a local college, you will find that there is an offering of courses for senior citizens.

Many senior citizens take art or writing classes and discover talents that they either never knew they had, or now have time to cultivate already established interests. It is a wonderfully fulfilling, invigorating experience to discover and to develop talents in your senior years.

Now that you are retired, you will find that you have a lot of time in which to do things that you never felt you could do before because of the responsibilities of work and family. The most frequently heard exclamation that I've heard from busy retirees is, "I don't know how I ever found time to work!" I'm sure there is some craft, game, or skill that you have always had in the back of your mind to learn that you now have the time to cultivate.

Perhaps you never had to use a computer on your job, but still wished to learn how to use one. Computers are a wonderful way to widen one's horizon and to keep in touch with what is going on. Most public libraries have computers and will show you how to use their system. Many school systems have evening adult courses that include computer classes, or you may be able to find a User Group near you that will help you learn. You can find such a group by calling your local computer store or the Association of Personal Computer User Groups at 914-876-6678. There are plenty of computer magazines and books; I particularly like the "dummy" books that are written in simple English and take nothing for granted, such as IDG's PCs for Dummies (1997, $19.95), and most large newspapers have computer columns. You may be able to find a private tutor through your local community college or even your local high school, since young people are so computer literate these days.

Recreation

Almost any town of any size has a Senior Citizen Center where hot meals and/or recreation are provided. For people who are new to an area or who for various reasons need and want socialization, the centers are a logical place to meet people who are their age, and where activities are provided. As an example, a retired artist friend of mine teaches a weekly art class at the Woodstock (New York) Community Center, where seniors meet every day for activities. Woodstock is a well-known artist's colony, so the activities of that center represent the artistic interests of Woodstock's citizens, and trips are taken to other areas to visit museums and historic points of interest. You should be able to find out about your closest senior center through your local Office of the Aging.

There are even travel groups that specialize in day trips for senior citizens. Apparently gambling has always been attractive to the elderly, so in some areas of the country there are tour buses that go to places like Atlantic City, Las Vegas, Laughlin, Az., Indian casinos, and riverboat casinos on the Mississippi River. Harrah's casino did a national survey that showed that twenty-seven percent of Americans over the age of fifty-five gambled at least once during 1997. A recent survey in Illinois found that forty percent of gamblers who visit the twelve riverboat casinos are over the age of fifty-five, thirty percent are retired. The gambling seniors may be living on mighty little income, but that dream that somehow they might hit the jackpot draws them after a life of scrimping.

SUMMARY

So, live it up if you can. Find what you enjoy doing, meet as many people as possible and figuratively spend your children's inheritance! Maybe people will then describe you as they described the musician, Dizzy Gillespie, as "68 years old, going on 22."

Chapter III

Abide With Me?
Sex, Marriage and Other Interesting Topics.

Abide with me from morn til eve
For without thee I cannot live
Abide with me when night is nigh
For without thee I dare not die
—John Keble

During the time that I have been writing this book, I have heard stories, usually second-hand, but sometimes directly about:

1. Sudden divorces of long-married couples
2. Eighty year old lovers
3. "Dr. Ruth" type sex columns for seniors
4. Many seniors living together sans marriage
5. Various ways of meeting new partners
6. Seniors remarrying
7. Seniors divorcing quickly after remarrying
8. Late gay and lesbian come-outers and gay and lesbian groups for seniors

9. Pre-nuptial agreements before later remarriages

10. Viagra, viagra, and more viagra

This list has not been arranged according to any logic, but only as I thought of issues that have come up. What I have found so surprising is that there are very few articles or books on any of these subjects except Viagra. I wonder why this is so. Is it because there are still too many stereotyped assumptions being made even by professionals about people over sixty-five? Many of these problems would have been unheard of thirty or forty years ago, but with increased longevity and a better quality of life during the later years, people are living very different lives with very different expectations for those later years. Therefore, the choices that older people now make in their most intimate relationships are very different than their parents would have made at the same age. Because there appears to be so little written on these subjects, this chapter will for the most part raise questions for the reader to consider.

SEX AND OLDER AMERICANS

According to reports on several surveys that I have read, older people still maintain an interest in sex and many are still sexually active. According to a report in the New York Times of September 29, 1998 of a mail survey of 534 men and 758 women commissioned and released by the National Council on Aging, many older Americans maintain an interest in sex. Nearly half of those over sixty still engage in sex at least monthly. The sample was weighted to match the sex, age, race, income and marital status of the American population over sixty. Thirty-nine percent of the respondents said that they were satisfied with the amount of sex they were having, while another thirty-nine percent said they wished they had sex more frequently. Active seniors were evenly divided on whether sex was physically better now or in their youth. Forty-three percent said sex is just as good as or better than in their youth, and forty-three percent said it is not so good. The respondents were also asked about their earlier expectations. One third of those surveyed felt that it was natural to lose interest in sex as one gets older, and others felt that sex would be physically impossible.

The same survey was discussed on the September 29, 1998 *Today Show* on NBC, which reported the percentages of activity in different age groups. Among the sample of people who were in their sixties, seventy-one percent of men are sexually active, and sixty-one percent of women. Among people in their seventies, fifty-seven percent of men and eighteen percent of women are sexually active, and among those in their eighties, twenty-seven percent of men and eighteen percent of women are active. The most common reasons given for the decline in activity were medical problems and use of prescription drugs for men, and lack of interest for women. Although four out of ten were not enjoying sex in their seventies, the conclusion was that sexual disfunction is not inevitable for older people.

In the past it was thought that impotence was more often than not an emotional problem. However, recent research has shown that over fifty percent of impotence has a physical basis, as examples, the aftermath of prostate problems and diabetes which can cause nerve damage. Medications are also often the cause of impotence, particularly some used for treating high blood pressure and heart disease. Other reasons for impotence are deficiencies of testosterone or of thyroid hormones, hardening of the arteries, poor circulation, spinal cord injuries and brain damage. If impotence is a problem, it is advisable to find the cause. If the reason is psychological, counseling can be effective; if physical, the specific cause can be found and then often corrected, through medicines or even a penile prosthesis. However, if the problem cannot be found or corrected, there are many ways other than intercourse by which a couple can express their affection.

Viagra

With the advent of the blockbuster drug, Viagra, which helps men get and maintain an erection, drug companies are wondering whether Viagra or some other drug would help women and are asking academic scientists what they know about women's sexual responses. As yet, it has been difficult to find a way of measuring women's erotic response to certain stimuli, and actually, there has been little research on sexual disfunction in women. For there to be the research on women, there would have to be general agreement that women's sexual desire is an important issue.

Viagra has not always been a simple and complete solution to a couple's problem. While men want to treat their impotence as merely a mechanical problem that can be solved by popping a pill, women want to address the emotions often associated with impotence. Frequently, the couple has found ways other than the most conventional ones of expressing sex and intimacy, or has avoided sex altogether. Making love involves much more than just the mechanical act of having sex. Often, when the possibility of sex resurfaces, the couple may have to face psychological problems that caused the impotence in the first place or which resulted from it and that have never been discussed or dealt with.

Many doctors say that even with the use of Viagra many couples still belong in therapy because of the many feelings that may have lain dormant because of their damaged sex lives and that do not disappear with the use of medication. But most men see the pill as an easy way out and are too threatened by the thought of discussing their sexual problems with anyone, especially a sex therapist. Some doctors are reminding men who take Viagra to take the time during foreplay to pay more attention to their partner's emotional and physical needs. Men need to communicate and express their affection more openly in order to interest their partners in making love again. For some men, this may require professional help . I have heard of marriages breaking up once the man was given Viagra. In such cases, the man expected the drug to solve all problems, and when such a miracle did not occur, he looked elsewhere or terminated the marriage.

Depression, Alcoholism and Domestic Violence

The rate of depression is high among the elderly. This can be the result of a variety of reasons, including illness, and often alcoholism is a way to mask depression. There are clinical signs of depression to heed, such as loss of energy and much less interest in people and things, feelings of sadness and hopelessness, and in more advanced stages, insomnia, and loss of weight. Any of these symptoms can be temporary reactions to crisis, but if they are extreme or last an undue length of time, consider them serious. Also watch out for excessive irritability, and sometimes overeating, for with many people these are the ways they deal with psychological stress. Domestic violence can be the result of agitated depression, alcoholism and even Alzheimer's, where with each there is loss of control. If you do observe signs of depression, or alcoholism and there have been incidents of abuse, do seek help from a qualified mental health professional. In almost any county in the country there is a mental health clinic or a social agency that can address these problems and help you deal with them.

Marital Breakups

Naturally, there can be many reasons other than sex for marital breakups after many years together. Once lately, when I was socializing with four other women, I was surprised to learn that I was the only one who was still on my first marriage. All of my acquaintances were perfectly ordinary, pleasant women in their seventies. Three had been divorced and had remarried within the past ten years. The fourth, after two divorces, was recently widowed from her third husband to whom she had been very happily married for fifteen years. Unfortunately, I did not know the women well enough to learn the reason for their late divorces. However, in any community there is gossip, and one learns some interesting reasons for breakups, without necessarily learning the identity of the couple.

All through marriage, there are adjustments that have to be made because of changing circumstances. Retirement is one of the crisis points in one's life. For those who have worked and have achieved a sense of satisfaction and empowerment through their careers, the sudden change to complete leisure can be traumatic. It seems as though a great void is created which has to be filled somehow, but often never is satisfactorily. Sometimes it is men who adjust more easily to retirement, seeing it as a relief after so many years of hard work, which they did not enjoy. Sometimes women who developed late careers after raising children and who found enormous emotional satisfaction from their work have told me they find retirement harder than their husbands, and resent having to retire when he does.

I have also talked with a number of women who never worked and previously had their house to themselves during daytime hours who quietly resent the amount of time that the retired and idle husbands are home, which is seen as an intrusion on their schedule and their privacy. In addition, if the partners move to another locality, they are apt to leave behind close friends and family on which one or both of the two have relied for emotional support and which sometimes may have been the ties that kept the couple together. Until an adjustment to the new kind of life is made by both partners, the changes made at retirement- leaving a career, the idleness of leisure time, the constant daily contact between a couple, and the moving away from previous long relationships- in and of themselves can be a source of stress in a relationship. New ways of communicating and negotiating each other's needs must be found and therapy or marital counseling may need to be considered.

Some couples have vehemently disagreed on where to live after retirement and sometimes one will take off. Other couples try a new location and find that the move suits one but not the other, and unable to resolve their disagreement, one returns home. In one particular situation, I learned of a couple, both widowed, who remarried quickly and then precipitously moved to the southwest. Within two months, the wife had moved back home to her cold state because she missed her seven children too much. Some remarriages have been unduly delayed or have not lasted because one partner's children did not approve of the parent's choice.

Then there have been some totally surprising breakups that have taken place after a crucial illness or surgery. The partner, who recovers from the ordeal realizes that he or she has come face to face with mortality, and decides to leave an unsatisfactory marriage to find some other partner or another lifestyle before it is too late. Often these are marriages that appear to be satisfactory on the surface but actually are seething underneath or behind closed doors and may have been for many years. Marriage and other kinds of love partnerships are so psychologically complex that none of us really knows what another person's relationship is or has been like.

Just as retirement is a major period of stress in a marriage, so is a major illness or sudden disability that occurs in one of the partners. Ideally, when such crises happen, the well partner should express love verbally but also by giving whatever assistance the ill partner needs. The one who is well corrects for the partner's disabilities: the one who walks well pushes the disabled one in the wheelchair, the one who hears well answers the telephone. But with some couples the stress of the illness and the change in roles that the illness imposes are too threatening to the well partner, who wants out. The equilibrium of the marital relationship has been upset so that expectations in the roles taken by the two partners and the activities they enjoyed either singly or together no longer hold. (Fortunately, it would appear that such an extreme reaction occurs more frequently in younger couples where vigorous health and activity are natural expectations.) If couples have enough money, outside help can be hired to do the nursing, the diapering, the shopping and the housework that the well partner may find so intolerable. This then allows him or her some time for personal activities, thus relieving the stress enough to maintain the marriage. You may even have a social agency in your area that offers an occasional day of respite care at a nominal rate.

For those couples who do terminate a marriage, especially if the relationship is one of long duration, the break can be difficult. Women I know who have decided to leave their partners after many years, say they have done so after long consideration and a weighing of the pros and cons. It has been done usually after the children are grown and have established independent lives of their own. As with any divorce, there are regrets that the relationship changed and did not meet expectations, and a kind of grief process is experienced, similar to what happens if one is widowed. (Actually one divorced friend grieved terribly when her ex-husband died, as she had many good memories of their earlier years of marriage.) They say that the decision was difficult, and that because of financial changes, their lifestyle necessarily changed, but they still do not regret the decision. Most do not intend to remarry, but they do see their freedom as a potential for a new and very different life.

On the other hand, retirement and its leisure time can become an opportunity for a couple to rekindle an earlier relationship. They are alone and are without the stresses of a job and the responsibilities of raising and educating children. They share memories and chores. There is now time for them to travel together, to share interests, to find a new kind of sexual partnership and a renewed respect and caring for each other. Also, severe illness that can happen so quickly in old age can bring a couple together who perhaps have taken each other for granted. Suddenly, faced with the possibility of losing the partner, the relationship takes on new meaning and sweetness.

SEX AND THE NURSING HOME PATIENT

Occasionally a married couple will end up in a nursing home at the same time. Yet I have never known a situation where putting the two together in the same room has worked out. It is hard to say whether this failure is caused by possessiveness or nagging by one or the other of the spouses, or by the nursing staff feeling their control is threatened. I also have not heard of a married couple who are either together in the same nursing home, or one is still in the community and visiting, attempting to have any kind of sexual relationship in the nursing home. My impression is that in most nursing homes, whether two patients are married or not and even if they are mentally competent, the idea of their having any kind of a sexual relationship is a taboo subject.

The greatest fear by both families and staff is that a patient who is not competent will be taken advantage of by a "lecherous old man" who is a patient. Often, such men will also make advances to staff, and will be firmly told that this is not appropriate behavior. Yet I have not encountered a nursing home that has a written policy allowing competent consenting couples to have the privacy and opportunity for a sexual relationship. This is something that really should be addressed and the staff given in-service instruction on normal sexuality for the aged.

Death of a Partner

Death is inevitable, and usually a couple does not die at the same time except in an accident. If one of the partners has been ill for some time, there is time to prepare psychologically for the death, but this does not negate the wrenching experience of widowhood. Even with preparation, I have known women to grieve for years. Fortunately, in most areas social agencies, churches or mental health services offer support groups for widows, which help them through the immediate crisis period and sometimes longer. One friend told me that her widow's support group has continued to meet over several years time, now going out to dinner every month in order to maintain the important ties made during the point of crisis. Support groups are set up mostly for women because it is men who usually die first.

Many women have chosen to spend months, sometimes years, taking care of their husbands at home, rather than placing them in a nursing home. A few women have told me that they could not have done otherwise, though it was both physically and emotionally exhausting. Some of these same women were able to express relief when it was over, which does not mean that they did not love their husbands, but that the process was too difficult for both to undergo much longer. Even women who have not had to take care of their dying husbands may feel some ambivalence. In addition to the grief that they feel, they may enjoy their new independence. The ambivalence does not mean that their love was less; it sometimes is a natural step in the grieving process.

The experience of widowhood varies according to the age when it takes place. Women who are widowed young find the experience devastating, partly because of the responsibility of raising young children alone, but it is young women who will recover from their grief the fastest and who are able to make a new life for themselves. Sometimes it is the women who have been happily married for four or five decades whose grief may be tempered by the realization that they are fortunate to have had so many good years together. But if these women are in their seventies or eighties and are in failing health they may not have the physical or emotional resources to easily rebuild their lives. Doctors should be especially sensitive to latent as well as overt depression that is felt by widows. One person I know who had been widowed for three years saw her primary physician for an annual exam. He must have picked up some clue that she was still depressed, asked her whether she was, and then very wisely urged her to take a mild anti-depressant even though she was not especially aware that she needed it. She reported that almost immediately she felt very much better and was grateful that her doctor had been that assertive. Although happily married people frequently feel that they will never find anyone who could possibly replace their first spouse, it seems to be the widowed who remarry faster than the divorced, for if they have been happily married they are more willing to return to the married state.

The Dating Game

Both men and women throw up their hands at the prospect of dating in their seventies or eighties, but I notice that plenty of people do find a partner or a second spouse. Very frequently, this turns out to be the deceased spouse's best friend, also widowed, who is already a good friend, and who helps the widow through the grief period. These marriages are often very successful, as the two people already know each other well, and may already travel in the same social circle.

There are many other ways for widows to meet men, often the same ways that are recommended for much younger people. One of the best is through some group that is not specifically set up for the purpose, such as a political club, senior citizen center, a bridge club, or book study group. This is where two people who are involved in a cause or an interest quite independent of their need for companionship will naturally meet someone with similar interests. There are personal columns where there are often ads for senior citizens, dating services and web sites on the internet, but one should be very careful of such means of meeting partners. A friend of mine who used a dating service several times told me that she always met her dates at some neutral setting, and never gave out her home address or telephone number until she felt that she knew the person much better. Such services do sometimes attract people who are dishonest about themselves and who turn out to be unstable and possibly dangerous.

In many large retirement communities, there are singles clubs and dating services. The NBC News program of November 28, 1998 had a segment on 80-year-old Dr. Helen Greenblatt who has an advice column in the *Leisure World Voice* on sex, romance and relationships, in the Laguna Hills, California Leisure World, retirement community of nineteen thousand people. The news program quoted her as saying, "Age is largely a state of mind". Because women outlive men, according to the census, at age 75 there are four women to every man. Consequently, singles clubs are overwhelmingly women, and a personal ad placed by a man may be answered by scores of answers. The women in such places are not necessarily looking for marriage, but are seeking the companionship of a man and possibly romance and sex. A friend of mine, widowed for three years, has been seeing a man for the last year, having met him through a club that both she and her husband belonged to. She and her friend, whom she describes as a "gentleman," socialize together a great deal and travel together, but she says she would remarry only if she found a man who would "sweep me off my feet" as her husband had. Many of the women in the retirement communities relish their freedom, feeling that they have spent their whole adult lives caring for other people. The men are always looking for younger women, but in retirement communities women who want younger men rarely get them.

"Shacking Up"

Many older couples prefer an arrangement of living together without bothering to marry. This may have financial advantages, as both can continue to receive social security checks, and also if the relationship does not work out it is much easier to terminate it than it is to divorce if one marries. In our youth we frequently used the expression, "shacking up" for a live-in relationship, which was far less common in the nineteen forties and fifties, but now is common to all age groups. Also, just as young people live together for a period of time before marriage, so do many older people to test out the viability of the relationship.

I have friends who have weekend relationships with men, which one widow I knew described as "the best of two worlds," as she had someone she cared for but did not wish to marry. He was her sexual partner, her companion, and her escort without her having to sacrifice her own independence. She made clear to him the limits of the relationship, which lasted nearly ten years until she moved to another state to be close to her children.

There are also passionate relationships that take place in older people, some as old as eighty. A New York Times article describes a widow who contacted her first lover after learning that he had lost his wife about the same time that she lost her husband. The writer describes the self-consciousness and anxious moments she felt before their passion was rekindled, and the joy they both then felt even though they were now old.

LATE LIFE MARRIAGES

Once in awhile, one comes across delightful wedding announcements of older couples who have married. They recount very happy occasions that perhaps are generally less formal than first marriages, but nevertheless very joyful occasions witnessed by family and friends. One couple whom I know lived together first before getting married, then returned to the east coast to be married where their children lived. It is surprisingly how often people who have loved each other as young people and who may even have been engaged years before but have not had contact in perhaps forty years, somehow meet again and quickly reestablish their old relationship and end up getting married. The National Enquirer reported such a story. A couple who had previously been engaged as college sweethearts but ended up marrying other people, met again in their eighties on a cruise ship, and before the cruise was over were engaged.

Often the married couples will divide their time between the two homes that are owned by each. Many times this is easier than sorting through possessions and moving into one house, and it also enables each of the pair to maintain contacts in their home communities. Prenuptial agreements are used very frequently to make sure that assets that are meant to go to children are protected, and spell out very specifically how assets will be distributed in the event of death or divorce. Lawyers have found that negotiating a prenuptial agreement provides a reality test for the relationship. The process can expose flaws in their relationship before it is too late, and can become a test of whether the couple can work out knotty problems. Especially, as laws differ from state to state on divorce and death, it is important to consult an attorney to draw up a prenuptial agreement, which will cost on the average $1500. Each of the parties should consult a separate attorney well before the wedding so that there is not a feeling of duress in coming to an agreement.

As well as providing companionship, love, tenderness and a sexual partnership, marriage brings many other benefits to a relationship. Researchers have found that statistics show that married people generally have better emotional health, live longer, and have more money. At the same time, marital stress over a period of time may make people more prone to heart attacks, as angry quarrels narrow blood vessels, increase heartbeats, and raise blood pressure, all of which lead to arteriosclerosis and coronary heart disease.

OLDER LESBIANS

A number of years ago, a lesbian friend told me there were a growing number of lesbians among older women, some of them women who had already been in heterosexual relationships, and others who were single and in long-term secret relationships with other women. Some of these women were coming out in their seventies. The coming out can be liberating and there is a support system among lesbians; for the former heterosexual woman it can be more difficult because of resistance by children or former friends who find it difficult to understand. There are a number of articles in periodicals on the subject of older lesbians, and I am sure there are web sites for such organizations as Older and Wiser (GLOW), a support group for older gay people, the Gay Women's Health Oasis, and Old Lesbians Organizing for Change.

SUMMARY

So, here in our most intimate relationships as in many other areas, there are many choices to be made. We are suddenly living in a time when there is much more tolerance of a variety of behavior, and we ourselves are healthy enough during our senior years to take advantage of the many options open to us.

Chapter IV

There's No Place Like Home:
Living Independently

Many older people who still own their own homes, or who have rented or owned one apartment for years. May wish to remain there if they are physically able to. A home is a place where people express their own individuality. If it is where they have lived for many years they have important associations there. Particularly, as one gets older, change can be distressing, more so to some people than others. Perhaps the person who chooses to stay is a gardener who gets enormous pleasure in seeing the growth of the same plants and trees each year, again an expression of oneself. In their community, whether small town, suburb, or city neighborhood, older people certainly have established many supports, including friends, religious affiliations, social and political groups, and professionals who serve them. All of these relationships may have great psychological meaning. These days most families are geographically separated, for very few children remain in the area where they were raised. They go where jobs are. Whereas before World War Two a family's social life generally centered around the extended family that lived in the same area, now because of geographical separation, family visiting is much rarer. It is now usually nearby friends who provide the emotional ties and social support which were formerly provided by families.

In some communities in New York, and I'm sure in other states, there are formal and informal networks that are developed to provide needed services to seniors who remain in their old community. For instance, in New York City there are many apartment buildings where people have continued to live from early marriage into their retirement years, and these buildings may end up entirely filled with older people who either cannot afford to move or do not wish to. Several years ago, I heard of one such building on the West side of Manhattan filled with seniors who decided to hire a social worker to provide needed counseling and referral services. A new term is being used for buildings and communities where there is a concentration of seniors who have just remained in their old neighborhoods: N.O.R.C.s, naturally occurring retirement communities.

Social agencies are targeting such areas so that needs and services can be anticipated, and local governments are doing all they can so that older people can remain independent. David Stern, the executive vice president of Jewish Association for the Aged in New York, feels that N.O.R.C.s could develop cooperatives through which to contract services such as transportation, home aid and snow removal, and because of their size they would secure less expensive and more reliable services. Massapequa, N.Y. on Long Island, provides free transportation for shopping, free or low-cost concerts and museum trips and a variety of educational and recreational services. Academic institutions offer courses at reduced rates, and for those people who are eligible, there is real estate tax relief and loan assistance for home improvement projects.

In February 2000, the Joint Center for Housing Studies at Harvard University released a two-year study, "Housing America's Seniors," which reported that people 65 and over with ownership rates of almost 80% account for about 25% of all home owners. Only 10% live in age restricted communities where housing accommodates the physical needs of seniors. This suggests that the majority of people are staying in homes they already own and where they may have lived many years. In addition to structural changes that may have to be made to accommodate increasing physical limitations, seniors who wish to remain in their own homes may want to take advantage of several fairly new financial options.

One possibility is the reverse mortgage for people 62 and older, who may be equity rich but cash poor, particularly in this economy when a person may own a house that is now worth twenty or more times the original purchase price. The reverse mortgage may be given in a lump sum or in monthly amounts; its advantage is that it does not require repayment until the owner dies or sells the house. Once the owner no longer occupies the home, repayment of the loan is due, along with accrued interest. In case the owner dies, the heirs may repay the mortgage either by selling the house or with other funds. The reverse mortgage enables people to remain in their own homes by giving them money which they may use for almost any purpose. With the money they receive they may repay large debts, do a major remodeling of their home, buy a less expensive mortgage-free home, or increase their monthly income. These "mortgages" can be complicated, so it is advisable to consult with a Fannie Mae approved reverse mortgage counseling agency. Your local Office of the Aging may do this counseling; if not, it should be able to direct you to an approved agency.

Most older people have saved money or invested in a home with the idea that their children will inherit at least the home, even if one or the other of a married couple end up in a nursing home on Medicaid. It is now possible to ensure that the children do benefit from the value of the home by transferring the home to an adult child, but the following "life-estate clause" must be included in the transaction: "the grantor reserves to himself a life estate in the subject property for his use and enjoyment for the entirety of his lifetime."[1] This clause also saves a great deal of money in capital gains taxes. If you consider doing this, be sure to consult an attorney.

Not all seniors wish to remain in the community where they have raised their children. Both the south and the southwest have mushrooming populations because of the number of retirees who have chosen to relocate there to take advantage of a warmer climate and cheaper housing. In a booming economy, they find they can sell their homes readily and often at a great profit; they may then sell all of their furniture or give it to their children, and start afresh in the warmer location. For some people, starting over in a completely different geographical area with a new home, new friends, and community supports, and sometimes totally different furniture can be rejuvenating, almost as if they are starting over their marriage. Their children visit them during the winter months, and they in turn go north during the summer months to visit families and old friends and to escape the heat in the new localities.

In addition to the burgeoning southern and southwest retirement communities, there is a trend to build such communities in the north for those people who do not wish to go too far from their roots. Wherever these communities are, what was formerly farmland or ranchland has been converted into huge retirement areas that include housing developments, apartment houses, and trailer parks. Their economy may depend largely on the building industry and all the various services that are secondary to it. Whole communities may consist of people who have come from elsewhere. Because everyone is new to the area and because

---

[1]Dennis Hevesi,"The Elderly Face Housing Choices,"*N.Y.Times*,5/14/00.

everyone is old enough to realize consciously or unconsciously that they do not have time for the formality of slowly becoming acquainted, friendships are made very readily, and support systems are developed.

In addition to the creation of retirement communities, there is a new trend to build intergenerational communities such as the town of Columbia, Maryland, built in the 1970's, and the more recent Disney-sponsored community of Celebration, Florida, built in the 1990's. These simulate established small towns where people remained most of their life near their family.

How to Remain Independent

What people who decide to relocate have in common with the elderly who still live in their old communities in non-institutional settings, is that they are for the most part still reasonably healthy. Moreover, whether they stay in their old community or move elsewhere, both groups have often chosen to remain strongly independent, even if their families sometimes see this independence as a problem. Families often worry that elderly parents living alone may have accidents or, because of increasing medical problems and frailty, they may not be able to care for themselves adequately. Sometimes they press their parents to move to institutional settings before they are emotionally ready to do so. If competent, elders have the right to decide to live where and as they wish to live. They may not yet be ready to consider continuing care or an assisted living facility or congregate living and certainly not a nursing home, and some are determined if possible to never go that route.

Adjustments and compromises often have to be made in order to maintain independence. This may mean moving to simpler quarters, and for disabled people, making structural changes to accommodate walkers or wheelchairs, and building ramps. This also includes finding ways of being monitored either by family, friends, neighbors, or by formal programs in the community, and of getting assistance with meals, shopping and perhaps housework. (See Appendix)

An example of fierce determination is Angela, now ninety-two, who like many elderly people fell and broke her hip several years ago and had to go to a nursing home, frequently the reason many elderly women end up there permanently. Angela, however, was bound that she would return home, even though she lived alone. She was discharged after three or four months and has remained home, walking without a cane and continuing to drive to her daily activities. Her daughter wishes her to move in with her, but Angela has refused, saying, "Why would I want to move so far from my church, friends, activities and the stores that I know?" She lives in a simple home, and neighbors and church friends keep an eye out for her.

Rose, a ninety-three year old widow with heart problems, continues to live alone in the house to which she and her husband retired in the 1960's. Some of her neighbors have lived there almost as long as she has, and they keep an eye on each other, telephoning or visiting each other daily. Rose does not drive, and is dependent on a walker, so she has a couple come in to clean and shop, a man to do yard work, and Meals On Wheels to provide daily meals and a little sociability when they come. She has things set up in her kitchen and her living room so that she can easily reach them without having to get up. She likes to read and still has an active mind, so her family sends her books, and she has people get books for her from the library. She remains cheerful and positive and cherishes her independence. But for people like this to remain independent, housing modifications sometimes have to be made, and community support services must be readily available.

As our older population grows, creative, informal, neighborhood volunteer systems for giving help are appearing in many communities. In one of the old historic districts of Tucson, one such program, the Old Fort Lowell Live At Home program has been developed. There, neighborhood volunteers provide a variety of services to elderly residents, such as friendly visiting, transportation, yard work and light housekeeping. The volunteers receive training, and at the beginning of their service they are given a contract which has been signed by the client and that lists specific tasks. I suspect that those people who do manage to remain independent and who have the necessary support systems are happier and in turn physically healthier.

Therefore, when it comes to independent living, it is a responsibility of the public and private sector to see that the elderly have access to community based services that will make it easier for them to stay in their own homes, or at least in their own communities. Those responsible include community planners, builders, public and private social service agencies, religious and service groups, transportation services and health care providers. Home equity conversion loans can also help older people on limited incomes remain in their own homes. Even if the home is mortgage free, home repair and modifications may be necessary to ensure safety and to improve mobility or to create rental space to make the home more affordable.

Every state has a state Office of the Aging, and area Offices of the Aging, usually located in each county. Nationwide, there are 57 State and Territorial Units on Aging, 655 Area Agencies on Aging, 221 Tribal Organizations and multiple service providers that may or may not have contracts with their state. Federal funds are provided to the states by the Administration on Aging under the U.S. Department of

Health and Human Services. In turn, the states must provide certain basic services, including nutrition programs, legal services, and information and referral services. The State Offices of the Aging determine statewide policies, procedures and programs, and provide money for and supervision of the local Offices of the Aging. States vary considerably in how much money is budgeted for services, which of course determines the number and breadth of services provided by the local office, or whether private agencies must provide the bulk of services. In every state, the area Office of the Aging, most often located in your county of residence, is where you would get information on housing and services for seniors that allow them to remain independent and even information on nursing homes and other kinds of institutional care in your area.

I have used Dutchess County, New York, and Tucson, Arizona as two communities that approach the problems of their aging population differently. New York State and its counties have a long tradition of using public funds either directly through their public agencies or through contracts with private agencies to provide a wide array of health and social services for their citizens (see Appendix). Arizona, on the other hand, is a conservative state that prides itself in its individualism and its low tax rate, so there are fewer public funds being used for programs for the aged.

My husband and I retired to Dutchess County, which is located on the Hudson River about one hundred miles north of New York City. Though it is a large rural area, its major employer has been IBM. In 1994, its population was under 260,000. The county Office of Aging, the official Area Office of The Aging, is a very active, well staffed public agency that helps plan and coordinate services to the aging population of the county, and provides a wide array of educational, legal, nutritional, counseling and referral services. In its outer office it has a large display of readable literature on public and private services available to county senior citizens. The pamphlets are there for people to take and use. Staff members see people for counseling and appropriate referral, and counselors who may specialize in a particular area of concern lead community meetings and train volunteers to work on programs offered by the county office.

Tucson, a city with a very fast growing population of three-quarters of a million, is located in Pima County, Arizona, sixty miles north of the Mexican border. Many recent Mexican immigrants and many retirees have moved there from other parts of the country. Also like many other warm areas of the United States, it has a large number of "snowbirds," most of them from the Midwest or the Mountain States, who live in the county for only part of the year. The Pima County Council on Aging, which stresses that it is a private, non-profit agency, is the Area Agency on Aging. It is funded through several sources: the federal Older Americans Act, and also through the Arizona Department of Economic Security, Aging and Adult Administration, Pima County, the city of Tucson, and various private funding resources, including the United Way. Of course, with its population, Tucson has many more services for seniors than does Dutchess County, New York. Medical services are excellent, as there are several large medical centers that are also teaching hospitals where a good deal of research is being done. Many services are offered to seniors through privately funded organizations, most of them religious centers, service groups, private social agencies, and some business groups. For example, one of the large department stores in the middle of Tucson, Robinson May's, in partnership with Tucson Medical

Center and Pima County Council on Aging, sponsors SAGE. a senior center at the store, where people can take courses and participate in activity groups. A large shopping mall, also in the center of the city, every other Tuesday hires a dance band to play "golden oldies" in the middle of the mall, to which seniors come in their best attire to meet other single seniors.

Certainly, Arizona is one of those western states that are anti-government in every way: very anti-regulation, and frequently rabidly opposed to using tax dollars for even the most basic services. On the other hand, I have not encountered in the East the degree of volunteerism that you find in the West, or also the degree of responsibility that families feel for each other in time of need.

In any county in the country it should be possible to get information on services and activities for senior citizens through the Area Office of the Aging. Look in the yellow or blue pages section of your telephone directory for its address and telephone number.

HUD Elderly Housing

For people who cannot manage complete independence or who do not wish it, senior housing is a good choice. For those with a limited income, federally subsidized housing is an attractive option.

In the early 1960s, through the United States Department of Housing and Urban Development, federal money became available for what is referred to as Title 8 subsidized housing for senior citizens. This is a good resource for those people who wish to remain independent, but who cannot afford to stay in their homes, or lack the strength to maintain them. In Dutchess County, there are seven Title 8 HUD sites. All of them have eligibility requirements that are determined by HUD: a minimum age of 62 and a maximum gross annual income in 1998 of $19,650 for an individual, $22,450 for a couple. All but two of the sites apply "federal preferences" in selecting tenants. These preferences are: displacement from your present living quarters, living in substandard housing, or payment of more than 50% of your monthly income on rent. A tenant's rent in the Title 8 housing is determined by HUD to be 30% of his or her adjusted gross income. Some rentals include utilities, some do not; other rentals allow a credit toward utilities. The sites vary in the number of apartments and other features. HUD decides on applicants and what rentals they will pay, and keeps a tight rein on the operation through the site manager. The sites that I know in Dutchess County are attractive, are located in safe neighborhoods, offer some socialization for residents, and provide some benign monitoring of them for health and safety. Your Office of the Aging should have a list of HUD sites in your county.

WELLS MANOR

Wells Manor in Rhinebeck, New.York is a good example of HUD housing. Rhinebeck has a very small but good community hospital with its own nursing home, as well as two religiously affiliated nursing homes. The hospital, which serves the northern end of Dutchess County, has always had a sense of responsibility to the larger community. It was the hospital that saw a need in the area it serves for affordable senior housing. Therefore back in the 1980's it became the sponsor of Wells Manor, a Title 8 housing on the outskirts of the village.

I visited Wells Manor twice, each time to talk to the coordinator, who showed me the grounds, two sample apartments, activities and meeting rooms. While she and I talked in her office some of the residents were socializing in the front hall while they waited for the mail to be delivered. They were mostly very attractive, neatly dressed women in their late seventies or early eighties who were not able to remain in their own homes. There were only seven couples listed on the mailboxes. At Wells Manor, there are 74 apartment units with an additional one for a staff member who lives on the grounds. Of these, nine are efficiency apartments, and the rest are one bedroom. In each apartment, there are handicap bars and emergency bell pulls, which connect to the manager's office during the day, and to the superintendent's apartment at night. The one room efficiency apartment is small by most standards (14 by 16 feet), but HUD considers this space large enough for one person.

The applicant is called when a vacancy occurs, and then has two chances to refuse. The one-bedroom apartments have a two-year waiting list, the efficiencies much less time. Even though Wells Manor is financially managed by a company in Massachusetts, HUD ultimately has control of all decisions. Though the manager interviews applicants who may come from anywhere in the country, information about them is verified and submitted to HUD for final decision.

The residents have their own Residents' Association, which discusses problems and plans activities. Residents may set up their own gardens, and transportation is provided twice a week to the village, and once a month to the nearest malls. Many of the residents have lived locally, and so maintain ties with churches and other groups. While the manager showed me apartments, she warmly greeted residents in her lilting Irish accent and especially gave attention to those people she was worried about or who needed to submit documentation for their annual HUD recertification. The resident's newsletter rightfully describes Wells Manor as

"An Independent Living Community Based on 'Respect for the Individual'."

CO-HOUSING

One of my friends told me that I must meet Ruth, a friend of hers whom she had known through the cooperative movement, and who now because of severe physical disability lives in the Fellowship Community, a very special kind of institution which I will discuss later on in the book. For years, Ruth had been intensely interested and involved in cooperative housing and cooperative communities, in which people either share one house and all of its responsibilities, or are part of a community in which the residents own their own homes but also share ownership of common land and perhaps a central building.

Cooperative communities are not a new concept, for during the 1930's and after World War II there were a number of such developments in the New York metropolitan area that attracted people who were particularly interested in promoting community through non-violent social change. Many of these people were active in the civil rights movement and in pacifist organizations.

Ruth was interested in developing shared housing for the purpose of saving money, but also for promoting community. In 1979 she bought a large house near her workplace, which she and her two children shared for almost twenty years with other people. It started with one couple and their child, and totaled 55 different people over the years. Ruth had a dual role of both owner and member of the cooperative. All of the residents shared responsibilities: financial, cooking, cleaning, "and to make it a good place to live." People were found through word of mouth, through bulletin boards, the cooperative movement and pacifist organizations. Ruth met with prospective residents, but ultimately, the whole group living in the home voted on whether the applicant would be a good candidate. Residents pooled their money for food, ate together and had weekly meetings to work out procedures and problems. This was an "intentional" community where people shared work and meals. The experience was meaningful enough so that some residents who left Ruth's cooperative returned after several years, and in the years since there have been reunions with old residents. Even though Ruth still owns the home and some cooperative members still live there, and she occasionally calls meetings with them, she knows that she should sell the house, now that she is living elsewhere. But selling is a wrenching prospect. In keeping with her idealism, she would like to sell to a non-profit group. Actually the second time I saw her, she thought she had found just the group she wanted in her house, which made it much easier for her to break her ties with her beloved co-op.

The *Boston Globe* on November 30,1997, and on March 26,1998 reported on the co-housing movement in the Boston area, where it is very popular. There are waiting lists for already established communities, and one Watertown architectural firm opened a special office to help co-housing groups get started. The current concept of co-housing is modeled after the 1960's Danish *Bofoellesskabers,* or "living communities," built in reaction to the "social sterility and isolating architecture of post-World War II suburban development."[2] A number of people, particularly in urban areas, say that they were attracted to co-housing because of a feeling of isolation and loneliness, and a strong desire to belong and be committed to a community. The usual co-housing design is a cluster of townhouses or free-standing houses with a

---

[2] William A. Davis, "Instant Community. In The East Coast's First Urban CO-Housing Project, 85 Cambridge Residents Will Share Space and Ideals," *Boston Globe,* 3/26/98.

common building centrally located for meetings and meals. The design is pedestrian oriented with parking spaces outside of the clusters and walkways and play areas inside to make the development safe for children. In the Boston area, where housing is generally very costly, townhouses in the co-housing developments can cost $120,000, and custom-built colonials $300,000; in a Cambridge, Massachusetts development, studios sold for about $85,000, and townhouses for $390,000 in the late 1990's. Generally in Massachusetts and elsewhere, groups have difficulty finding available and affordable land, sometimes because of zoning problems, or because the neighbors do not want co-housing, which they see as "radical," or as creating potential traffic problems.

The following are examples of co-housing that I visited. I decided to give a description of all three projects because each one has a distinct character.

Simeon Center

Co-Housing is now increasingly intergenerational. Simeon Center is one such group; it specifically advertises itself as intergenerational, though actually most of the people who have already committed themselves to it are over 65. The Center, which started its planning in 1992, is associated with a Rudolph Steiner community in rural Columbia County in upstate New York. The Steiner communities which originated in Europe are based on the teachings of Rudolph Steiner, an Austrian philosopher, who developed systems of education, agriculture and aesthetics. (See Chapter V. for a more extensive description.) The communities are mostly self-sustaining and include their own schools.

The Simeon plan calls for seven, three unit clusters of townhouses surrounding a common house that will contain shops, a library, child care rooms, guest rooms and an office. Residents will have the option of sharing meals in the common house. In 1998, prices for condos with 900 square feet were $114,885, which is a high figure for that county, and the young people are finding it hard to make the financial commitment.

It's a lovely setting, however, and the connection to the Steiner community is a plus. Harlemville is a very stable, settled community of farmers, teachers and professionals, who do organic farming, have a well known produce and bakery store, and operate a Rudolf Steiner school. The Simeon Center land will be owned by a Community Land Trust, and condominium ownership will be provided for each residence, including a share of all common elements such as the Common House and other facilities. As with most of the co-housing groups, the Simeon Center wishes to provide the care and concern once provided by extended families. It specifies in its brochure that in joining the community, people commit themselves to giving assistance to their neighbors.

CANTINE ISLAND CO-HOUSING

Just across the Hudson River from the Simeon Center is a mostly completed co-housing development in Saugerties, New York. Saugerties is an old conservative Dutch town, which is lately getting an overflow of New-Age people from neighboring Woodstock, the adjoining town; the contrasting life styles make the town especially interesting. With only 12 households, Cantine Island is smaller than most co-housing developments, but its members hope to add two or three houses. It started in the early 1990's and has an interesting history. The property was donated by a wealthy woman whose husband was interested in Aikido martial arts, and whose original desire was to see the land used for an Aikido center. This did not work out, but the owner's stipulation in donating the property was that it would not be sold piecemeal or to a developer, and eventually the original settlers came upon the idea of co-housing. The owner approved, as long as there were to be no more than around twelve houses, in order to preserve the integrity of the land.

Even though the land had been donated, it took Cantine Island a long time to reach the construction stage. They struggled to attract people through ads, posters, booths at fairs, slide shows and open houses, and, of course, word of mouth, but it was difficult to get people to commit. The resident I talked to who had been involved with the project from almost the beginning felt the cost of $130,000-$190,000 for the houses was on the low side, but too pricey for the area. In 1998, there were 18 adults and 10 children among 12 households, with a number of single adult households. The adult age spread was from about 38 to 66. The homes are modular, six of them free standing, and six built as three pairs. Each house was owned fee simple by paying cash or by securing a mortgage. The front yards are small; the back yards give a little privacy. When I last saw it the total construction still was not finished, as the common house had not yet been built. Parking was separated from the housing to provide safe space for walking and playing. Residents will have to pay $50,000 for shares, which will cover professional fees and the common house and land for two or three additional houses. A homeowner's monthly fee is about $100 to cover the cost of insurance, plowing, maintenance of the parking lot, and utilities for the common house. When the development was looking for membership, people could join initially for $40.00, which gave them a packet and three months' membership; with this they were expected to come to meetings, to join committees and contribute to the project as "participating members." At the end of three months, people could fill out full membership forms and make their application to a local bank for a mortgage. If members did not approve of an applicant, their dissatisfaction had to be resolved through meetings.

Before construction began in 1997, there were many disagreements over design and money, resulting in a number of members leaving. In reaching a vote on an issue, whether a new membership application or an issue of design, an attempt is made for a consensus vote. If consensus is not reached with three separate votes, then the meeting can go to a majority vote. My informant told me that in the eight years since she has been involved in the project the co-op never had to go to a majority vote. She said, "the process of doing co-housing is a powerful growth experience, but very taxing. You have to be willing to give it your whole life during the development phase!"

Sonora Co-Housing

Another co-housing group I visited was the Sonora Co-Housing in Tucson. I was particularly interested to know whether, as with the Boston groups, urban co-housing groups are able to attract prospective members more readily than those groups in more rural areas. The Tucson group has a web site, advertises in the newspaper and over public radio, and uses all of the other methods already mentioned. Every Sunday, they have an open house on the property site, at which time they give a slide show, answer questions, and find out a little about the people who are attending the open house. In September 1998 they bought their land consisting of almost five city acres in a modest neighborhood, and by the following winter had already sold 26 of the planned 36 units. This was the 70% needed for the builder to be able to get a loan of $5,000,000 with which to start the project. The neighborhood is convenient to the University and other central locations, with bus service in all directions. The units are clustered with nice views of the Catalina Mountains. Parking spaces are on the perimeters and winding pedestrian walkways and "gathering" nodes are located throughout the property.

There is an area for an organic vegetable garden, another for a meditation grove and space for a swimming pool.

Both the visitors at the open house we attended and the investors were obviously environmentally conscious, as there was a good deal of discussion about the construction of the houses. At first, the investors had wanted to use straw bale construction, but there were not enough large straw bale production teams available to work on a project this size. So recycled steel was to be used with the roofs made of corrugated iron to provide easy runoff in some of the sudden wicked summer rainstorms you can get in the desert. There was a great deal of discussion about the placement of windows as Tucson was still undergoing 100 degree weather in October, and windows on the west side in such a climate let in unbearable heat. We were assured that the main windows would face north and south. The units range from 650 square feet to 1600 square feet, are from one to four bedrooms, and will sell for $85,000 to $140,000 a unit. Because space is left on the land for so many different purposes, 60 % of the total cost is for other than construction of the individual homes: purchase of the land, hookups, burying of the electrical and telephone lines, and, of course for the building of the common house where communal meals, meetings and social gatherings will be held.

As we sat there at the open house, we all were asked to give biographical information. Most of the people were professionals, many associated with the university, others were writers, artists and craftspeople. Those who had small children wanted a safe place and ready playmates for them, as well as a diverse group of adults as role models. Many of the single people, who owned homes already in the city, spoke of a need for community and an opportunity to know their neighbors better than they could in their present neighborhoods. Both the young couples and the retirees were looking forward to the intergenerational character of the community. Sonora Housing, now built, is a lively, idealistic, committed group of people, who had many of the problems that other co-housing groups had, but were able to move toward construction and settlement much faster.

For all their differences, the co-housing communities have many things in common. Environmental issues are a main concern of all of the groups; therefore, more open space is used, making the cost of construction higher. For that reason, co-housing is apt to attract mostly white middle class professionals, who can afford to buy the land and the houses. All of the groups were struggling, but some more so. All of them lost people along the way because of disagreements, lack of commitment, or personal reasons necessitating a move away from the community. Also, trying to get consensus on vital votes can be very difficult. Yet a number of people I spoke to said such struggles made for individual growth and a greater appreciation of what a group is all about. It would seem as if the urban co-housing developments are able to attract investors much faster, probably because there is much more disengagement and loneliness in cities, and so many single people there are searching for a caring community. Admittedly, many times people move to suburban and rural areas just to gain privacy, and people who really cherish privacy would not be happy in a co-housing development. However, the opportunity for seniors to live in such idealistic communities is very exciting. This is a housing choice that provides close contact with younger adults and children, all three generations benefiting from familial type relationships, in an age when generations can be so widely separated.

RETIREMENT COMMUNITIES

In 1959, the United States Department of Housing and Urban Development (HUD) made available federal funds for the construction of retirement communities that would provide age-restricted housing for senior citizens. Such housing had to provide recreation and verify that at least one of each housing unit's occupants was at least 55 years old. Children under the age of 18 were not allowed as permanent residents. An amendment to the Fair Housing Act of 1968 exempted "housing for older persons" from the act's prohibitions against discrimination because of familial status provided it included the following requirements:

—At least 80% of the housing units must be occupied by at least one person who is 55 years of age or older.

—The housing must provide facilities and services designed to meet the physical and social needs of older persons.

—The owner or manager of the housing must publish and adhere to policies and procedures, which demonstrate the intent to provide housing for people 55 and older.

Theoretically, 80% of a residential area can be owned by people younger than 55, but the residences can only be considered housing for older persons if at least one resident of a unit is 55 or older. In other words, the residence could be owned by a non-resident under 55 but would have to be leased and occupied by someone 55 or older. In Green Valley, Arizona, one of the early retirement communities built in 1964, there are now 69 age-restricted developments and about 29,000 residents with as much as one third of the population part-time residents. The major real estate developer in this unincorporated geographical area is now offering 20% of new development housing to people 45 or older. However, when that housing is resold, it must be sold to a buyer who can insure that one of the residents will be at least fifty-five.

In the 1960's and 1970's retirement communities were built in the warmer areas of the country such as Florida and the Southwest where land was plentiful and the climate was more attractive to older people. Now such communities are mushrooming in all areas of the country, warm and cold. Those people who do not wish to relocate from a particular area still may choose to move into a retirement community to take advantage of the amenities it offers.

Usually, housing is more affordable in these retirement communities and people feel safer isolated from urban problems or behind secure gates. Another reason people choose to live there is because there are no children. They want an uncluttered, tidy community without the noise that goes with having more than one generation living in a neighborhood. Retirement towns are homogeneous, one-class communities.

Such communities often resist incorporation and the responsibilities it entails. For instance, Green Valley, Arizona has had a vote for incorporation come unsuccessfully before the voters four different times. The residents who were more opposed to incorporation were afraid of increased taxes; others said that they were tired of being involved in complicated governmental structures and just wanted to spend their last years taking it easy. Leisure World in Laguna Hills, California a retirement community that was built in 1964 when Green Valley was, but is a little more than half its size, also went through several unsuccessful attempts to incorporate. Finally in 1999, it voted to incorporate as a city. The impetus for such a vote was the threat of a proposed nearby airport which the voters felt they could fight more effectively as a city.

There are many good things to be said for retirement communities. Housing is designed for the elderly-mostly on one level, with doors wide enough to accommodate wheelchairs, and often with built-in grab-bars in bathrooms and sidewalk ramps for easy accessibility of wheelchairs and other conveyances. There is also a variety of recreational activities of all sorts, such as golf courses, swimming pools and exercise rooms; it is often the recreational life that will draw people to a retirement community rather than the housing alone. Many seniors decide to take up new hobbies, learn new subjects, hone some skill they already have, or pursue an intellectual interest now that they have the time to do so. In Green Valley, where there are many retired teachers and professors, the recreation association will help them set up courses. It is especially interesting to take classes where there is free discussion, as the participants enrich it with varied life experiences. Green Valley residents for the most part agree that they have never been so busy as they are presently and that such an active life style helps keep them young.

Generally, in retirement communities, residents are economically comfortable, physically well and busy and happy. However, things are not always so rosy and problems may be hidden. Remember, this is a generation that has been fiercely self-sufficient, that lived through the Depression, made sacrifices during World War II, raised itself economically during the post war years and saw that its children had an even better life than it had. Though couples twenty-five years ago were able to retire on the husband's small Social Security benefits with perhaps a small pension and maybe a small nest egg, they might not have realized that the wife would probably survive her husband into her nineties. More often than not, the pension does not survive the husband, the nest egg has been spent long ago and the social security benefits remain small. This may mean that the widow cannot afford the diet or medicines she needs, or the electrical bill when the temperature goes over 120 degrees as it can in the southwest, or sundry other necessities. She may be too proud to ask for help from family if there is any, from neighbors or friends or from social agencies. So, in a community like Green Valley, she becomes part of the hidden poor concealing her problems behind closed doors. In 1996, I heard Hal Myers, the Executive Director of the Green Valley Assistance Services give a talk entitled "If Everyone in Green Valley Is Rich, Then Why Is Your Neighbor Eating Catfood?" The title was chosen as a result of a telephone call to his agency from a supermarket reporting that one of its regular customers who had no cat was buying only cat food. The agency's social worker found that the woman was not buying the cat food from choice but because she was poor and was too ashamed to ask for help. But in such a community, store clerks and neighbors do keep an eye on such people and tactfully give help where needed or call the appropriate agencies in town.

As well as social agencies, there are many grass roots organizations that give concrete help, informal networks that keep an eye on people and many churches and synagogues that are very active in providing needs in the community. In Green Valley, the Green Valley Assistance Services, along with the churches in the community, has developed the Interfaith Volunteer Corps to provide respite care, light home maintenance, shopping, meal preparation and friendly visiting among other services to those people who need these services. There is no charge for the services of the volunteers. In November 1998, the Arizona Governor's Council on Aging announced that it was going to introduce in the legislature a "Gatekeeper Program." This project would train key people in local communities such as mailmen, meter readers and others familiar with people on a block to call a specific telephone number to report any suspicions they may have about residents.

Arizona continues to be a prime retirement destination for many people. On October 3, 1998, the Arizona Republic, a Phoenix newspaper had a feature article on retirement communities that emphasized that developers are selling a lifestyle more than they are selling a home. Retirees now make up more than twenty percent of the population of Arizona. Developers are aggressively pursuing the "active adult" market: those retirees who are well enough to play golf very frequently and who also wish to spend their time doing so. Therefore more of the big developers are putting up active adult communities with such amenities as golf courses, tennis courts and swimming pools. The news article mentions thirteen large retirement communities around Phoenix that have been or are in the process of being built. Such communities represent nine percent of the housing market.

The first of the Phoenix area retirement communities, Sun City, was built in 1960 by Del Webb, who has continued to develop other Sun City communities across the sun belt and even recently in the Chicago area for those retirees who wish to remain near family and old friends. Sun City, northwest of Phoenix, has twenty-one thousand residences, about forty-two thousand homeowners, and about four thousand renters. It has all of the usual amenities, but also a symphony orchestra, an art museum, an outdoor Sun Bowl for entertainment, twenty-one shopping centers, a four hundred bed general hospital, the largest cancer hospital in the state, and the largest Alzheimer's research center in the world.

An ABC News program on retirement communities on December 8, 1998, stressed that an increasing number of them are being built in college towns, where the college or colleges allow seniors to take courses along with the regular students. The intergenerational mixture is stimulating to both age groups. Some alumnae return to their college towns to live in a retirement community, and consequently end up with even more of an incentive to endow their college. This means that the partnership between the college and the retirees is of benefit to everyone.

The Summer 1998 issue of *Consumer's Digest* contains an article on twenty-five of the best retirement communities in the country, including Green Valley. Most of them are in warm states because that is where most retirees settle if they decide to move out of state, but there is one in Bloomington, Indiana, another in Durango, Colorado, a third in Boise, Idaho, all three cold states in the winter months. There are also several in Oregon and Washington. For the most part, they are located in small towns where the pace is more relaxed and cost of living low and where there may be a university. These are all communities where you can get acceptable housing for between eighty and a hundred thousand dollars. They point out that although Florida, Arizona and California remain the most popular states for retirement, people are now retiring at an earlier age and therefore are choosing to settle in communities for many more reasons than just the comfort that older retirees are seeking.

Sometimes some of the best retirement communities have not kept up with the changing demographics of the aging population. With medical advances and changing life styles, people are living much longer than they did in the sixties when the first retirement communities were built. Because of extended age, residents need even more amenities to help keep them as independent as possible, or at least they need the community to include assisted living facilities for them to move into when they cannot maintain complete independence. The following community has apparently not kept up wholly with the needs of its aging residents.

LEISURE WORLD

In Laguna Hills, California, Leisure World, one of seven Leisure Worlds in the United States, has been operating since 1964. It now has more than eighteen thousand residents with an average age of seventy-six living in 12,736 cooperative and condominium housing units on over two thousand acres. According to newspaper ads in 1999, prices ranged from about sixty thousand for a two bedroom, two bath cooperative, to the upper three hundred thousand dollar level for a three bedroom, two bath manor home. Monthly fees range from three hundred to five hundred dollars, which include most recreational activities; in addition, the Golf Course and Equestrian Center charge user fees. Leisure World is a gated community with very strict twenty-four hour security measures taken to screen people who drive through. There is a free bus system with fifteen buses that drive through the complex from 8 a.m. to 6 p.m. to transport people to nearby shopping centers and a shuttle bus from 6 p.m. to 11:30 p.m. There are more than two hundred and thirty-five Leisure World clubs and organizations and one hundred and forty-five classes offered there by the local community college. In addition, trips are taken to Los Angeles museums and cultural events. This is an attractive settlement and a lively one. On one of my visits to Laguna Hills in 1986, I noticed some of its residents picketing on the beach regarding some political issue.

Betty Friedan, in The Fountain of Age talks a great deal about Leisure World, since her own mother lived there for thirty years. She felt that there was a great deal of denial of age at Leisure World, but also an obsession with it. Several residents she interviewed said that the establishment at Leisure World still sees it as a center for vital, swinging adults, and refuses to face the realities that the more elderly people there might need services other than the busy activities. These additional services might include panic buttons, neighborhood teams to keep an eye on the more frail residents, or a day care center for those with disabilities. There is no facility at Leisure World to take care of residents who need more care, and there, as in other retirement communities, there are a lot of lonely, frail people hiding behind closed doors. Betty Friedan's own mother had to leave after thirty years because of increasing heart problems that left her too debilitated for the resources at Leisure World.

Gays and Retirement Communities

Because most retirement communities are economically, socially, and racially homogeneous, with conservative social attitudes that go back to the fifties, it is my impression that homosexuals and lesbians would not feel comfortable in them. After years of openness, many homosexuals who have moved to such communities or to assisted living or nursing home facilities, feel very alone and fearful of condemnation. Therefore, there is a new move to build retirement communities and assisted living facilities especially for gays and lesbians. Of course, these communities and facilities would also have to be open to non-homosexuals, so that they could not be accused of discrimination. Cities that are planning gay retirement communities are Fort Lauderdale, Florida, Boston, and the Palm Springs area.

Mobile Home Communities

A very good place to look for affordable and attractive housing is in mobile home estates, which are increasingly being used for full or part-time living, particularly in the warmer climates. Mobile home parks are not the same as trailer parks, which are disparaged by many people. Remember the remark made by James Carville, advisor to President Clinton, using the phrase "trailer trash," in conjunction with a certain female ex-friend of Mr. Clinton? These relatively new mobile home estates are as attractive as homes in many tract developments, but are far less expensive.

Mobile home developments were preceded by trailer parks for what was then called trailers used by temporary or itinerant workers during the depression of the 1930's. They then became temporary homes for war workers in factories during World War II. After the war, during the 1960's, the trailers were changed in design so that there were two uses for them. Some continued to be used as recreational vehicles, while others which were widened to 10 or 12 feet, then were made into double and triple widths and put on concrete foundations and began to look like split level or Cape Cod style development houses. These houses then become movable only when they were delivered to the mobile home park from the factory.

Chiori Santiago, the author of a June 1998 Smithsonian magazine article entitled <u>House Trailers</u>, traveled over the country to look at mobile home communities. One, Cooperative Santa Elena, in Soledad, California, is now owned by farmworkers who, after being tenants there, bought it in the 1970s having felt mistreated by its owner. Each household pays $150 a month rental to the cooperative, and takes a good deal of pride in its property. Another rather more luxurious community, <u>Tahitian Terrace</u>, near Santa Monica, California, charges $1000 a month to its residents, who are largely Hollywood artists and writers.

The community that both Ms. Santiago and Betty Freidan, author of <u>The Fountain of Age</u>, liked a great deal was <u>Trailer Estates</u>, in Bradenton, Florida, near Sarasota, which did not become age restricted until 1993. There are 1400 families in the community, which is large enough to have its own post office, firehouse, volunteer ambulance corps, marina, and a very busy clubhouse. In the 1980s when Betty Friedan visited, 65% of the residents were married, 29% were widowed; the mean age was 70, and one third were over 75. Three quarters of the residents had a high school education or less, one quarter had some college or a graduate degree. They mostly came from small towns or urban areas of the Midwest, where they had owned their own homes. They were an exceedingly active group of people, participating in karate classes, crafts and sewing groups, bike riding or using a kind of tricycle with a basket set on the handlebars for shopping. They were often off by day for garage sales or consignment sales, picnics, and at night dancing at a local ballroom, or at the nearby Gulf of Mexico to watch the sunset. The homeowners led all of the activities, and the Recreation Director was also a volunteer resident; in fact, 99% of the work was voluntary. In the 80's, the cost of the homes and land was between $25,000 and $45,000

I talked with one of several people I know who live in a particularly attractive mobile home age-restricted (55 years and older) community of 150 homes on the west side of Tucson, high enough to have spectacular views of the sky and the city at sunset. My friend found the community in 1988 through a realtor who specializes in mobile home communities. She and her husband wanted to be out of the city, have a good view, and live in a park-like setting. Aesthetics was an important consideration. At that time, they were still living in the East, and were in Tucson only two or three months of the year. Their first home cost them only $15,000. Six years later, after they had decided to live full time in Tucson, they bought a larger 24 foot double wide home in the same park with much more property. It had been there for twenty-five years, and needed work, so they were able to buy it for $25,000. They had the walls redone with plaster-board, added a third bedroom and workroom, and landscaped the property themselves with desert plants and stones. In the living room they have hung Mexican rugs and used Mexican pottery and lamps they bought in Oaxaca on one of the many Elder Hostel trips they take. They rent the land that the mobile home is on for $270 a year, and pay a mobile home tax to the county of $250 a year. The development has a swimming pool, a hot tub, a clubhouse where crafts and exercise classes are held, movies, Wednesday morning breakfasts and periodic pot-luck dinners. There are both a library and a laundry in the clubhouse. Many of the residents are single, many are retired teachers, and one third of to one half of those who live there live elsewhere for half of the year.

According to the Smithsonian article, mobile home estates are affordable, neat and homogeneous and offer "the promise of suburbia to those who cannot afford to move from the city." But for people who wish to remain in the city, with all of its conveniences and cultural opportunities, mobile home living is an affordable, attractive alternative to apartment living, or more expensive housing. Betty Friedan found great sociability and vitality in the community of mobile homes she visited. According to her, residents "opted for a moving life, not (for) care. Death happened (there) in the midst of life."[3]

SUMMARY

For seniors who want a safe, quiet life without children, and who wish to be separated from the problems of urban

---

3. Betty Freidan, *The Fountain of Age*, (New York, Simon & Schuster, 1993)

areas such as crime, smog, traffic and overcrowding, the retirement communities would be the right place. Such places are built with the needs of senior citizens in mind, with many physical amenities and recreational activities available. Housing can be very inexpensive, simple and comfortable. However, these communities can be very isolated from the rest of the world, both physically and psychologically, and social attitudes can be extremely conservative. They may be located in suburban or rural areas or behind gates, which only adds to the "ghettoization" of the elderly. They are apt to be exceptionally quiet and dark at night, and sometimes one has the feeling that an awful lot of people are just sitting around waiting to die.

Many seniors do not want to be isolated geographically or in age-restricted neighborhoods. They feel a strong need for inter-generational contact, for ethnic diversity, for proximity to museums and other cultural activities, to universities, and to centers of government. They want to be involved in the "real world" and to feel that they have a vital part in it. They feel that this involvement helps keep them young and healthy. They therefore choose to remain at home in the towns or cities where they have already lived or choose to go into intergenerational communities, including co-housing such as those described in this chapter. Or if they choose to move to more comfortable climates, they deliberately choose housing or apartment developments that have children.

Many seniors do not wish to move from their old neighborhoods, either because they cannot afford to or because their ties to community and friends are too strong to wrench themselves away. Simpler housing such as apartments or condos can be found that make daily living easier for seniors, or houses can be adapted to their physical needs. If one cannot afford to make the necessary changes, there are community programs to do so for seniors with limited incomes, and the local Office of the Aging should be able to direct you to such programs.

The Office of the Aging in your county should be your primary resource for all local services for senior citizens. Please refer to the Resources section for national resources, which in turn can direct you to more local ones.

APPENDIX I:
SENIOR SERVICES IN DUTCHESS COUNTY, NEW YORK.

The following is an example of the services that can be offered in a county such as Dutchess County, New York. You may wish to contact your Area Office of the Aging to find out what services are offered in your area. See the Appendix at the rear of the book for the address of all state Offices of the Aging.

1.HOME MAINTENANCE & REPAIR SERVICES.

This includes basic maintenance, upkeep, weatherization, and ways of making the home more secure, accessible and accident free. The Office of the Aging can direct a client to local groups that do rehabilitation and repair. The following kinds of modification may enable a senior to remain in his or her own home: ramps, railings, proper lighting for exterior accessibility, a downstairs bedroom and a bathroom with grab bars that can accommodate a wheelchair. The program that covers this is the Senior Citizens Owner Occupied Rehabilitation program through the Department of Planning, which offers loans up to $15,000. If a loan cannot be repaid, the county takes a lien on the property.

In addition, there is a volunteer program in the county, which is sponsored by trusts, unions, banks, IBM, other industries, churches and some alumni groups. On the last Saturday of April as many as six hundred volunteers rehabilitate homes of lower income people, particularly the aged and disabled, to make them safer and more comfortable. Funding, which is tax deductible, comes from individuals, foundations, clubs, service groups and religious groups. Another group in the county, one of thirty-eight Centers for Living in New York State funded by the State Department of Education, provides architectural barrier consultation to people with disabilities. More than 75% of its staff is disabled.

2. REVERSE MORTGAGES:

The Office of the Aging can counsel people on reverse mortgaging, which is a new concept not yet available everywhere. With this loan you dip into the equity that you already have in the house that you own, which must be free and clear, or have a low outstanding mortgage, and you must be at least 62 years old. What you claim as equity cannot exceed $155,200. If you should consider this plan, it is advisable to contact a lender to find out whether you can take the money in a lump sum, in a line of credit, or in monthly payments. The amount you can get depends partly on your age; the older you are, and the larger the value of your home, the more money you can get. Out of the loan, you are allowed to pay for renovations to the house and/or home care. Interest rates are generally higher than on conventional mortgages, so you would need to weigh the plan against your financial needs. Before anyone can receive a reverse mortgage, he or she must receive what is called a "certificate of counseling," which can be done by the Office of the Aging, or a referral can be made to another resource for the counseling. The reverse mortgage is a business arrangement involving fees and interest, and if appreciation on the home occurs, you may have to share with the lender a percentage of the home appreciation during the term of the loan. The loan need not be repaid until the recipient dies or permanently moves from the home.

3. REAL ESTATE TAX EXEMPTION:

There can be up to a 50% real estate tax reduction to those people over sixty-five with low incomes. The income limit varies with the community, but there is no limit on assets allowed. There is also a Veteran's Property Tax Exemption; with both of these, property owners should check with their town office to see whether they qualify.

4. HEAP: HOME ENERGY ASSISTANCE PROGRAM

Under this program, financial assistance with bills and emergency help is available; even a furnace can be replaced at no cost to the client. There are income eligibility requirements but no limit required in assets.

5. WEATHERIZATION REFERRAL AND PACKAGING PROGRAM (WRAP)

If a person is eligible for the HEAP program, he or she is eligible for this. The Office of the Aging will make referrals for this help.

6. NUTRITION SITES

There are ten in the county, with additional ones located at senior citizen housing sites. Good nutritious meals are provided at a nominal charge along with social activities. Nutrition counseling is provided with a nutrition newsletter.

7. MEALS ON WHEELS

This is a volunteer service for homebound seniors which delivers daily nutritional meals for a nominal charge. A home visit is made to determine need and eligibility.

8. FOOD STAMPS, S.S.I. AND MEDICAID

These are available if the client's Social Security payment is under a certain amount. Under the Food Stamps Program, coupons are used as cash for buying food in stores, to pay for home delivered meals, and for meals in Senior Citizen Centers or Nutritional Sites. Also, limited income Medicare eligible individuals may be able to have Medicaid cover their Medicare monthly premiums, deductibles and co-insurance. For income eligible individuals, Medicaid can also be used to pay for health care services not provided by Medicare, such as home care, prescription drugs, dentistry, eyeglasses, and hearing aids.

Under S.S.I., monthly payments may be made to low income disabled or blind people over 65 over and above what they already receive under regular Social Security and other income.

9. Are you O.K?. Program

This is a particularly helpful program offered through the Sheriff's Office to people who live alone. Every day at the same time, a computerized call goes out to a subscriber of the program. If the person fails to answer after fifteen minutes, emergency data already given by that person is retrieved, and the Sheriff's Office then dispatches a designated friend or family member, or a police officer to check on the person.

10. Personal Emergency Response System (pers)

This a program arranged through the Office of the Aging. The client wears a pendant around his or her neck; in an emergency, a button on the pendant is pressed to summon help. There is an initial installation cost, and a monthly rental.

11. Lifeline Telephone Service:

Telephone services are provided to low income families of any age. Senior applicants must be receiving any of the following services: Food Stamps, Medicaid, SSI, HEAP, Veteran's Disability Pension or Veteran's Surviving Spouse Pension.

12. EPIC (Elder Pharmaceutical Insurance Coverage)

A New York State drug program for low income residents who are 65 or over. Premium costs and deductibles are determined by income and marital status; payments are determined by the cost of the prescription.

13. MASS TRANSIT REDUCED FARE on all bus lines for those 65 and over.

14. DIAL A RIDE

Eligibility for this program is based on age (60 or over) or disability. The client must register and receive a card and always reserve a ride in advance. The service is funded by participating townships. There are a number of other transportation services listed on a brochure put out by the Office of the Aging.

15. TRANSPORTATION FOR MEDICAL APPOINTMENTS

These are provided through the Red Cross and various religious and charitable organizations.

16. SENIOR CITIZENS RENT INCREASE EXEMPTION.

This program exempts rent controlled, rent stabilized, or Mitchell Lama middle-income housing as well as hotel tenants from certain rent increases. Clients must be income eligible, though there is no required limit on assets.

17. VETERANS BENEFITS:

Pensions are provided under the U.S. Department of Veterans' Affairs for low income and disabled veterans; additional benefits are health care and prescription drugs, home loans, disability compensation, burial benefits, etc.

18. LEGAL SERVICES FOR THE ELDERLY.

The Office of the Aging contracts with a private attorney to provide part time legal services for residents 60 or over. Although there is no financial eligibility requirement, the service is intended for those senior citizens who would not otherwise be able to afford the services of an attorney. Emphasis is on legal advice regarding problems that result in an immediate threat to income, shelter, patients' rights and health care, advance directives, and assistance on Medicaid and Medicare eligibility, etc. The Office of the Aging also has a list of law firms that provide legal assistance pro bono or at a reduced rate.

19. HOME CARE NEEDS ASSESSMENT AND CASE MANAGEMENT through CASA, the home care division of the Office of the Aging.

Chapter V

You Better Get In While You Still Can!
Institutional Living

Even though most people prefer to live independently, there often comes a time when, because of changed conditions or circumstances, they or their families decide that they no longer can completely manage on their own. There are of course those people who are so sick that they need twenty-four hour nursing care or the rehabilitative services that are offered in a nursing home. Also, there are increasingly lonely people who decide to enter a less supervised level of institutional care, where they would find companionship more easily with people of the same age and in the same circumstances. People also enter institutions when they need more supervision because of increasing physical or mental frailty, for example early stage Alzheimer's patients who may wander and then are unable to find their way home. Some people are unable to get their own meals, do simple household tasks, take their own medication or keep themselves clean. Usually, these people do not have a family nearby to help them, or the family is too preoccupied with its own responsibilities to take on the constant care of an elderly parent. There are occasionally families where a serious rift has taken place resulting in no contact at all. There are also people, usually widows or widowers, who enter continuing care facilities while they are still relatively well, anticipating that they will need greater supervision later. They wish the security of knowing that when they need assisted living or nursing home care, they will remain with their friends in the institution that has become their home.

Whatever the level of care, if the applicant is competent, he or she should be fully involved in making the decision to move toward institutional care and in the choice of the particular senior residence, assisted living facility, continuing care facility or nursing home. This should include visiting the institutions, if that is possible. Unless there is very serious illness that necessitates an immediate move, it is often better to wait until the person has had time to weigh the reality of the situation and the various choices so that he or she is more cooperative and psychologically ready to make the change. This chapter will discuss the various levels of institutional care, their cost, the services one should expect to receive and some examples of very good institutions.

Adult Homes & Assisted Living Facilities

Unlike nursing homes, adult homes or assisted living facilities are not medical facilities. Henceforth, I will use the term assisted living facilities to cover both. They do not have nurses or doctors on staff, as residents in adult homes do not need the close medical supervision that nursing home patients do. The difference between adult homes and assisted living facilities is in the degree of assistance that the resident needs. In both of these institutions there are fewer workers than in a nursing home, because it is assumed and required in some states that adult home residents will have more ADL skills than do nursing home patients. ADL is an acronym for Activities of Daily Living, which include feeding oneself, bathing and dressing. Generally, residents are fully mobile or only dependent on a cane or walker, but even if that person is in a wheel chair, he should be able to wheel himself and to transfer himself from wheelchair to bed or toilet. In many assisted living facilities, it is expected that the residents will be mostly continent, but I would think that occasional "accidents" would not be frowned upon. From my experience, only beginning stage Alzheimer's patients can be managed in an assisted living residence as more advanced patients tend to wander and get lost. Thus, many nursing homes keep them in locked units.

The patient who does not have serious medical problems but is mildly confused does well in an assisted living facility, which provides structure, supervision, and some assistance. In these institutions, a staff member must give out medications. There must be some sort of activities program, and to hold a license, the home must meet certain standards of nutrition, cleanliness, structure and maintenance. In each state, a state agency is responsible for regular surveying to determine that residents are well cared for and that the building meets standards of cleanliness and safety; you should be able to ask to see the results of the last state survey. Your local Office of the Aging should have a list of adult homes and assisted living facilities in your area.

No decision to place a person in any institutional setting should be made without visiting the facility you are considering for yourself or a family member. A person without family should have someone visit who holds power of attorney and is responsible for that person's welfare. If it is possible and the patient is well enough he should also visit and be involved in deciding whether he wants to live in the institution.

Observe carefully as you move around the home. How does staff relate to the residents? Are they polite and respectful?

Even without actual disrespect, is staff indifferent to residents? Do staff members handle residents gently? Is the residence clean, without a strong smell of urine or disinfectant? Are rooms attractive, and are residents able to have some of their own possessions? If they are well, are residents out of bed and dressed in street clothes and are they clean and neat? Is there some sort of activities program? A schedule should be posted, and residents should have a choice to participate in activities or not. However, if you observe a roomful of residents asleep in front of a television set, you should wonder how adequate the recreational program is. Are the residents going to be congenial? I mention this because some institutions take discharged psychiatric patients whose behavior can sometimes be intimidating to more reticent, shy residents, or in other homes very confused residents are mixed with relatively alert ones. Is there a council where residents can air complaints and make suggestions, and is there a formal grievance procedure that the resident and his family are informed of?

Once the person has been placed in the assisted living facility, family and friends, especially in the beginning, should visit frequently to demonstrate that the new resident has not been abandoned and to help in the initial adjustment. Make contact with staff to find out how they see the resident adjusting. Take the resident out to lunch or shopping or to his or her home church or synagogue, so that he or she can maintain ties with the home community if he or she wishes. Continue regular contacts, and see that the resident has whatever he needs in the way of clothing and personal items. The resident's family or friends will always mean more than anyone at the residence, and there is nothing sadder than an elderly person who feels abandoned, whether this is actually true or not.

Communities in New York State have two kinds of adult homes. For instance, Dutchess County, N.Y. (see chapter IV) has 7 Adult Care Facilities, ranging from 18 beds to 175 beds, and 13 Family Type Homes with four or fewer beds. At least one of the Adult Care Facilities in the county takes psychiatric dischargees and other people with behavior problems. For contrast, another 58 bed residence that obviously was originally set up for genteel, conventional and conservative ladies still offers a very gracious life style. A woman I know, who was an outspoken political radical, was unfortunately placed by her family in this adult home. The home was lovely, but she and it were a mismatch. Because she was so different from other residents, she was teased by them, and after a period of great unhappiness had to be transferred to another facility that was less of a culture shock for her. This demonstrates how carefully a prospective residence must be looked at to decide whether it is the right place for a particular person.

Many institutions have a religious or ethnic affiliation, which appeals to some people. In Westchester County, New York, there is a Danish Home and a Swiss Home, and in Rhinebeck, New York, a Baptist Nursing Home, and Ferncliff Nursing Home on the old Astor family property, a Roman Catholic nursing home run by the Carmelite Sisters. In Brooklyn, where there is a large orthodox Jewish community, there are a number of orthodox nursing homes.

The following home is unusual in the way it fills the bill for a particular segment of the population.

Sunset Hall

Sunset Hall in Los Angeles is an example of an independent, non-profit residence for the elderly that caters to a particular group of people. The home was started 75 years ago by women from the First Unitarian Church of Los Angeles as a home for religious liberals; now it is a home for aging radicals and other free thinkers. It is a two-story stucco building with 36 apartments in a neighborhood of Central American immigrants. The residents are still very politically and intellectually active, preferring discussion groups, watching CNN news programs, and reading both the L.A. Times and the New York Times to bingo and the other usual activities found in institutions for the elderly. If they feel strongly enough about some local political concern, they will gather their wheelchairs and walkers and using the residence's van join a march in protest of or support of the cause. Issues that are still important to them are support of workers and trade unions, women's issues, and national health insurance. Residents are frequently vocal about any changes in Sunset Hall. For instance, they have objected to the raising of the fees, and to using tablecloths to muffle noise in the dining room, which they felt was a needless expense. What most distressed them was the possibility that liquor would be removed from their weekly wine and cheese party on the recommendation of a local physician. According to one of the residents, at one time, they even had a Republican resident who left, but not because of incompatible politics, but because of dissatisfaction with the food. She wanted white bread. The residents who decide what food they want served have chosen to have egg bread, rye bread and whole wheat, but no white bread.

There is room for 40 residents. Even the residents are members of the Sunset Hall organization, and help elect the Board of Directors. The staffing includes an Executive Director, office staff, caretaking staff, dietary workers, a consulting nutritionist, an activities director and a social worker who sees residents for individual and group therapy. Speakers and classes are offered, and frequent trips are made to surrounding museums and parks. Children from a local elementary school as well as college students are often at the home, and residents have participated in developing a local community garden. In 1998, the monthly rates ranged from $1,295 for a fully independent resident living in a studio apartment to $2,475 for a resident who needs personal care in a suite. The rate includes meals, housekeeping services and varying degrees of personal care. How gratifying to see a residence that so encourages continued meaningful activity and political involvement for its elderly residents, activities that help maintain the residents' sense of identity and intellectual acuity.

Many times, small homes can offer a family atmosphere more easily than can larger institutions. The following is an example of this.

Nan's Hacienda

In Sahuarita, Arizona, located just north of Green Valley, I visited Nan's Hacienda that was recommended by a friend. Actually, Nan's is four separate residences, owned independently by different family members and licensed separately. They are attractive houses with cool patios and landscaped yards located in pleasant developments. The homes were originally built as part of the development, and now there is no way of telling from the outside that they are small adult homes, with a capacity of 6 to 10 residents for each home.

Most of the residents are in single rooms, the lower paying ones in semi-private. The homes are extremely attractive, clean and homey, and the residents' rooms are individually decorated with fresh paint and good quality, pleasing furniture, draperies and bedspreads, and the residents' personal possessions, the sort of room that you would want for a family member. If the resident or his or her family is not satisfied with the decoration, they are free to change it at their own expense. All of the bathrooms have grab-bars and there are tile floors in bedrooms where incontinent residents sleep. Baths are given three days a week, and skin care for incontinent residents whenever needed. The food is home cooked, and when necessary, special diets are prepared. Each of the houses has pet cats or dogs, and some residents have brought their own animals with them to the adult home. The presence of Nan's eight year old niece with the elderly residents seemed very natural. This was the same home where a resident sat in the back yard continually stroking a pet cat sprawled on her lap. As was the cat, the resident was completely satisfied and needed no other entertainment. One of the homes had an activity room that contained a pool table and an organ; this was where a family was visiting. Two other of Nan's homes had private rooms for family visiting. In 1998, the fees ranged upward from a minimum of $1700 a month, depending on the size of the room.

In each of Nan's homes, there are a manager, a caregiver for each of the three shifts, a housekeeper and a yardman. Staff must meet state continuing education requirements, and while on duty are expected to do whatever is needed. Each of the homes has a blackboard with instructions in both English and Spanish for the care of some of the residents with special problems. Both therapists and doctors are willing to make house calls, if necessary, hospice serves residents in the facilities and a nun from the local Catholic Church comes in to give communion to Catholic residents. I noticed oxygen canisters in a closet, and was told that the state of Arizona allows the use of oxygen, allows caregivers to give injections, and allows gastric tube feedings. The attending physician must give written permission for the staff to administer medications, which are kept in a locked closet. When I was introduced to a blind resident who was alone in his room and still in bed at ten-thirty a.m., I was told that the state required a resident to be out of bed only a minimum of three hours a day. This was a man who had just previously been in a nursing home where he was aggressive, but he was also a person with an advanced degree and a professional background who seemed appreciative of some sociability.

The residents generally seemed contented, were friendly, and a number of them had a rich sense of humor. The staff seemed to treat them as if they were elderly relatives, and I suppose that this attitude is more possible in such small adult homes. Both the homes and the residents were clean and attractive, and there was no odor of either urine or disinfectant. Staff obviously cared about the residents, who appeared in turn to feel at ease with the staff. Residents generally stay there two or three years, some as long as six. One out of ten returns home, and the adult home tries to do some follow-up when residents leave.

Nan particularly likes taking care of what she calls dementia residents, but if they become too aggressive she must refer them elsewhere. She was very open and above-board with me, even discussing a recent complaint made to the state by a family of one of the residents who had an advanced bedsore. She was distressed about the complaint, knowing the power that the state has over her operation. At the same time I had the impression from reading blackboard instructions that there were a number of incontinent residents who needed skin care. It would be very difficult for one caregiver to keep up with the problems presented by so many incontinent residents. In turn, Nan told me that the local nursing homes refer to her some of their problem patients. In accordance with state law, when a resident is admitted, his or her family is told the complaint procedure, and is given the telephone number for the office of Adult Protective Services, and the Governor's Advocate for the Aging. I liked these homes very much, as did my friend, but I do feel that Arizona regulations allow a level of care in the adult homes that would not be acceptable in New York.

CONTINUING CARE RETIREMENT COMMUNITIES

As people live longer, and our economy remains healthy, all over the country there is a great demand for what is referred to as life-care or continuing care retirement communities. Over the last six months of 1998, when I was poring over newspapers every day, the New York Times featured a number of articles on the amount of building in the Northeast of such developments and facilities for senior citizens, particularly for the affluent elder population. In a New York Times article dated September 13, 1998, the following statement was made. "Diverse requirements for people age 55 and older, in various states of physical and financial health, have produced a profitable alliance between developers and health service providers, and a bewildering array of choices for customers."[1] A great many of the continuing care facilities, which provide a continuum of care from independent living to assisted care to nursing home care, are lifetime care communities, which require a large down payment and a signed contract. The contract guarantees that the resident will be cared for in the facility the rest of his or her life. Although generally a person can only enter at an independent living level, once there he or she will be given whatever level of care is needed. Of course, the presumption on the part of everyone is that if a person enters the facility pretty well physically, he or she will remain so for some time. As well as a down payment, there is also a monthly fee that covers

---

[1] Eleanor Charles, "For Affluent Elderly, An Array oif Housing Choices," N.Y.Times, September 13, 1998.

maintenance, meals, activities and administrative expenses. The monthly fee varies with the size of the apartment or suite and with the amount of care that is needed. If residents are receiving assisted living care, they are given one or two meals a day and assistance in bathing, dressing and the taking of medications. Because in many states there is a moratorium on the building of nursing homes, more assisted living facilities are being built, rather than the continuing care facilities that must include nursing home beds. For the affluent, the construction of both assisted living and continuing care facilities has suddenly become big business for profit-making developers. As a matter of fact, one developer thought that it would be feasible to build continuing care or assisted living communities every thirty miles in heavily populated areas. In addition to the for-profit facilities, there continue to be built some very good non-profit communities.

Back in the 1960's, some life-care communities that were guaranteeing that there would not be an increase in the fees went bankrupt. Even with large down payments, because people were living longer than expected, the facilities could not provide the medical benefits that they had promised. I remember a New York nursing home patient who in the sixties or seventies had given her lifetime savings as a down payment to a Florida lifetime care facility that eventually went bankrupt. She and other patients in the Florida facility had to leave without receiving any refund on their down payments, a most traumatic event in their lives. In New York State, such bankruptcies led to regulations that made it very difficult for profit-making developers to feel they wanted to build. The state also requires that revenues be set high enough to cover the cost of extended care, including possible future nursing home care, making the monthly fees more than most middle class people can afford. In addition, for many years the New York

State Department of Health has been very careful to approve new nursing home beds only if there is a demonstrated need for them.

Even non-profit homes anywhere are generally not promising that fees will remain the same, and all of the communities I visited refunded a percentage of the down payment should a resident leave or die. I would strongly advise anyone who is considering entering either a continuing care or an assisted living facility to have an attorney review all of the financial arrangements, especially the contract.

I visited four continuing care facilities, all non-profit, three of them with Quaker affiliation. All four are well known for their exceptionally high quality of care.

Duncaster

In the summer of 1997, a friend invited my husband and me to visit her at Duncaster, a Connecticut non-profit continuing care facility near Hartford to which she had moved a year before at the age of 69. When Joan was widowed fifteen years earlier, she had returned to upstate New York, to the home which had been owned by her family for 76 years and where she had lived as a child. Her two children and their families lived in Connecticut and Massachusetts, and she found that she had developed few close friends in her hometown, where she had not lived for more than forty years. She also felt she was too removed there from cultural activities. Although she was still active, her medical problems were such that she decided to consider a continuing care facility. There was no longer anyone living near to her whom she could call on in case of an emergency, as close friends had moved away. She also wished to live nearer to her children. She especially wanted to make the move while she was still active enough to enjoy it, and she did not wish her children to later have the burden of having to make the decision for her.

Joan invited us to have lunch with her and about six of her close Duncaster friends, who were really very charming and welcoming. Almost all of them, in trying to persuade us to consider the move, used the expression "You better get in while you still can!" This referred to the requirement in most of the facilities that you can enter only at the higher levels of functioning, independent living, and sometimes assisted living, but the caution also alluded to the reality of long waiting lists. Joan showed us her one bedroom apartment with balcony overlooking some gardens planted by first floor residents outside of their residences. She had her computer and drafting board set up in her bedroom so that she could continue to do the drafting work that she trained for several years before. The apartment had good-sized rooms for a single person, and was light. Residents on all of the floors made use of hall space outside their apartments for an overflow of beloved antiques, paintings or prints, all of which also added an individual touch.

Joan showed us the medical clinic and the nursing care section. As we toured Duncaster we met personnel and other residents and observed activities that were underway: people working in the greenhouse, others painting in the art studio, still others preparing for a play-reading, two women working in the second-hand shop, others in the library. One woman who lives across the hall from Joan was bringing in her dogs after a walk outside. For many years Joan had been a hiker and wished to continue to do so on the grounds of Duncaster. Therefore, just after she moved there, with the permission of the administration, she bushwhacked a trail in woods on the property so that people like herself and her neighbor would have a place to walk. In the previous spring, professors from the University of Hartford had given a course at Duncaster for a small charge. Joan likes the companionship and activities at Duncaster as well as the on-site medical care. She also does volunteer tutoring in an inner city school in Hartford and attends church there.

Duncaster has studio, two different sized one-bedroom apartments, and two-different sized two-bedroom apartments. In 1997, there were three refund plans for each size apartment. Plan I refunds 90% of the entrance fee at any time; Plan II refunds the entrance fee in an amount that diminishes it by 1% per month after occupancy, and Plan III refunds the entrance fee in an amount that diminishes it by 2% per month after occupancy. Therefore the entrance fee and monthly fee for a studio range from $61,400 and $1,670 for Plan III to $117,500 and $1,450 for Plan I. The largest two-bedroom apartments range from an entrance fee and monthly fee of $95,700 and $3,010 for Plan III to an entrance fee and monthly fee of $271,000 and $2,490 for Plan I. Some people have been able to combine adjoining apartments, or have chosen to rent a one or two bedroom apartment and a studio elsewhere in the complex to use as an office. The complex consists of 216 apartments housing more than 200 residents in three wings. It is located on the outskirts of Bloomfield , Connecticut, just a few miles from Hartford, a two hour drive from both Boston and New York.

Residents obviously care for and look after each other, for one friend at the lunch table asked Joan if she would drive him to his nearby town to see his stockbroker, as he can no longer drive, and people inquired frequently about residents who were not feeling well. Most of the residents had lived and worked locally and had family nearby so that they still had strong ties to the community, but they also generally seemed content with this particular kind of institution

The Kendal Continuing Care Communities

The Society of Friends has a long tradition beginning in the 19th century of caring for the elderly, and each one of their residential facilities has a Statement of Mission which follows Quaker principles and is taken seriously by both staff and residents. Great stress is placed on respect for the dignity of each resident, regardless of infirmity or frailty, and a conviction that all people have strengths to be supported and nurtured. In all of the Kendal homes, there are very high standards of care and concern. As an example, no physical restraints are ever used. A philosophy is followed in each that "dignity, autonomy, and a sense of control become more precious as older adults face emerging limitations and personal losses."

Over the years, my husband and I have visited three Quaker directed non-profit continuing care communities: Pennswood Village, in Newtown, Pennsylvania built in 1977, Kendal at Hanover, in Hanover, New Hampshire built in 1991 and Kendal at Oberlin in Oberlin, Ohio. There are eight retirement communities owned by the Kendal Corporation in Kennett Square, Pennsylvania. Pennswood and Kendal at Hanover and Oberlin have received accreditation from the Continuing Care Accreditation Commission of the American Association of Homes and Services for the Aging.

Pennswood Village is located 45 minutes from Philadelphia and 90 minutes from New York City by train, so that residents can take advantage of events in both cities. Another of its assets is that it is located next to the George School, a Quaker secondary school and near the Newtown Friends School, a Quaker elementary school, allowing for intergenerational activities. Bucks County Community College holds several courses each semester at Pennswood. Although there are 365 residents, and 252 apartments at

Pennswood, more than there are at Duncaster, the buildings are only two stories high so that one does not feel quite so overwhelmed as one does at either Duncaster or Kendal at Hanover, where there are three or four floors to a building. However, with both Pennswood and Kendal at Hanover, the size of the apartments and the fees are comparable to those at Duncaster.

We got a very comfortable feeling when we visited Pennswood in 1987, for everyone was very friendly and seemed to be "doing their own thing." At the time we visited, the big annual flower show was being held in Philadelphia. One of the ladies we met who was formerly one of the judges at the show was planning to attend it that afternoon. Before she left for Philadelphia, she was arranging flowers in one of the living rooms, having been given this assignment. We were told that another woman was off on a trip to Europe. Volunteering within the facility, but also in the outside community is encouraged in both Pennswood and at Kendal at Hanover. When we visited Pennswood in 1987, there was a twelve-year waiting list, probably not the case now, as many more Quaker continuing care residences have been built since then.

Kendal at Hanover would appear to be the elite of the elite. In the summer of 1998, we visited relatives who have lived there since shortly after it opened in 1991. Although winters are very long and very cold in Hanover, New Hampshire, the advantage of Kendal at Hanover is its closeness to Dartmouth College. The college has the Institute for Lifelong Learning, a Center for the Creative and Performing Arts, as well as an art museum and very good library. It also has The Dartmouth Hitchcock Medical Center, the largest medical facility in northern New England; associated with it are the Dartmouth Medical School and a large cancer center. Kendal at Hanover has 300 apartment units and 75 nursing units, and at the time we visited was building an Alzheimer's unit.

In keeping with the cold climate, Kendal at Hanover has an indoor garage. It also has an indoor pool, a low-impact aerobics gym, (as do the other aforementioned facilities), art studios and an excellent library that is so good that book dealers from long distances arrive early in the morning for their annual book sale. As we waited for our relatives, I noted on various bulletin boards upcoming events: a meeting on conserving the land in the area, a concert by the Hague Baroque Ensemble, good quality movies, and meetings on a variety of topics. There are chapters of Amnesty International and the World Federalists. The residents themselves plan and conduct the activities programs, act as guides to show visitors around, and volunteer in the nursing home. The residents we spoke to were very proud of and loyal to Kendal.

Kendal at Oberlin, built in 1993, is smaller, with 144 cottages, 48 apartments and 66 beds in their health center; because of the cottages, which are built in groups of four, there is a less institutional feeling. In addition, it has a day care program for the children of staff members and local citizens, which brings an intergenerational mix. Residents speak with enthusiasm of this opportunity to continue to have normal contact with children. There is also a close relationship with Oberlin College, students from which participate with Kendal residents in various educational projects.

All of the continuing care facilities that I have visited are very attractive and very similar. Residents of such communities feel great security because they know that they will be cared for during the rest of their lives without having to move. A variety of services are provided onsite;

the apartments and grounds are attractive and well maintained; housekeeping and linen services are provided, and residents may choose various types of meal plans, so that what a resident has to do is kept at a minimum. The recreational and activities programs are excellent and are certainly directed at keeping residents physically fit and intellectually stimulated. However, continuing care communities are much too expensive for the average middle class person, as both the down payments and the monthly maintenance fees are extremely high, although not unreasonable, considering what is offered. The communities are located in areas removed from the center of a city or town, and may be gated, so that one has the impression of isolated enclaves of very affluent elderly people who are removed from the rest of the world, unless they quite consciously fight this possibility. Betty Friedan in her book, *The Fountain of Age,* speaks of "institutional retreats", a kind of ghettoization of the elderly that takes place in retirement towns and communities. She remarks that many people are drawn to such communities out of loneliness and a need for identity as well as an anticipated need for care which they feel cannot be met in their own communities.

NURSING HOMES

A great deal has and is still being written about nursing homes in the United States. Since the mid 1970's, when there were major nursing home abuses in New York, there have been periods when stricter regulation and monitoring to ensure greater safety and better care of patients have occurred. Then there have been periods when the state felt that it was more important to reduce Medicaid and Medicare. Costs. After the abuses of the 1970s, regulations were strengthened and expanded to improve the structure and maintenance of nursing homes, to determine that patients were getting the physical care they needed and that the rights of patients were honored. It took regulatory staff to see that these new regulations were implemented. Interdisciplinary teams consisting of several professionals went out to do annual surveys of the nursing homes for state licensure and for federal Medicaid and Medicare recertification. Followup visits and sometimes daily monitoring had to be made to see that deficiencies had been corrected within a stipulated time period. If satisfactory conditions still did not exist, fines would be levied. Many homes that presented major problems were closed.

Just in the last few years, when cost containment has become the overwhelming consideration, regulatory staff has been cut and offices consolidated. As a result, I believe that we are increasingly going to see laxness, indifference, neglect and abuse, and perhaps dangerous structural problems in nursing homes. As a example, The *New York Times* of October 29, 1998 had an article describing a Queens nursing home whose 282 patients had to be moved out in the days following a big rainstorm over the Labor Day weekend. According to city officials, the storm *exacerbated the facility's (already existing) structural problems.* The evacuation of patients had to be done so quickly that "some (patients) were given just a few hours notice before they were handed plastic bags filled with some of their belongings and (were) scattered among various health care facilities around the city." How is it that the facility was allowed to reach the point where patients were endangered because of existing structural problems? Where was the regulatory agency, the New York State Department of Health? In a society where money becomes the overriding value, and with a health care system where profit is the bottom line, it is especially important to keep a close eye on health care facilities that have responsibility for our more helpless citizens.

For this reason, anyone who is considering a nursing home should be especially alert and thorough. As with adult homes, take a tour, observe how the staff treats patients, whether they are respectful and attentive, or just show indifference, which can easily become neglect. Are there personal possessions in patients' rooms? Look at the activities calendar. Are there activities scheduled for each day? Is there provision for religious services? Are the scheduled activities in fact taking place, or are there large numbers of patients sitting in front of a television set or dozing in front of the nurse's station? Are patients clean, and dressed in street clothing? Is there an odor of urine or feces or a strong odor of disinfectant? Are restraints used; if so, do you see staff checking the restraints and periodically releasing them? Menus should be posted, and does the patient have a choice of food? Is there an active therapy program in place? Do you see patients undergoing physical therapy, and are aides ambulating patients? How does the facility handle patients' spending money? Are the results of the last survey posted, and what sort of items were problems during the survey? Were they "paper deficiencies" or did they seem to be items that involved serious patient care problems? Is there some way that a patient can make a complaint without reprisal? What is the role of the social worker in the home? Is his or her role only to support the expectations of the nursing home, or will the social worker act as an advocate for the patient? How much is the patient involved in the admission process? (This is a clue to how much he or she will later be involved in decisions affecting his or her care.) How much help is the family going to have in preparing the patient for admission and in helping with the ongoing adjustment of the patient once he is admitted?

The admission of someone to a nursing home is a terribly difficult event for both the patient and his family. In addition to losing his home, and the disruption of moving to an institution, the patient loses many freedoms and many relationships. Any institution must have a certain amount of regimentation for things to go smoothly, especially if there are many patients in residence. This means that patients must get up at a certain time and eat their meals with a lot of other people at specified times. There is no such thing as choosing to stay in bed just because you want to or because you just feel a little tired. If you should want to do that in a nursing home, it would be seen as a sign that something serious is the matter, and the charge nurse would be called. Although pets may be brought into a nursing home for "pet therapy," patients are not allowed to keep their own pets with them, a major trauma for some people. If the nursing home is too regimented, the patient may not be allowed to make choices for himself.

There is just the beginning of what may become a trend: to release patients in nursing homes from the tyranny of schedules. In one upstate New York nursing home, patients are asked at admissions what time they prefer to get up in the morning and when they like to have breakfast. Another upstate home four years ago decided to break the usual rigid schedule, so when it did reconstruction, it planned for nine to twelve residents to live in single rooms clustered around big open kitchens, living rooms and dining rooms. With this setup, the residents are allowed to eat and sleep and dress according to personal preferences and each unit has its own staff to give all the necessary care to patients. There is a homier atmosphere established with plants everywhere and children and animals allowed to visit. The staff has found that the noise level, the wandering by confused patients, the use of restraints and drugs are all down. It is not yet known how these humane changes will affect operating costs, but at least for-profit nursing home chains are visiting homes where changes have been made.

If the facility's policy is to encourage continued decision-making, then staff will be trained to take the time and patience to allow the patient to make some decisions in his daily life, and to be actively involved in his care plan. After all, those who are admitted to the nursing home are adults, not children. Even confused patients can be involved to a degree. Often the most difficult patients are those who may be angry and demanding, but they are the ones who get attention and are often the ones who survive the best. It is the good, passive patient we should worry about the most.

The few friends who are left to the patient may not visit, for it may be too far or too expensive for them to do so, or they may feel threatened by the sight of an old friend so sick or debilitated. If family relationships have not been close, the family may visit only infrequently, and when they do, the visit may be fraught with tension. The family must realize how important their continued relationship with the patient is; otherwise, the patient can very easily feel abandoned. Because of all of these changes and trouble spots, it is only natural that the patient would feel considerable depression at the beginning of his placement in the nursing home. The role of the social worker in the nursing home is to facilitate the patient's and the family's adjustment through individual and family counseling.

Once the patient is placed, his or her involvement in a support group helps provide mutual support, socialization, and a reference by which he can lessen feelings of helplessness and improve his self-esteem. I have observed more often than not that nursing home patients do not choose to make close friendships with other individual patients, but socialize better in small groups. A nursing home social worker surmised to me that a patient's reluctance to make close friends serves to protect him or her against the loss of one more close relationship. By the time people are in a nursing home, they have already suffered many losses, and are physically and psychologically too frail to make the effort.

The professional social worker is the one who is specifically trained to identify adjustment problems and to help in their resolution. The cost of not addressing the social and emotional components of health care is high and is paid through increased medical problems, patient and family suffering and a greatly diminished quality of life. With all of this in mind, at the time of admission you may want to find out what help will be given to the patient and his family to facilitate his adjustment.

Of course, when you consider admission, you will be expected to discuss finances. The costs of nursing home care are extremely high, and Medicare provides very limited coverage. In New York, the cost in many nursing homes amounts to about $6000 a month, which means that even with nursing home insurance which does not cover all of the cost, the savings and other assets of the average person are soon depleted, and application for Medicaid must be made. Most people of the generation that is in nursing homes have saved diligently, with the expectation that their savings and other assets will be their legacy to their children. In order to avoid losing all of those assets to nursing home costs, some people will try to give it to their children before their death. However, in New York during the Medicaid application process a thorough investigation is done by the Department of Social Services, and if it is found that assets were given away during the three years prior to the application date, a review is made based on certain criteria. There is a possibility that a penalty will be imposed. The patient is allowed to keep $3500 and $1500 in a special burial fund. From their income, they will be allowed to keep $50 a month for personal expenses, and any income above that must be applied to the cost of care. If the person is single and owns his or her home, the home must be sold and the proceeds used to pay for care before the person becomes eligible for Medicaid. If the patient is married, and the spouse continues to live in the home, the home and one car become exempt assets. What is called the "community spouse" may retain a monthly income of $2,019 and assets of $74,820. Twenty-five percent of the income above the $2,019 and all assets above the $74,820 will have to be applied to the spouse's cost of care.

Even in the best of nursing homes, and there are many good ones, patients experience many losses such as privacy, freedom to use one's time as one pleases, old friends including beloved pets and money, to name just a few. There are many people whose medical condition is such that they can only be cared for in a nursing home, but there are others who could be cared for at home if only our home health care system were developed to a greater degree.

THE FELLOWSHIP COMMUNITY

I have left a discussion of the Fellowship Community until the last, as it is a unique residential choice located in Spring Valley, New York, in one of the suburban counties thirty miles from New York City. This is a community founded in 1963 by several Anthroposophists, one of them a physician, who saw a need for an alternative to the usual institutional care for the elderly. The founders followed the ideas of Rudolph Steiner (1861-1925), an Austrian philosopher, scientist and spiritualist, who was the father of Anthroposophy (the wisdom of the human being), a way of life that synthesizes the scientific and spiritual. Steiner, certainly a brilliant and creative thinker, developed practical applications of his "spiritual science," including medicine, education, biodynamic gardening, architecture, art and music. He had very definite ideas about each of these areas, and wrote extensively about them and also about "the cultivation of the soul's inward life and the opening of the eyes to a spiritual world." His teachings are still followed faithfully in the Waldorf Schools that exist all over the world, by Anthroposophists, and in Steiner communities of various kinds. Many regard Steiner as a Western occultist and Christian mystic; however what he valued the most were "the qualities of a warm, awake human being living freely and compassionately in the world..."[2]

Dr. Paul Scharff, the Fellowship's principal founder, set out to develop a whole social framework around the care of the elderly, a "socially responsible experiment," in which medical care of the elderly would be "integrated into the processes of everyday life." Healing includes everything that the community does, all of the work needed to sustain the community, and the interrelationships between all, workers, their families, and the elderly residents. The central idea behind this community is that "for true fellowship to exist, the aging and dying people of the community must not be isolated from the active processes of living nor from the concerns of the middle-aged and the young."[3] The elderly are surrounded by and if possible included in a range of activities: weaving, collating newsletters, planting seeds, preparing food for canning or freezing, setting and clearing tables, to name a few. The elderly and the young work and eat side by side. Even those residents who are most ill or are dying are close to the hub of activity, unlike in nursing homes and hospitals.

---

2. Richard Levitan, "From The Cradle To The Grave," *Yoga Journal*, July-August 1993, reprinted in pamphlet published by The Fellowship Community, 241 Hungry Hollow Rd., Chestnut Ridge. N.Y. 10977.
3. ibid.

The community consists of about 150 people from infants to people in their nineties. There may be sixty-five to seventy older people, thirty children and the rest are the staff or "co-workers" as they are called. There are about 80 acres including farmland and orchards, which allows the community to be self-sufficient as far as fruits and vegetables. The co-workers care for the sick elderly, prepare food for the whole community, tend the vegetables, herbs and flowers and the orchards, and prepare bread and crafts that are sold in their store. Those of the elderly who are able to do so look forward to working alongside the younger people. Co-workers move back and forth between different activities. The simplest tasks are shared by everyone, from physician to gardener.

When co-workers join the community, their financial needs are assessed by the Executive Circle, and each co-worker is then paid a monthly stipend based on that information. Housing, food, transportation and medical care are automatically supplied. One co-worker remarked that the loss of high remuneration can be remarkably liberating, as you find yourself free to work, not compelled to by necessity. He said, "We make every effort to render service as a gift."[4] Adjoining the Fellowship property is a Waldorf school which co-workers's children may attend on scholarship. There are also many faithful volunteers at The Fellowship, some of whom are trying things out before making a commitment to becoming a co-worker. Ann Scharff, also a founder, said that not all of the co-workers were Anthroposophists, but that the role of co-worker appealed to many young people who were looking for a spiritual movement and a new vista.

The elderly live either in independent living apartments in a separate building, or if they need more care in Hilltop

---

4. *ibid*

House, which holds 33 residents. This is the central building, which has the dining rooms for the entire community and the Goethe Room, a large circular room where meetings, concerts and other activities are held. The Fellowship Community has three fees. The Life Lease Fee is a one-time fee given at the time of entering the community; this fee varies from $18,500 to $35,000, depending on the size of the living space. This fee accrues to the community at the rate of 10% a year, and is used for construction and large durable expenses. At the time of death, the total amount goes to the Fellowship. The second fee is the Monthly Fee. For those living in Hilltop House, the fee is either $685 or $800 depending on the size of the room. This fee pays for general maintenance, food and its preparation, utilities, transportation to medical appointments and weekly shopping trips. For a person who lives in one of the apartments the monthly fee is between $400 and $650, depending on its size, but meals are extra. The third fee is the Support Care Fee, which is in force when a person develops increasing needs for care, and ranges up to $880 when a person must have complete or nearly complete care.

I visited Ruth, who lives in Hilltop House, as she needs a wheelchair and some assistance. (See the discussion of Ruth's interest in Co-Housing under that section.) The first time I met her, I picked her up at the Fellowship of Reconciliation in Nyack, ten miles east of Spring Valley where Ruth volunteers one day every week. We returned to Hilltop House around two-thirty in the afternoon, when people were walking in and out of the building and there was a young volunteer playing the cello in the Goethe Room, with several residents as his audience. Ruth's room was very homey, with her computer and her telephone, notepaper and address book, those things that keep her connected with old friends, placed close to where her wheelchair is put. In the short time that I was there, she had a number of telephone calls. In the middle of the afternoon, after the children had returned from school, the community gathered for a snack, elderly people arriving from the apartments, co-helpers from their various tasks, and the residents of Hilltop House, all ages mixed together, happily chatting about the days' events. The second time I visited, Ruth invited me to lunch. She was on the telephone when I arrived, so I waited in the Goethe Room where several young girls in pigtails and dresses were doing craft work with their mothers and some of the elderly residents. The little girls were completely comfortable with the older residents.

We sat at a table with several ladies from the apartments, one of them an ex-colleague of Ruth's. At the table, there was also a volunteer who had been helping out for several years, traveling a long distance to the Fellowship, a co-worker who had come in from the fields, and another co-worker who was in and out, busy helping in the kitchen and clearing tables. Our food, which had been grown there, was delicious. There was a pleasant buzz in the room as people were catching up on the day's business, and a four year old girl was excited about her birthday, which was celebrated with a birthday cake and a rousing cheer from young and old. There was also excitement because a large number of residents and co-workers were going to a Shakespeare festival in New Jersey that evening. The women at the table said that they were happy to be living at the Fellowship; two of them specifically said that they were especially relieved that they would be able to die right there rather than in a hospital, a fear that many nursing home patients have. Those who were Anthroposophists used the term "crossing over" for death.

I found the Fellowship Community very remarkable, as it answered many of the problems that are so often seen in the usual institutional setting. Elderly people were not being separated from other generations; they were an important part of a working community; their own skills and assets were used and appreciated; and at the same time they were treated with loving, gentle care. I heard none of the whining or yelling that is so frequently heard in nursing homes—not to say that people there never complain, but each time I visited I had the sense that everyone was pretty generally contented. The community was born out of tremendous idealism, and it has successfully survived thirty-three years without the spirit waning.

SUMMARY

Institutional living is usually considered only as a last resort when people can no longer completely care for themselves or cannot afford the home care that they need. Nevertheless, some people are entering life-care communities before they absolutely need to only so that they can take advantage of an opening or to save their children the burden of moving them later on. Institutional living can provide some measure of security, but it also has many negatives. People who cherish their privacy find congregate living hard, and the over-scheduling of everything can be very annoying to some people who are used to a freer life style. If you have a choice about moving into institutional care, be sure to visit any place you are considering and carefully weigh the positives against the negatives. If you still feel that you need that care, then enter the institution remembering that you have certain rights. These include the right to be a partner in making decisions about your care, that you must be treated with respect, and that you should be given every opportunity to remain as physically active as you can, and to be socially engaged and intellectually challenged.

Chapter VI

Doctor, Please Listen!

Deem me worthy of seeing in the sufferer who seeks my advice, a person neither rich nor poor, friend or foe, good or evil. Show me only the person.
—Maimonides

My husband and I have often commented that at some point in social gatherings with close friends, discussion has almost always centered on those personal concerns that were of most importance at that particular age. For instance, when we were young, and still without children, discussion would center on our careers. Later, as young parents, there would be a good deal of talk of childbirth, child-rearing practices, nursery schools or what were thought to be the best of the public schools. As our children reached late teens the topics would be colleges and their cost, therapy for us or for them and cheap travel escapes. Still later, we would talk of children marrying or not and where we had traveled, or what our next destination might be. In our early sixties, the topic was retirement and various options, and where we might be considering settling after retirement.

Now that we are in our seventies, the topic we hear most frequently is declining health, what treatments we have had for particular medical problems, doctors, hospitals and

HMOs. Sometimes people try to avoid the subject of medical care, which seems very strange indeed and makes us wonder whether there is some terrible problem that they are hiding. However, the subject that has run through every period of our lives is doctors: who are the ablest, who are the most approachable, who are the most caring, and why the hell we can't call our doctors by their first names if they call us by ours.

Doctors And Nurses

At one point after my husband and I had moved to a new community we found a physician who was unusual in several ways. As well as being a highly recommended doctor who knew his medical science and was a thorough practitioner, he liked his patients and came to know them as individuals and friends and was not afraid for them to come to know him in the same way. Often, he talked about what you were reading and about what he was reading; and always he was concerned about and kind to his patients. He seemed to know that he must establish a relationship of trust and cooperation from his first contact with patients, and was not afraid to let them know that he did not have all the answers. For example, the first time I saw him, he did a thorough history and examination and then took my husband and me into his office for a conference. Before he expressed any medical concerns, he told me what my rights as his patient would be, among which was permission to call him by his first name. He also stressed that he expected that our relationship would be a partnership. I had mentioned to him my concern about the sudden atrophy of one of my kidneys and my wish to prevent this from happening to the other one. To date, none of my doctors had suggested any way of avoiding a recurrence. He did, but before starting me on a course of treatment, he said, "In cases like this, I turn to God!" Some of my atheist friends said they would never have confidence in a doctor who said such a thing, but my reaction was, "Here is a doctor who isn't so arrogant that he feels that he has all the answers." Thereafter, with good care and compassion, he saw us through a number of serious medical problems. Unfortunately, he moved away from the community several years later, leaving behind a number of very devoted patients. What I am saying does not mean that I expect a doctor to be my personal friend, but the doctor-patient relationship is helped considerably if the doctor shows compassion and is willing to show himself or herself as another human being.

Sharon R. Kaufman, a researcher at the University of Wisconsin, did a study of the development of medicine over the past seventy years by examining the medical practice of seven physicians in their eighties who had been trained in the 1920's and 1930's. At that time, there were few drugs, so the role of the doctor was to try to cure and to be there at the patients' bedsides to provide comfort and to relieve their pain and suffering. They hoped to make a correct diagnosis through observation and through the use of the stethoscope, a flashlight and the ophthalmoscope. People stayed in the hospital until they felt better, which sometimes meant they were there for months or perhaps as long as a year. House calls were routine. Sulfa was not used until the 1930's so many people died who might have lived ten to fifteen years longer.

One of the physicians in the study admitted that the ward rounds in the intensive care unit have not changed very much, as some doctors are still discussing the patient without including or making eye contact with him, as if he is not present. They do so despite the patient's right to privacy, to disclosure and to participation in decision making.

Radical changes in treatment have come about since the discovery and use of sulfa and antibiotics, and there have been many technological developments, which means that life threatening diseases can be diagnosed and cured. According to Ms. Kaufman, these rapid changes were not adequately evaluated, and therefore have produced unexpected moral dilemmas.

Above all, interviews with these elderly physicians, most of whom were nationally known specialists, revealed doctors who loved their profession and kept up with changes, but who were also exceptionally human and kind to their patients. So many doctors today seem to have become as mechanized as their technologies.

When I was touring a continuing care facility, I saw lying on a physician's desk *In The Country of Illness* by Robert Lipsyte, and having already read a review of it decided to get it out of the library. Lipsyte had had two bouts with testicular cancer and his wife two with breast cancer. This history obviously meant he had contacts with many doctors and other medical personnel in what he refers to as that place called "Malady." In several parts of his book he discusses what patients need from doctors. He says it helps patients to keep in mind that most doctors are ordinary people with special skills they learned in school, skills that were not given to them as a divine gift. We are their "customers, ...not the lucky recipients of their munificence"[1] I think so often people in my generation were raised to consider that doctors were not ordinary people but some sort of divine being whose word was not to be questioned, who must not be criticized and whose diagnosis and treatment must be accepted without reservation. On their part, doctors in their conceit can withhold information and be incredibly protective of each other, sometimes at the cost to patients.

---

[1] Robert Lipsyte, In The Country of Illness, (New York, Alfred A. Knopf, 1997), page 47.

The following is an example of several physicians' arrogance and poor communication with a patient. In 1988, over New Year's weekend, I developed severe chest pain on the right side and went to the emergency room of our local hospital to have x-rays taken. Although the final diagnosis was pleurisy, the x-rays revealed a lesion on the left lung. This x-ray was then followed up over the next few weeks with a series of tomograms, which were viewed by an oncologist who declared that I did not have cancer. Because the lesion was located in a part of the lung where tuberculosis is usually found, my doctor decided that I had probably been exposed to that disease. She started me on a course of TB drugs after I showed a sudden positive TB skin test although my sputum test for TB was negative. More than a month later, after I had requested in vain to be referred to a lung specialist, I made an appointment with a pulmonologist, whose name I secured from a friend. My husband wrote a letter to my internist, which I signed, expressing our dissatisfaction that she had made no referral to a lung specialist and asking that my record be sent to the doctor I had made an appointment with. In response, my doctor telephoned me, furious that I questioned her judgment and screaming that I had thirty days to find another doctor. This was neither professional nor compassionate treatment. The first time I saw the specialist he declared that if the lesion was not reduced in size after several weeks on the TB drugs he would consider it cancer. However, when it remained the same size he would not follow through with a biopsy, despite having agreed with my new internist to do so. The lesion did turn out to be cancerous, but several doctors along the way either protected or made excuses for the decisions made by the first internist. Cornelius Ryan, author of *A Private Battle*, written in the 1970s had comments about the arrogance of doctors, their lack of communication with each other and also with their patients.

Norman Cousins in *Anatomy of an Illness as Perceived by the Patient* says that time is the one thing that patients need from their doctors: "time to be heard, time to have things explained, time to be reassured, time to be introduced by the doctor personally to specialists or other attendants whose very existence seems to reflect something new and threatening"[2] Unfortunately, in these days of managed care, doctors are so pressed for time that they frequently check their watches as they consult with you. Managed care has taken a great deal of autonomy away from doctors and has also made it more difficult for them to establish trust with patients. Lipsyte observes that HMO doctors are often restricted in what they can tell patients about procedures and protocols that may not be covered. He suggests that a patient go to a doctor with a written statement of his medical history and current complaints, and a list of questions he may have. He also recommends bringing a friend or family member along to take notes. He adds that you should be pleasant and tactful with a doctor but firm and focused. My husband and I have begun to take notes with us to doctor's appointments, both because of our aging memories but also because it does help to focus a meeting with him. A friend who was a nurse also recommends taping an interview with a doctor, as it is hard to get down everything that is said and to remember it all.

Jerome Groopman, author of *The Measure of Our Days*, who is Professor of Immunology at Harvard Medical School and a world-renowned researcher on cancer and AIDS, takes patients who have been shunned by other doctors and who are frightened and alienated. He shows himself to be an extremely kind, sensitive man who takes a great deal of time to get to know his patients as people, asking them about their work and interests and about their

---

2. Norman Cousins, <u>Anatomy of An Illness as Perceived by The Patient</u>, (New York, W.W. Norton Company, 1979).

personal backgrounds. As a result of this exploration, he uses metaphors that are most understandable to them. He also looks behind their behavior to the feelings within, openly expresses empathy to his patients and is unafraid to share himself with them. He will also adapt treatment when necessary to people's preferences, for instance going along with one patient's insistence that she would not again undergo radiation treatment, and accepted her decision to use a Tao healer. As I read Dr. Groopman's account of his work with eight patients with advanced cases of AIDS and cancer, I wondered how nowadays he could take the amount of time he did with them. I also wondered whether he had had some personal therapy to help him become so very sensitive.

I personally do not think you can train people in the classroom how to be compassionate. If they don't have sensitivity to people in need by the time they have graduated from medical school, they're just not going to get it. Over and over again, I have heard people say that as a result of the terribly demanding training of medical students and residents, doctors for their own self-protection must necessarily become hardened. Yet there are plenty of doctors who have been practicing for many years who have not lost their ability to empathize. Now medical schools are taking on the task of helping to improve medical students' interpersonal relationships and sensitivity. They can at least teach techniques for working more sensitively with patients and give tips on what not to do, but patients can immediately tell the difference between technique and genuine empathy.

In response to our growing senior population, at Mt. Sinai School of Medicine in New York City, all students spend a month in their last year learning to care for elderly patients. They are taught skills in comfort care, pain management and communication. In order to help develop more empathy in the medical student, the school uses actors to set up difficult experiences which the student may later have to face. The interactions between students and actor-patients are videotaped for later examination by the student.

All residents in internal medicine at Johns Hopkins Bayview Medical Center are required to take training in geriatrics. House calls, which are central to the training, bring residents into contact with healthier, more vigorous elderly people in their own homes. According to Dr. John Burton, director of the division of geriatric medicine and gerontology at the Hopkins School of Medicine, which helps direct the program, "suddenly, the residents aren't the benevolent dictator. They're the invited guest."[3] With about twelve months out of their three years of training devoted to geriatrics, residents see elderly people in a variety of settings, including retirement communities and nursing homes as well as their own homes. Unlike other areas of medicine which concentrate on curing disease and extending life, geriatrics monitors medications and sees that people are kept comfortable and dignified, according to one of the geriatricians in the program, Dr. Eric DeJonge. Therefore, goals are necessarily limited. Dr. David B. Reuben, chief of the geriatrics division at the U.C.L.A. School of Medicine, has said that "geriatricians are the Labrador retrievers of medicine. We're warm, fuzzy people."[4] According to the American Geriatrics Society, there are eight thousand, eight hundred physicians certified in geriatrics. By 2030, the United States will need thirty-six thousand physicians to care for about seventy-six million older Americans.

---

3. Sara Rimer, "New Frontier For Medicine: Treating the Elderly," N.Y. Times, 9/24/98

4. ibid

Students who are now entering medical school can expect that at least half of their patients will be over sixty-five. There are seventeen clinical geriatricians on the Hopkins Bayview faculty and thirteen fellows. According to Dr. DeJonge, most specialties concentrate on one organ, whereas geriatrics concentrates on the whole person. Another of the geriatricians in describing one patient said "...she does have a life. This is an education for anyone who wants to open their heart. The human spirit is amazing."[5]

Forty years ago when our oldest child was very small, our pediatrician would make house calls when our son had one of his severe strep infections. Since then, I have heard of almost no house calls to any patient at any age. However, recently the New York Times featured a Bronx pediatrician, associate professor of pediatric medicine at the Albert Einstein College of Medicine, who makes house calls part of his weekly routine. In his clinic, he offers home visiting to some of his sickest patients and their families, most of whom say they want him to visit. In the home he can find clues to continuing medical problems and social and family problems that bear on treatment. Dr. Okum often takes interns and pediatric residents with him, and home visiting will be a major part of care when Montefuiore Hospital builds a new children's hospital in 2001. Unfortunately managed care short-sightedly does not see the value of home visiting, and so does not reimburse for it.

Doctors do make mistakes, but attempts are being made to change conditions that lead to them. Back in 1984, there was the famous case of Libby Zion, who landed in the emergency room of New York Hospital severely agitated and running a high fever. Eight hours later she was dead and to this day the exact cause of her death is unknown. However, the case aroused public debate about the number of hours that residents had to put in before getting time

---

5. *ibid*

off, and whether resident fatigue contributed to her death. In 1987, a special commission was established to review residency programs and to make recommendations for change. As a result of their study changes in residency programs had to be made in New York State. There had to be more supervision of residents and they could not work more than twenty-four hours straight and not more than eighty hours in a week. These recommendations became law and were adopted by other states. As a result of the new regulations, night floats were created - residents who worked night shifts for a specified period of time, usually a few weeks. However, it has now become apparent that the new regulations and the use of night floats have brought new problems. Since the night floats have not had daytime responsibility for a patient, they are apt to be unfamiliar with his problems, and important information can be hidden in records, leading to delays or to the wrong treatment. Although residents like the new system, it seems as though there needs to be an improvement in the transmission of information at the beginning and end of the night shift.

Doctors are human and they do make mistakes. The February 1, 1999 issue of the New Yorker magazine carried an "Annals of Medicine" article on mistakes that even good doctors make and what hospitals are doing to try to prevent these from recurring. Research has shown that medical malpractice suits have not reduced medical error rates. One reason is that as a result of the lawsuit pointing out how badly the doctor may have performed, it is unlikely that he will thereafter acknowledge and discuss medical errors. Hospital lawyers warn doctors that they must discuss complications that have occurred with patients but must do so in such a way that a lawsuit is not brought. As a partial solution, in almost every academic hospital in the country, there is what is called a Morbidity and Mortality

Conference held weekly to discuss problem cases where errors have occurred. Most states have laws to protect the proceedings from legal discovery so that physicians feel quite free to review mistakes and deaths behind closed doors with the goal of determining how to prevent such an error in the future.

Despite some distressing encounters I've had with one or two doctors, I still have a great deal of admiration and respect for them as individuals and professionals. They work terribly hard, and for the most part are dedicated to their profession and to their patients.

I have even had a doctor apologize to me for a mistake he had made. I'm sure that most patients see that doctors are human and that they unintentionally make mistakes. However, most people I know cannot understand and strongly resent the arrogance of many physicians. It does not build trust with patients and at times can lead to cold, unkind and uncaring treatment of people when they are most emotionally vulnerable. Anatole Broyard, author of *Intoxicated By My Illness*, says, "Not every patient can be saved, but his illness may be eased by the way the doctor may see himself…he must see that his silence and neutrality are unnatural. It may be necessary to give up some of his authority in exchange for his humanity. He has little to lose and everything to gain by letting the sick man into his heart. If he does, they can share, as few others can, the wonder, terror, and exaltation of being on the edge of being, between the natural and the supernatural."[6]

Most of my doctors accept Medicare assignment, meaning they will not charge above what Medicare allows for a procedure. However, I am appalled when I see on my

---
[6] Anatole Broyard, <u>Intoxicated By My Illness</u>, (New York, Clarkson N. Potter Inc. 1992), pg. 57.

Medicare statements how little they are paid for their services. I also feel indignant that Medicare does not reimburse them for all of the time they put in talking directly to patients on the phone or to others on behalf of them. I can understand that they might feel angry at Medicare, and I can also understand a growing unionization of doctors, although I would not wish to be very ill and unable to reach my doctor because he was out on strike. Even though I worked for a regulatory agency, and believe that regulation has its place in the health care system, I would think that doctors must be very resentful of the autonomy that they have lost with managed care. They should also be resentful of how much HMO profits and losses have become the overriding consideration, rather than the welfare of the patient.

Nurses used to be called the "handmaidens" of physicians, and did not have the professional respect and power that they have gained over the last fifty years. Now most registered nurses have bachelor's degrees and many have gone on to earn master's degrees or have trained to be nurse practitioners, who are increasingly being used in HMOs. The arrogance that I see in some physicians can carry over to their relationship with nurses. I've seen doctors publicly and loudly berate nurses who had the temerity to disagree with them or to suggest something. I think this happens less these days, but when it does the nurses still often accept the abuse as if this is the way things are between doctors and nurses. On the other hand, these days nurses with advanced degrees can readily move into administrative positions, and nurse practitioners can either practice independently or in a group medical practice where they can do pretty much everything done by a general practitioner in many states, including prescribing medication. There is a term used for nurses with a master's degrees in a primary care specialty such as pediatrics or family medicine—Advanced Practice Nurses, or APNs. There are now 140,000 APNs in the United States. In New York City there is the Columbia Advanced Practice Nurse Associates, the first APN practice to be reimbursed by insurers, primarily because the APNs from the group have hospital admitting privileges at New York Presbyterian Hospital. Other kinds of APNs are nurse anesthetists, certified nurse midwives who provide obstetrical and gynecological services and clinical nurse specialists who train and develop hospital nursing staff. APNs devote a lot of time to educating patients to existing or potential medical problems, the preventive focus of which appeals to insurers.

The Psychology of Illness

Robert Lipsyte in his book *In The Country of Illness*, says that when we are very sick or are taking care of someone else who is very sick, we feel as though we are suddenly drawn to another place which he calls Malady. We the patients become quite removed from everyday life and from all but our caretakers and those with whom we are most intimately involved. If we are seriously ill, our whole life revolves around our illness, especially if we are hospitalized. There is almost nothing else that we think about for there is nothing else that is quite so important to us. We become self-absorbed, and often what would be ordinarily considered a trivial thing is exaggerated and takes on undue importance. We become intensely sensitive, sometimes unduly suspicious or critical, we feel that the sickness is an unjust punishment and that others have not been meted the same fate that we have. We are convinced, and it is often true, that the only people who could possibly understand us are those who have undergone the same disease or the same treatment. We regress to terrible dependency on those close to us, and rage if we feel that they aren't giving us what we need. Often we feel that things will only get worse.

Of course, though our behavior may be a real pain to those caring for us, it is really self-protective behavior. At the time of serious illness, we may need to be taken care of like a baby and we may get what we need only if we demand it. At times we feel that we are unlike other people or that some people are shunning us, as there is still a primitive reaction to many serious illnesses. For instance, there continues to be such fear of cancer that sometimes, people react to cancer patients as if the cancer is contagious and always fatal. "It took illness to make me feel powerless and to eventually offer some insight into what it might really mean to be black, a female, gay and have to grovel, flirt, cakewalk, conceal," wrote Lipsyte.[7] Susan Sontag in *Illness As Metaphor* remarks that "dreaded diseases bring out both people's worst and best."[8]

When you are seriously ill, you very quickly learn who your close friends are. They rally around and try to help as they can, or try to just be there. Merely the presence of someone who cares means a great deal. There is often a sorting out of relationships that takes place even with family members. When you are seriously ill, those of your children who have really matured will put aside other things to be with you, to help and to express their empathy and appreciation for you. A friend of ours struggled with lung cancer for two years before he died at home. During those years, his son regularly flew out to Arizona from the East to visit and help care for his father, and then at the end spent several weeks with him. From interacting with his father's friends when they visited and from working on his memoirs, Jim's son gained increased appreciation and a deeper love for his father. That time together was very precious to both of them.

---

7. Lipsyte, page 57
8. Susan Sontag, <u>Illness As Metaphor</u>, (New York, Vintage Books, 1979) page 39

There will always be people who have their own stories to tell or who try to persuade you to pursue some particular treatment or doctor or to indicate that what you are feeling isn't legitimate. When this happens, a patient feels as if the remonstrator is placing a notch in his gun. The sorting out of friends certainly took place in 1988 when I was coping with the long period when no accurate diagnosis was arrived at before it was finally decided that I had lung cancer. During the time that I was on tuberculosis drugs, an old friend was to stay overnight with us enroute to another destination. We felt a moral obligation to call him to explain that I was on the TB drugs and his response was that he would call us back. He did call to say that he felt he should not stay with us, but never again was he in contact, never did he send a note, and never did he make another phone call. Perhaps he was terribly ashamed afterwards, but his behavior clearly demonstrated to me that the friendship meant little to him. At the same time, there were many other old friends who came from long distances to visit or to take me out to lunch when I was better.

Susan Sontag in *Illness As Metaphor* makes the point that when the causes of illnesses like tuberculosis and cancer are still unknown they become mysterious and it is then that they are looked at metaphorically. When the treatment of tuberculosis was ineffective, it was seen as a disease that was insidious and merciless, the only end to which was death. Cancer, which is still very much of a mystery, is seen in much the same way and will continue to be until it too is understood. There are also more subtle cultural beliefs that surround these two diseases, some of them similar for the two illnesses, others quite dissimilar. TB at an early stage has visible symptoms - a cough, fever, progressive emaciation and languor, whereas cancer is insidious, invisible, often discovered by chance and then can be far advanced. TB is a disease of poverty, cancer of the affluent, often the result of a high fat and protein diet and of toxins. TB was considered to be painless, and cancer excruciatingly painful. In the nineteenth century, tuberculosis was romanticized and was thought to be an index of being genteel, delicate, sensitive, and creative. It was felt that some passionate feeling provoked or found expression in tuberculosis, and now it is felt by some that cancer is generally caused by a repression of feeling- that cancer patients are not sufficiently sensual or not in touch with their anger. Punitive notions of disease are especially expressed around cancer. We speak of a "war on cancer," that cancer is a "killer", and that people with cancer are "victims". People who have cancer are often heard to say, "what did I do to deserve this?" The romantic view of the disease is that it is an expression of one's character and it is one's character that causes the disease because it has not been expressed directly. People sometimes directly, but more often by suggestion, place the blame for the cancer on some weakness or deficit in the patient who then erroneously feels that with the onus on him, he must master this weakness in order to cure the disease. Lipsyte writes about "New Age Hustlers" who imply that serious disease comes to those who deserve it, "who bring it on themselves by some issue or attitude festering beneath the surface of their lives"[9]

Suggestion enters into the areas of disease and treatment. Doctors in Texas are conducting a study of arthroscopic knee surgery in which patients are assigned to three groups, in one of which sham surgery is done. Two years after surgery, the patients in the sham surgery group reported that they had as much relief of pain and swelling as did those patients who had the real surgery. Other studies have shown that placebos and anti-depressant drugs worked just as well. Also, it has been found that placebos work about

---

[5] *Lipsyte, page 209*

as well as aspirin and codeine in relieving pain. They can bring changes in pulse rate, blood pressure, skin conditions etc., the explanations for which can be found in "expectancy theory", based on past experience leading to certain expectations. A gastroenterologist at Yale suggested that a placebo might work successfully with diseases that develop slowly and gently.

There are gender differences in the incidence and morbidity of disease, and in how diagnosis and treatment are accepted. Every woman knows that men are worse patients than they are. A telephone poll conducted by CNN reported that whereas seventy-six percent of American women had had health exams in the last twelve months, only sixty percent of men had. Some people attribute this to men fearing that they will be seen as dependent and vulnerable, while women are the traditional caregivers for children and the elderly and are therefore more sophisticated about medical matters. Women are used to seeking treatment for family members and asking questions of doctors, and they know the right questions to ask. They also talk among themselves to gain information about diseases and ways of treating them. By talking they are able to face the medical crisis more openly. Some people feel that men associate good health with sexual functioning, so perhaps new ways have to be found to reach men so that they are more ready to confront their physical and psychological fears in order to improve their health and therefore live longer. Natalie Angier, in a *New York Times* article, makes a point that men, whose life span is seven years shorter than women's, are much more self-destructive. They are apt to be four times more successful at suicide, they are twice as likely to be alcoholics, have three and a half times more fatal auto accidents, are murdered eight times as much as women, and gamble more rashly. Men continue to assume the role of the Marlboro Man - tough, action-oriented and resilient, with a very narrow range of feelings, and I must add a greater need to use denial.

We need to be more sensitive to the feelings engendered by illness, and the metaphorical meaning of certain diseases. Perhaps if we better understand these, we can move beyond them to a more honest confrontation of medical issues, disease and treatment.

In considering the aging process, my experience suggests that people age in very different ways and at different rates.

Years ago, a colleague of my husband's, Ross Alexander, wrote and directed a play called *Coming Apart* that opened at a theater at the State University of Albany. Ross was then in his fifties and died shortly afterwards, but he was able to write a simply hilarious comedy about aging, which I've thought about many times since seeing the play. As the title indicates, every system in the protagonist's body was fast falling apart; the reaction of the viewer was to laugh uproariously, but also to wonder if that was what was going to happen to him. I do think that some people age over a long period of time with one system after another faltering and failing. Then there are others who have one defective system in the body, such as people who are quite ill with heart problems for many years without much else wrong with them. Also, there are people who remain in comparatively good health until their late seventies, eighties or even their nineties and then die very suddenly of a heart attack or stroke. The following sections are on the three most dreaded diseases of old age and some of the new knowledge and treatment that have emerged over the last year or two.

CANCER

Even more than heart disease and stroke, cancer is still a dread disease. Perhaps this is because there are so many cancers and except for lung cancer we still don't know the cause of most of them. Cancer can be very insidious, be discovered by accident, and many times be beyond control by the time it is diagnosed. Because the cause is still misunderstood or unknown, many myths still surround the disease. Many people either deny or exaggerate the presence of cancer. For many, it is an automatic death sentence. For others, it becomes a kind of crusade against evil forces. They will go to any length and bear the long ravages of chemotherapy treatment that may last for months and even years, just because they want so desperately to live. These are the tough fighters who don't give in to death. Instead, death takes them.

Patricia was one of those fighters. In the spring of 1998, she was told that the breast cancer for which she had had surgery five years earlier had spread to her bones and liver. She was put on strong chemotherapy that made her desperately sick, she lost forty pounds, and there was little time between her treatments when she felt well enough to do much of anything. Six months later, when the course of chemotherapy was over, and there was no change, her oncologist told her that she would live only another two months without more chemotherapy. She was determined to go on and felt she had no choice, so she decided to continue chemotherapy and the combination of drugs was changed.

Neurological damage set in, but she found she could manage to drive short distances and continued to get herself to her treatments that involved five different chemicals and lasted five hours. By the winter of 1999, she had found a healer who used touch and prayer at the same time, and by scheduling the healing sessions just before her chemo treatments she found them easier to take. She was able to manage at home with home health care and the assistance of friends and family. Still alert and chipper, she said that her doctor told her that she could probably remain at the same level by continuing the chemotherapy. She did so for another year.

Another crusader was the superintendent of the Seattle school system who was featured in a New York Times article. He, too, was described as a crusader in his fight with a rare blood cancer, myelogenous leukemia. Even after his chemotherapy was determined to be unsuccessful, he underwent an operation in which cells taken from a sister were injected into him, although the odds were not great for such a procedure. From his hospital bed, Mr. Stanford carried on his work as superintendent. He said he was not giving up and would return to work.

There have been remarkable strides in the treatment of cancer in the last forty years. At that time, we had a young friend die of Hodgkin's Disease that is no longer fatal. At that time, many people with leukemias also died at an alarming rate, whereas now many people with the diagnosis either survive with it as a chronic problem for years or they are treated successfully and are "cured." The five-year survival rates for the ten most deadly cancers: lung/bronchus, colon/rectum, breast, prostate, pancreatic, non-Hodgkins lymphona, leukemias, ovarian, stomach, and brain/nervous system have increased as dramatically in the last twenty-five years as the mortality rates have decreased. In March 1998, the government announced the first drop in the number of new cancer cases since 1930. Chemotherapy has been pushed to the limits, and the use of some chemotherapy in high-risk patients has been successful in delaying or even reducing the incidence of breast cancer without raising the risk of uterine cancer, a side effect of tamoxifen. As a result of many tax dollars going into research, many oncologists think that they are at a critical point in the treatment of cancer. They feel that laboratory advances in molecular biology and genetics will lead to new treatments. Also, clinical trials have found new uses for older drugs, meaning that some cancers can be turned into manageable chronic diseases, just as the use of insulin keeps diabetics alive for years. Cancer drugs used in combinations have been found to be more successful than if used singly. Some scientists feel that cancers are possibly genetic diseases, not that cancer is inherited, but that behind all cancer cells are genetic alterations, the causes of which are still unknown.

BREAST CANCER

For women, the greatest fear is breast cancer, although for them there is a greater incidence of deaths from lung cancer and heart disease. Breast cancer seems to sneak up on you; there still is no definite known cause, so often by the time it is discovered it is pretty well advanced. We all know many cases where breast cancer metastasizes, and the side effects of chemotherapy can be devastating. All of these considerations make women feel helpless. For several years, the use of estrogen has been recommended for women at risk for cardiovascular disease. Some women who could benefit from its use turn down estrogen because they fear the small increased risk it presents for developing breast cancer, instead, taking a greater chance on a heart attack or stroke. "Taking blood pressure medicine and nitroglycerin doesn't sound so bad. But chemotherapy is frightening"[10]

Some women who are at high risk for breast cancer will do almost anything to avoid it, especially young women who have breast cancer running rampant in their families and as a preventive measure have both breasts removed. It is thought in such families the individual carries genes that

---

[10] Denise Grady, "In Breast Cancer Data, Hope, Fear and Confusion," N.Y. Times, 1/26/99.

predispose them to breast cancer. In the last ten years, it has been found that a mutation takes place in two genes that produce a lifetime risk of cancer as high as fifty to eighty percent. It is recommended that women with this gene mutation have more frequent breast examinations and mammograms. It is also thought that women who have a history of breast biopsies should be examined more frequently, as the need for biopsies may indicate a tendency to develop breast cancer. Although the overall risk of cancer is still one in eight women, or twelve and a half percent, the risk varies from one age group to another, and getting breast cancer does not mean automatic death. When the disease is found and treated early, ninety-seven percent of patients are still alive five years later. If the cancer has invaded the lymph nodes, the five-year survival rate is reduced to 26%, and if the cancer has reached into the bones or other organs, then the five-year survival rate is only 21%. Among all women who have had the disease at any one of the stages, 50 to 60% survive fifteen years. Naturally, women who are treated early are the ones who survive the longest, evidence of how important it is for women to do self-examination and to have annual mammograms. Some doctors are convinced that every lump that is found should be biopsied, as mammograms alone cannot distinguish between a cyst and a cancer. Ultrasound can distinguish if the cyst is filled with fluid, and guided by ultrasound, the needle can be used to drain it. Between 1990 and 1994 the death rate from breast cancer declined by an encouraging 5.6 percent.

Elderly women should be prepared for follow-up testing on their mammograms, for if women are prepared in advance for the need for follow-up testing they will be far less anxious when the need emerges. Almost 10% of women in their late sixties and seventies are sent for additional testing, although the number who are then actually found to have cancer is small. Even though the highest rate for breast cancer is in women in their seventies, some doctors feel that sickly women in their seventies and women over 85 need not have mammograms, as they are more likely to die of cardiovascular problems. On the other hand, vigorous women in their seventies should have the test.

WHAT YOU CAN DO TO HELP PREVENT CANCER

There are many things that you can do to help prevent or at least reveal cancer early. Most doctors stress the importance of certain annual tests to detect cancer. These include mammograms after the age of 50 (in addition to monthly breast self-examination) to detect breast cancer, occult rectal blood tests and colonoscopies for colon cancer, and a rectal examination and the PSA test to detect prostate cancer. Dentists will usually exam a patient's mouth for cancer as a routine part of their exam, and internists will look for skin lesions that might be cancer, especially in those parts of the country where people are exposed to the sun a great deal. Be sure that if you find any abnormality such as a lump or bleeding or change in bowel or urination habits or unusual discoloration of the skin to tell your physician.

There have been many articles and programs on television about the role of diet in helping to reduce the risk of cancer. Diet alone cannot prevent cancer. However, studies suggest that changing American eating habits to place more emphasis on fruits, vegetables, whole grains, fewer red meats, less total fat but especially saturated fats and less alcohol will reduce the likelihood of developing common cancers. These include such cancers as colon and rectum, lung, bladder, stomach, esophagus, mouth, throat and breast. Of course, these same diets can help fight heart disease, high blood pressure, diabetes and obesity. A number of studies have shown that a diet high in tomatoes and tomato products can lower the risk of a number of cancers, including prostate, lung and stomach.

The following is an example of how valuable it is to detect a cancer early. Colon cancer appears third on the list of cancers with a high incidence rate. A new Dutch study shows that colon cancer patients in the early stage of the disease who receive a vaccine after surgery double their chances of remaining cancer-free for five years. The vaccine is custom made from a mixture of the patient's own cancer cells and bacteria and is successful for those colon cancers that had not spread beyond the bowel wall. The vaccine presumably triggers the immune system to find and destroy cancer cells.

Doctors recommend colonoscopies regularly for those over 50, and some insurance companies including Medicare are beginning to pay for them. With the use of colonoscopies, colorectal cancer can essentially be prevented, as polyps can be picked up through the test before they develop into cancer. This is a cancer that is symptomless in its early stages, so having periodic colonoscopies is advisable.

How You Can Get Help In The Event of Cancer

With any cancer, gathering as much information from a reliable source is an aid in reducing anxiety. The internet can be helpful for both information and support. Onco Link (oncolink:upenn.edu) at the University of Pennsylvania is a credible source for information, but do be careful, as there are a number of sites that promote unproven methods. Personal sites can be of help for some useful and practical information, for example, the side effects of particular chemotherapy treatments. The Food and Drug Administration has said that the internet has much good information but that people should learn to sort out the true information from the wacky, and that they should beware of cure-all claims. The National Council of

Reliable Health Information has said that if there is to be a health break-through, people aren't going to read it as a secret message on the internet; instead, people will be able to read it in all the newspapers.

Many people find support groups beneficial in getting through the cancer treatment and even afterwards. Such therapies can be offered at medical sites, through social agencies or private therapists. Patients who are undergoing the same symptoms, treatment and psychological distress can find great comfort in each other. It always seems to lessen the severity of a problem to know that other people are experiencing the same thing and often very helpful tips are shared. This sharing can also be done on a more informal basis with friends or acquaintances who are experiencing the same problems. However, it is more beneficial to have a professional present who can act as facilitator of the group and also determine if a person needs more help than the group can give.

Above all else, ask many questions and share fully with your doctor how you are feeling physically and emotionally. If you are in pain do not hesitate to ask for pain medication, and ask for an increase in the dose if that is necessary. Most doctors are understanding about this and wish to make you as comfortable as possible.

SUMMARY

There is obviously a great deal of cancer research going on now, and more public money is being used for it. Progress is being made, though small, the incidence of cancer is being reduced. There are studies of the relationship of genes to cancer. There are also cancer cluster studies in many states to determine whether there is a correlation between an abnormally high incidence of a particular cancer with a particular environment.

Though we may not know the exact cause of a number of the most frequent cancers we do know from studies that diet has some bearing on reducing the risk of cancer as it has for heart disease and stroke. Exercise also seems to have a bearing on some cancers. In addition to the internet, there are other sources for information, counseling and support. If you have a local chapter of the American Cancer Society, it should be able to direct you to appropriate help.

We must take an active part in cancer prevention. There are particular tests that are recommended for people over fifty that will detect cancer early. The earlier the detection the better one's chances for recovery and survival

Heart Disease and Stroke

I was three when I remember seeing my grandfather huddled in the corner of his dining room, a blanket wrapped around him, a grimace on his face. He had a history of heart problems and had had a stroke three years earlier which left him unable to move or to speak. He was a very frightening spectacle for such a young child, and I'm sure that the effects of his stroke made a terrible existence for him, for he had been an articulate, intellectual man who took great pride in his philanthropic work. He was only 57. Later, more than twenty years ago, I knew two men in their 40's who developed strokes which left them paralyzed and unable to talk. One had been an editor, the other a private school headmaster, both of them intellectuals. Interestingly enough, they found each other and were able to visit and play chess together once a week, and perhaps they found a way of communicating with each other. But their incapacities were tragedies for them and their families.

These days we are so conscious of lowering blood pressure and preventing heart problems by giving up smoking and adhering to a proper diet and exercise that we hear much less about strokes that leave people quite so disabled. Also, many drugs are now used effectively to treat heart disease, high blood pressure, high cholesterol and triglycerides, all of which can lead to further heart problems and perhaps also to stroke. In addition, coronary by-pass surgery is now used for many men with clogged arteries who after the surgery go on to lead fairly normal lives. (Why is it we hear of just men who have this surgery?) After surgery or a heart attack, patients are given help in making the transition from hospital to home with education on diet and exercise, and then afterwards out-patient help is given with stress management, weight control and smoking cessation, if that has been a problem. Evaluating medications is an important part of the rehabilitation of a patient who has had a heart attack or heart surgery. Cholesterol-lowering drugs, aspirin and beta blockers can prevent further problems and save lives. Some physicians are afraid to refer patients for rehabilitation programs, particularly the sickest and the oldest, because they fear the risk with exercise. However, statistics show that any risk is slight, and some studies of heart transplant patients who enter rehabilitation programs show a definite improvement.

A heart attack is a form of cardiovascular disease that occurs when blood stops flowing to the heart muscle, causing damage or death to parts of the heart. Sometimes blood flow can be stopped on its way to the brain rather than the heart; this event is a stroke. A stroke can also be caused by a blood clot in the brain, or a clot that forms elsewhere in the body that travels to the brain, causing an embolism. A third cause for stroke is a bursting of an aneurysm, a sac formed by an enlargement of the wall of an artery in the brain, which causes hemorrhaging. In men, signs of a heart attack can be an uncomfortable, sometimes excruciating squeezing pain in the middle of the chest lasting more than a few minutes, pain spreading to the shoulder, neck or arms, lightheadedness, fainting, sweating, nausea or shortness of breath. Indications of a heart attack in a woman can be very different and many times very subtle. If you are in a great deal of discomfort and suspect a heart attack, call your doctor immediately or even an ambulance.

Symptoms of a stroke are a sudden weakness or numbness of the face, arm or leg on one side of the body; sudden dimness or loss of vision, especially in one eye; loss of speech or slurred speech; sudden severe headaches; dizziness; and unsteadiness or sudden falls, especially if they occur along with the other stroke symptoms. If any of these symptoms of a heart attack or stroke or both should occur, you should get help immediately, as fewer deaths occur when appropriate drugs are given within one to two hours after the onset of symptoms.

High blood pressure damages blood vessels and weakens the heart, so controlling it is essential in preventing coronary artery disease and heart failure. Blood pressure is the force applied by blood against the walls of the arteries as it is pumped from the heart. When pressure is applied in greater than normal force for great lengths of time, there is trouble. High blood pressure is a sign of an abnormal pumping action. There are two readings: the upper or systolic pressure, which is the measure of the peak force of the blood as the heart pumps it out, and the diastolic pressure or the lower reading, which is the measure of pressure when the heart is at rest between beats. Readings will vary. Measurements tend to be lowest in the morning before rising and show a rise during the day and after exercise and stress. If my doctor, for instance, takes a patient's blood pressure and gets a high reading, he will take it again in a few minutes after the patient has had a chance to relax. If a person's pressure is consistently higher than 140 over 90, there is reason for concern. What will help lower the blood pressure is weight loss, exercise, intake of less salt, and moderation in the use of alcohol. If these alone do not work, anti-hypertension medication can be prescribed by a doctor.

Globally, women have two and a half times the risk that men have for heart problems, although men develop them at an earlier age. Studies have shown that the use of oral contraceptives for more than ten years does not increase the risk of a heart attack. Now it is thought that the delay in onset of cardiovascular problems in women is because of high levels of estrogen in the body before menopause. Birth control pills and smoking continue to be a risky combination, but the moderate use of alcohol is helpful. Excess weight is an especially significant factor in women, for just twenty or thirty pounds extra weight increases by 80% the chance of a woman having a heart attack. Women with much higher intakes of vitamin C and vitamin E in addition to beta-carotene have a much lower incidence of heart disease. Also, women with close friendships and ties with family seem to have fewer heart attacks. A recent report in the American Journal of Medicine reported that, contrary to popular thinking, studies show that estrogen plus progestin therapy for post-menopausal women do not prevent heart attacks, but instead open the door to clot formation in the veins and lungs. This was shown to be true despite the many advantages that hormone replacement therapy offers.

Interestingly enough, another study reported in the *New York Times* declares that estrogen supplements both improve a women's cholesterol levels but also reduce other substances in the blood that raise the risk of a heart attack or stroke. This would seem to contradict the earlier report in the American Journal of Medicine. Check with your doctor on the use of hormone replacement therapy and its relationship to heart attacks or stroke.

In the health care field there are certain gurus, and Dr Dean Ornish is one. His programs to prevent or reverse heart disease are rigorous. In addition to following his very stringent low-fat diet and giving up smoking, patients on the program attend exercise programs, support groups and classes in stress management based on yoga. With the few studies he has done, he has found that patients who followed his program ended up with lower cholesterol levels, less chest pain and improved heart function. He has critics among other doctors who question whether research supports his claims, especially since there have been so few studies with so few people. Yet people who have undergone his programs swear by them, some claiming that they were able to avoid surgery as a result of faithful adherence to his regime.

Despite all of the information that we have available on heart disease and strokes, there are over 700,000 people each year who have strokes, which are the third highest killer and the highest disabler in the United States. Only 5% make it to the hospital in time to be helped. The National Institute of Neurological Disorders and Stroke wants strokes to be given a new name, "brain attacks," and to require the same attention given to strokes as is given to heart attacks. People should know the warning signs of stroke so that they can get immediate help if they suspect they have had one. If people have one or more of the following symptoms they should call 911: loss of sensation on one side of the body, loss of the ability to speak or to understand speech, loss of vision in one or both eyes, loss of balance, and even headaches. Any one of them can be a sign of possible stroke. Taking an aspirin a day can lessen the chances of getting coronary artery disease or stroke.

Doctors are now just beginning to treat strokes very differently, enabling patients through the use of amphetamines and intense physical therapy to recover speech and movement of limbs in the first weeks and months after the stroke. However, these may not be the appropriate treatments for elderly people who have heart or other serious problems. Strokes are caused when blood flow in the brain is suddenly blocked or an artery ruptures.

Half of the 700,000 who get strokes will end up with some degree of permanent damage. A professor of psychology and neuroscience at the University of New Mexico discovered through experiments that rats with brain injuries similar to strokes were able to walk twenty-four hours after receiving a single dose of amphetamine.

There are now three ways to fight strokes. The first is to prevent them by reducing people's risk factors. The second is to treat the stroke within the first three hours with the use of clot busters, or what are referred to as TPAs to restore blood flow and help avert brain damage. In February 1999 it was announced a new drug, proukinase, had been found to reverse massive strokes within six hours of the first symptoms. It is released by the use of a catheter threaded through an artery directed into the brain.

Many people, however, do not get treatment that quickly. Therefore, the third way is to intervene within days or weeks after the stroke has occurred. New findings from neuroscience research show that, contrary to what most people think, help can be given during this period of time. Many neurons in the brain are left temporarily stunned rather than dead after a stroke. They may have been connected to cells that have died so that messages do not get through, and eventually some of those stunned cells die, while others find new hookups and start functioning spontaneously. Amphetamine works by causing the brain to release noradrenaline. This substance, which is the basis for learning and memory, helps cells wake up and respond. Other drugs, including Ritalin, also release noradrenaline. These drugs are ineffective by themselves, so physical therapy is also essential. (There is no evidence of increased blood pressure or heart rate with the use of amphetamine.) Patients on this regime achieve in six weeks what usually takes six months, and studies have shown that a year later after the amphetamine has been stopped, those patients are far ahead of those who did not take it. The people for whom this treatment has been used have been badly damaged by the stroke, but they improved enough by amphetamine or other drugs so that they did not need nursing home care. However, it has been and probably will be used only on a small number of patients, for the risks of the drug are uncertain, and amphetamine is known to be addictive. It also is an old, inexpensive drug that can no longer be patented, so drug companies have no incentive to test it in clinical trials on stroke patients.

As with heart disease, it is important to know the importance of preventing strokes. Heart disease and artherosclerotic cerebrovascular disease that lead to stroke often occur at the same time. Yet statistics show that stroke patients are more apt to die of a heart attack than another stroke. Patients must change their life style by stopping smoking, reducing alcohol consumption and cholesterol and treating high blood pressure.

At the age of 42, Robert McCrum, editor-in-chief of the British publishing firm of Faber & Faber, woke up one morning to find that he was unable to get out of bed. Alone in the house, he managed to get out by falling to the floor and then by slipping in and out of consciousness and taking all day by half-crawling, half-falling down the stairs, he got himself to a telephone on the first floor where he called for help. He had had a stroke without any apparent cause such as elevated blood pressure or an aneurysm. During the next year while he recuperated both he and his wife kept memoirs of his progress, and he found that during that time he took stock of his life, and became renewed in his understanding of family and the immense value of love.

Ways We Can Prevent Heart Disease and Stroke

Again, diet and exercise are of prime importance in preventing heart disease and stroke. In addition to keeping our weight down, we need to eat a diet that is low in fat, particularly animal fat, and high in fiber. It is also felt that a higher intake of vitamin C and beta-carotene reduces the incidence of high cholesterol and triglycerides, which clog the arteries. Smoking in particular is a prime cause of heart disease and stroke and a combination of it and birth control pills in younger women is especially damaging.

After you have tried all of these, if tests show that your cholesterol and triglyceride levels are still too high, your doctor will probably prescribe one of the new drugs that can dramatically reduce cholesterol and triglycerides.

Be aware of the symptoms of a heart attack and stroke so that you can get immediate help. The earlier one gets help, by way of ambulance, hospital or one's own physician, the earlier a regime can be started and in turn the greater your chances are for survival.

However, remember, you are very much the captain of your fate and it is not too late to change your life style to improve your risk factors for heart disease and stroke. So get off your duff and exercise, and remember one of the most effective exercises is to prepare the right diet and to push away from the dinner table.

Alzheimer's Disease

We have a friend in Green Valley who identifies his momentary memory lapses as a "Green Valley moment," and everyone laughs when this happens, as we all have those moments. However, they are moments of great frustration and sometimes embarrassment, for the disease that all of us fear most is Alzheimer's Disease. It is a disease that kills the essence of a person, can last for years, and wreaks havoc on a family, on its energy, patience and resources. There is still no definite known cause, and only a few drugs for treating it have been approved by the Food And Drug Administration.

Researchers are still trying to find the cause of Alzheimer's. In seeking the possible genetic components they are looking at three chromosomes associated with it, 21, 14 and 19. But little is a known yet and therefore prevention of the disease is not yet possible. Dementia is a generic name for the loss of intellectual functions. It is not a disease in itself but a group of symptoms that may accompany a disease such as Alzheimer's, the most common cause of dementia. Although research is being done on predicting Alzheimer's, it can still be best diagnosed with an autopsy.

Approximately 4,000,000 Americans had the disease in 1992; by the middle of the next century, perhaps 14,000,000 will have it. One in 10 people over the age of 65 and nearly half of those over the age of 85 have Alzheimer's. More than 7 out of 10 with the disease live at home; of those almost 75% are cared for by a family member. The rest of those living at home are looked after by a paid helper at an average of $12,500 a year. Over the country, half of nursing home residents suffer from Alzheimer's or a related disorder such as Parkinson's disease, Huntington's disease, or other dementias. The cost of caring for an Alzheimer's patient in a nursing home in 1992 ranged from $42,000 to over $70,000 a year depending on the area of the country. Since Alzheimer's patients can live many years, the average lifetime cost for each patient is $174,000. After cancer and heart disease it is the third most expensive disease in the United States.

Warning signs of Alzheimer's can include the following: recent memory loss that is not just occasional; difficulty performing familiar tasks; problems with language, which may lead to an inappropriate sentence; disorientation to time and place, which leads to patients getting lost even in their own neighborhood; poor judgment such as putting on inappropriate clothing; problems with abstract thinking; misplacing things; rapid mood swings; changes in personality, and loss of initiative. A doctor must make the diagnosis so that the family can face the problem and start planning for care.

For the past 20 years, scientists at New York University's Silberstein's Aging and Dementia Research Laboratory Medical Center have studied the brain during the aging process, from normal live brains and healthy behavior through dementia to autopsy. Using magnetic resonance imaging to scan a subject's brain, they can tell from the size of the hippocampus, a kidney shaped structure in the brain, what a person's memory capacity is. At this point the lab is focusing on the entorhinal cortex, which is a memory processing center of the brain that funnels information to the hippocampus. Subjects in the study are seen every two years for the rest of their lives. For three days they are put through a battery of tests: the M.R.I., psychiatric, neuropsychological and memory testing, as well as thorough neurological and physical examinations. They are given numerous word memory tests, finger tapping tests, as there apparently is a correlation between cognitive impairment and poor motor control, and tests for spatial relations. In addition, subjects are tested on their ability to recognize angles of lines, and are even given computer tests that resemble computer games. The head of the laboratory has been able to develop the scales used worldwide to measure the losses of abilities in Alzheimer's. Presumably, from the M. R. I., the researchers can find in the brain premonitions of the disease, for the entorhinal cortex is 27% smaller in people with mild forms of Alzheimer's, and 45% smaller in people with severe Alzheimer's.

On September 6, 1998, the National Broadcast Company *Today Show* gave a good deal of useful information on drug treatment for Alzheimer's. Naturally, when parts of the brain have shrunk cells have died as a result of the accumulation of toxic proteins called amytoids. There are two F.D.A. approved drugs on the market for use with

Alzheimer's patients: Cognex, which has side effects for older people, and Aricept, which can cause some gastric side effects but has shown cognitive and memory improvement in 25% of patients. Two thousand units a day of Vitamin E is recommended, but it may cause clotting side effects. Women who have been on estrogen are less likely to develop Alzheimer's. Gingko Biloba, which is reputedly helpful in improving memory, has been found to have little effect. Anti-psychotic and anti-depressive drugs can be used to improve behavior.

Wandering becomes a considerable problem as Alzheimer's disease progresses and the patient loses the ability to recognize his neighborhood or home. (In developments where every house looks like the next one I sometimes think it doesn't necessarily take something like Alzheimer's for someone to get lost at night!) Because the wandering becomes dangerous, patients often have to be put in institutions such as nursing homes that have locked Alzheimer's units. Almost every local newspaper has stories of lost patients with Alzheimer's who may be gone for days. One such resident of Green Valley, Arizona, was gone for more than a day, driving with his poodle three hundred miles east to Las Cruces, New Mexico, and then from there west another four hundred miles to Why, Arizona in search of the graveyard where his wife was buried—except that his wife's ashes had been sent to New Jersey for burial. "Safe Return" is a nationwide identification, support and registration program. When a person is missing, "Safe Return" faxes the registrant's information and photo to the local police. When the patient is found, the law official calls the 800 number and "Safe Return" notifies the listed contacts. On registration, the participant receives a bracelet with his name, his Safe Return identification number and a toll free telephone number. If you are interested in this national program, call 1-800-272-3900 or your local Alzheimer's Association chapter.

Most Alzheimer's patients are cared for at home by a spouse, other relative or by paid help. The task is both demanding and draining, physically and emotionally. In many communities, there are day treatment programs offered through nursing homes or social agencies, and support groups for caregivers. Both kinds of groups are helpful, especially the day treatment programs, as they give the family a respite. I have sat in on two conferences in Green Valley for caregivers, and have been enormously impressed by their love and dedication. Each of the conferences stressed how important it is for them to get away regularly and to try to maintain some independent life for a few hours a week. If the responsibility becomes too much for the family, or the patient has reached a point where the behavior or physical needs are too overwhelming, it is time to consider getting in home health care or nursing home placement. The following is a solution found by the family of one Alzheimer's patient.

A Special Kind of Caretaker

For a number of years, an artist friend of mine has been caring for elderly people in their own home or in hers. She is naturally a warm, caring person who enjoys what she is doing. At this point for seven days a week, twelve hours each day, she cares for an 86 year old Alzheimer's patient who is still only mildly impaired. Although Bill lives with a relative, he is considered part of Maria's family and enters into their family life. He has been on a new drug for three years, which has successfully maintained him at his level without any dramatic deterioration. He is sociable and is appreciative of what is done for him, and Maria uses a great deal of creativity to keep Bill busy. At no time does she patronizingly treat him as a child, as I've seen done in so many nursing homes with Alzheimer's patients. She and Bill follow a pretty regular routine, each day doing something special. One half-day each week they attend an art class taught by an artist at the local senior center. Another half day they volunteer to teach arts and crafts to a kindergarten class. Other days they visit friends or Maria's mother, take care of the vegetable and flower gardens, and attend community events. Everywhere they go, Maria takes pictures of Bill with other people, so that he has a reminder of the person and the event.

Maria and Bill once visited my home, and my husband was able to converse with Bill in his native language. During that visit with us, Bill was able to recall his youth and early adulthood and carried on a pleasant conversation with us. Yet he was unable to remember things that he had been told a few minutes earlier, so his caretaker had to repeat the same instruction to him many times, and many times had to prepare him for what was coming next.

Bill and Maria spend much time reviewing the album of pictures they have put together showing all of the activities they have been involved with. Over the three years she has cared for him, he has made the adjustment to a move to a new area, to Maria as a new caretaker and to her family and friends and a new way of living. He is given constant attention and stimulation, respect and loving care by Maria, her family and friends and is holding his own. Maria feels that nursing homes fail to see Alzheimer's patients as individuals with their own life histories.

I agree with Maria that institutionalized patients are not seen as individuals with a history of their own. In my visits to many nursing homes and as director of social service in one, I have found that confused patients can be reached and communicated with if more flexibility and imagination are used. There is a way of looking for and responding to confused patients' feelings that lie underneath what they are trying to say. As an example, I was once reviewing charts at a nursing home unit set aside for confused patients. In front of the nursing station where I was working was a very neat, clean, prettily dressed patient in a wheelchair. She was trying to say something to me in German. I responded to her by saying how pretty she looked, and her answer to me was to say in English with a smile, "You speak German, don't you!" I had given her special attention, and it was evident that she felt that I "spoke her language" and understood her.

Alternative Medical Treatment

Robert McCrum, in *My Year Off*, describes turning to a Chinese acupuncturist about halfway through his treatment and recovery from a stroke (see Heart Disease and Stroke section of this chapter.) He secured permission from his neurologist to use acupuncture and did see some improvement after several weeks of treatment, but was never sure whether this was because of the acupuncture or not. Later, when he was depressed he used St. John's Wort herb, finding he had more satisfactory results from it than from Prozac.

A friend of mine who has been a diabetic since the age of fifteen and became blind almost twenty years ago found ten years ago that she was unable to move her legs from her knees down. She consulted with a Tibetan healer who examined her and prescribed a combination of herbs, which she continues to take and feels they have measurably improved her condition.

Another friend who was diagnosed with prostate cancer was scheduled for surgery. He immediately consulted a Tibetan Buddhist healer who prescribed herbs and exercise and urged him to get another x-ray after following the regimen. The new x-ray showed no cancer and he cancelled his date for surgery. Several years later, he was diagnosed with colon cancer and once more sought the services of a herbalist. Again, tests showed no cancer after he had followed the herbalist's prescription. Both times his doctors were astounded.

We all have heard many stories similar to these of people who have taken herbs or followed some other alternative medical treatment such as a diet, special exercises, massage, acupuncture, chants, or meditation and were healed or saw a change in their condition. Often there was no rational or scientific explanation for the improvement, which was at times quite spontaneous, or even miraculous. Were they misdiagnosed in the first place? Was the improvement only temporary? Were these people intense, even fanatical believers in the unconventional treatment they were using? Did these people improve only because they wanted to so much, and so the expectation became the reality?

There have been studies on the relationship between mind and body, but we still know little of the power of the mind over the body, and much less about the role of the spirit. Most holistic doctors believe that conventional doctors attend only to the physical body and neglect the other two parts of the being. Yet over the past few years conventional doctors seem to be more open to the use of some herbs and some vitamins as preventive medicine for specific problems that might become something much more serious. I have had two doctors prescribe herbs and vitamins in the treatment of high cholesterol, at the same time urging a low fat diet and regular exercise. The University of Arizona Medical School has set up a department of integrative medicine with Dr. Andrew Weil, author of *Spontaneous Healing* as an associate director. However, most doctors feel that alternative medicine can sometimes be risky because the herbs are not designated as either food or drugs and therefore have not been properly tested by the Food and Drug Administration. Therefore, there is no real scientific proof for claims made.

Faced with an extremely serious illness such as cancer, most people will follow conventional medicine that is proven treatment, even as brutal and as toxic as the chemicals are that may be used. Yet how harmful are massage, acupuncture, yoga, prayer or meditation if they are used along with the conventional treatment? If these practices seem to work without our knowing the reason, then why not "go for it," as long as we do not rely on these treatments alone?

Summary

Certainly the relationship between doctors and patients and between doctors and nurses has improved in the last twenty years. Doctors are involving patients more directly in their treatment plans and are showing more respect and humanity toward them. In turn, patients must not put doctors on a pedestal, and must be more assertive in asking for information and making known their own wishes. In turn, nurses have come into their own. They are no longer the handmaidens of doctors, but are respected in their own right, and are moving on to many administrative positions.

As people survive chronic illnesses for longer periods of time and face very difficult terminal illnesses, health care professionals, particularly doctors, must understand what psychological meaning their illnesses have for their patients but also what metaphorical meaning society has given to their diseases. All of us who cherish those patients must also try to understand.

Chapter VII

A Better Death

> *No one knows whether death, which men in their fear apprehend to be the greatest evil, may not be the greatest good.*
> Socrates, in the <u>Apology</u> of Plato

Death is an inevitable part of life. However, as small children, or perhaps as adults during our happiest and most exhilarating moments, we may have wished for eternal life, for that particular moment to stop and last forever. Yet in many stories, classical and modern, a character is assigned eternal life, or he wishes for it, without specifying that he or she actually wants perpetual youth and health; and so in effect the character is cursed with endless aging and all its attendant frailties.

For instance, in the Greek myth, the goddess of dawn. Eos carried off Ganymedes and Tithonus, human brothers. When Zeus subsequently robbed her of Ganymedes, she begged Zeus to grant immortality to Tithonus, but forgot to ask him to grant eternal youth. Day by day, Tithonus became older, grayer and more shrunken and his voice became thinner and reedier. Eventually Eos, tired of caring for him, locked him in a room where he turned into a cicada.

In Jonathan Swift's *Gulliver's Travels,* the struldbrugs are human beings who live forever without being given eternal youth. They just get older and older, lose their memory, lose interest in their families and in life itself.

Aldous Huxley's *After Many a Summer Dies the Swan* is about an American millionaire who discovers how to achieve immortality. He learns of an 18th century lord who decided that one could achieve immortality by eating carp intestines since carp live to such an old age. The lord ate a great amount of carp intestines and ended up living to be about two hundred years old. However, he first became a moral degenerate, then retreated to a castle where he gradually turned into an ape. At the end of the story, despite knowing all of the degeneration that has taken place, the American millionaire is tempted to go the same route that the lord had.

In Par Lagerkvist's *The Sibyl*, a narrator in the story is cursed with eternal life by the Christ figure carrying the cross, whom he would not allow to lean against his house. Before he moved on, Christ said to him menacingly, "Because you denied me this, you shall suffer greater punishment than mine: you shall never die. You shall wander through this world to all eternity, and find no rest."[1] The old man continued to suffer from the curse forever.

All of these stories show what a living hell it would be to have eternal life as they did. In that state, they continued for eternity to degenerate physically and morally in one situation. They became more wizened, more frail, more bent, and more lifeless without the blessing of death. Even if one were to remain a youth forever, without the changes that take place with natural aging, life could become very tedious. According to Dr. Sherwin Nuland, there is plenty of evidence to support the idea of a specific time limited life span for each species. Rather than seeking the Fountain

---

1. Par Lagerkvist, <u>The Sybil</u>, (New York, Vintage Books, 1958)

of Youth, we should reconcile ourselves to our mortality and replaceability and accept that there is a new generation that should replace us. The process of life from birth to death as we know it is what is right.

> *That which has been born must die. The two are one: birth and death are one event which happens to a being, but which is cleft in twain by a little fissure we call life.*
>
> Sir Edwin Arnold, *Death and Afterwards*, 1901
>
> *To every thing there is a season, and a time to every purpose under the heaven: a time to be born, and a time to die*
>
> Ecclesiastes, Chapter 3, Verse 1-2

WITHDRAWAL OF TREATMENT

Over the past thirty years, in this country and in Canada, there has been a long history of events and court decisions leading up to the routine use of and respect for living wills and health care proxies. In the 1950's, most Americans died at home with relatives and the family doctor in attendance. Since then, a revolution in medical care has taken place so that in the 1980's as many as eighty percent of the 5,500 Americans who died each day did so, "wired and incubated, in an institution where the expensive technology [was] arrayed and controlled by specialists, who likely [knew] little about the patient beyond the medical problem"[2] Often a subrosa understanding based on trust would take place between the attending doctor and patient and family so that if some methods of life-prolonging treatment were used and did not work, they would be quietly removed and the cause of death would be given as the underlying disease.

---

[2] *Andrew H. Malcolm, "A.M.A. Rule: Step Toward a Social Policy on Dying," N.Y. Times, 3/17/86.*

The Karen Quinlan and Nancy Cruzan cases were crucial in determining legislation that would define the circumstances under which life- sustaining equipment could be terminated. In New York, it was not until July 1, 1987 after a long and heated debate that the State Senate approved guidelines for deciding when physicians should and should not resuscitate terminally ill patients. The guidelines followed recommendations made in 1986 by the State Task Force on Life and Law which stipulated that all patients facing cardiac or respiratory arrest would be resuscitated unless the attending physician had been given the patient's consent not to act. The consent, given in advance by a competent patient, would absolve the physician of civil or criminal liability for the patient's death.

As I urged in the first chapter, it is immensely important to prepare an advance directive called a Living Will long before you are sick and may need one. This form is often available at the time of admission to the hospital, but filling it out should not wait until that point; it should be done at your leisure when you are still of sound mind and are under no emotional stress. What is under consideration is your body and therefore it is your right if you are competent to make independent decisions without duress. The Living Will especially designates in advance your desires for end-of-life treatment, should your attending physician and a second physician determine that there is no possibility of recovery or that death is imminent. At that time, you may be unable to participate in medical decisions.

If it is your desire, on the form you should be as specific as possible in communicating that you do not wish artificial life-support procedures to be used for the purpose of prolonging the dying process. You should also specify that you do not wish cardiac resuscitation, artificial respiration, antibiotics, blood, infusions or tube feedings, but that you do want maximum pain relief. The form should be witnessed by two people, and notarized. A copy should go to your doctor(s), to the person you have named as your Health Care Proxy, and possibly to your minister. When you are hospitalized, you should take the Living Will and the Health Care Proxy along, and nowadays many specialists to whom you may be referred will ask for a copy.

A Health Care Proxy, also called a Health Care Power of Attorney, should always accompany the Living Will. This is also a legal document that designates who will be responsible for making medical decisions for you, should you be so incapacitated that you are unable to make or to communicate them yourself. On the same form, you should designate a second person to act as health care agent in the event that the first person is either incapable or unwilling to do so. This form also has to be witnessed, but in Arizona it can be notarized rather than witnessed.

Both forms can be purchased in a stationery store, and they are generally respected except under unusual circumstances. For instance, I have heard of some ambulance corps that will attempt to revive a person even if there is a "Do Not Resuscitate" order. I also understand that many doctors will not abide by all of the stipulations in a Living Will if there is not total agreement by the family members.

Facing Life and Death With Courage And Grace

My husband and I are at an age when a number of friends are dying, some of them very close friends of many years, and more than our own death, we fear losing such people with whom we have been closest. Several of these people have shown special courage and grace over long periods of fighting cancer, and can be examples for us.

In 1993, Patricia had a lumpectomy for breast cancer, and it was also discovered then that at least one out of fifteen lymph nodes that were removed was affected. Four years later, her husband, who was ten years her senior, died in a nursing home after a number of years of various illnesses including prostate cancer. After his death, she remained in their northeast home, to which they had retired some fifteen years before, since she had friends and family in the area. Both of her sons lived at great distances, one in Europe, another on the West Coast. After her breast surgery, Patricia was seen periodically by her oncologist, and there were some problems found, but nothing major until the end of January 1998, 4 1/2 years after her surgery, when it was discovered that her breast cancer had metastasized to her bones and liver. As if she had not suffered enough, another sudden tragedy hit her with the news that her older son had died three weeks after a diagnosis of leukemia. This, of course, delayed her own medical treatment.

With characteristic humor, when her oncologist gave her a 40% chance of surviving, she bargained with him for fifty percent. In April she started another six months series of chemotherapy from which she suffered such severe side affects including extreme nausea and anemia, weight loss and fainting that the chemicals had to be changed and the strength weakened. Her oncologist made house calls to inject her with drugs to fight her anemia and to strengthen her immune system. She insisted on driving herself back and forth for her chemotherapy, but could use help from family and friends if she needed it. Even though she was in bed most of the time, she would not consider employing someone to come in to help her, feeling that she must do whatever she could for herself. There was only a small window of a few days between chemotherapy and injections when she felt well enough to go out to shop and to visit with people. At one point she mentioned to me that the experience had absolved her of the obligation that she always had to please other people.

We had lunch with her in July between her treatments when her son and daughter-in-law were visiting from Europe. She was hardly recognizable because of the wig she was wearing and a weight loss of 35 pounds. The loss of her eyebrows was the most startling change, for this alone completely changed the character of her face. But she was as ebullient as usual, talking about the shopping she had done with her daughter-in-law, and reminiscing with us, as well as discussing current events. She was hopeful. However, in October the results of the latest tests showed that there was more disease. She was then told that she would live no more than two months without another six-month course of chemotherapy. When I mused that I would be unable to do it, she said emphatically that she had to.

Patricia lived for two years after the recurrence of the cancer. At her memorial service her son said that during those two years when she was so ill "she managed to find moments of pleasure in each and every day of that period, right up to the end....She could not understand those for whom life was a veil of tears or a burden of sorrows. For her, each day was a chance to speak with people, to meet them, to listen to them, and yes, to have them listen to her....She delighted in the view from her bedroom window, rather than bemoaning the weakness that often kept her from getting up and out. She lavished attention upon her flowering plants, finding them to be kindred spirits in their celebration of the wonder and joy of life. She always sought out the pleasure rather than settling for the pain....She has left this life that she loved so much. But she only left after taking as much from it as a person possibly could."

Another friend in 1994 at the age of 42 was found to have advanced breast cancer, which she had not discovered until she readily felt the tumor herself. Priscilla was self-employed without medical insurance so that she had not had regular physicals and certainly had not had a mammogram. She was advised to start chemotherapy immediately, but as a follower of holistic medicine and of other New Age systems, she decided that she did not want to use chemicals and instead turned to a Western clinic that used alternative methods to treat cancer. As I remember, from her explanation to me, the clinic used injections of gamma globulin over three weeks time to attempt to stimulate the immune system to fight her cancer, but the treatment failed and she returned home to the East Coast to die within three months. Priscilla had a much shorter illness then Patricia had but she too was valiant through several very painful months. During those last months, she had many friends rally around to take care of her. This and her very unique funeral will be described elsewhere in the book.

During the summer of 1998, I attended a seminar at the Omega Institute in Rhinebeck, New York, entitled *Conscious Life, Conscious Death*, led by Stephen and Ondrea Levine, internationally known thanatologists. There were about three hundred people in the weekend workshop, many of them professionals who work with the dying in hospices and other settings, and other people with terminal illnesses who had been given only so long to live. Through many meditation and breathing exercises and interviews with patients, they showed us how they help people honestly come to terms with living and dying, how to cope with pain and fear and how to have a peaceful death, especially through forgiveness, mercy and reconciliation with themselves and others.

One study done at Sloan-Kettering Institute in New York showed that 85% of cancer patients have terminal delirium, including agitation and auditory and visual hallucinations. According to Dr. William Breitbart, a world-renowned psycho-oncologist at Sloan-Kettering, the difference between a hallucination and a near-death experience, or dead relatives talking to you is a matter of perspective. To control behavior, he will prescribe psychotropic drugs. In nursing homes, I have sat with dying patients who appeared to be hallucinating. One elderly patient, in particular called out for days to her dead parents who appeared to be very present and comforting to her.

Theresa Schroeder-Sheker, a musician who lives in Missoula, Montana, has founded the Chalice of Reposes clinical practice and school in Missoula, which trains musicians to play the harp to dying hospice patients in hospitals, nursing homes and their own homes in order to calm them. The music is synchronized to their breathing. The technique was developed by French Cluny monks in the 11th century as a way of calming patients and helping their souls escape. The same music that was used by the 11th century monks is used by these 20th century practitioners.

Marilyn Webb avers that the "good death" has more to do with the decisions we and our health care providers make about our medical treatment and terminal care than with fate or good luck. She believes that dying well can be defined only by how the patient defines it, but that every good death has the following elements in common:

— Excessive treatment that extends the process of dying is <u>not</u> given.
— Pain medication is given appropriately and aggressively.
— The dying person is shown respect and is given as much power to make decisions as he or she wants.

— Emotional issues are addressed.
— Family and friends get all of the psychological, spiritual and physical help that they need.

I would like to add another element to a good death. Patients, if possible, should not die alone, even if it means using a sensitive volunteer to sit with the patient to hold his or her hand if this makes the patient more comfortable.

First and foremost, pain must be dealt with. I have heard of doctors who refused to increase doses of morphine to dying patients who were obviously suffering tremendous pain only because they feared the patient might become addicted to the drug. What kind of foolishness is this? Also, doctors must give full disclosure and not minimize the risks of certain procedures or surgeries. According to Dr. Sherwin Nuland, doctors often feel that they must "rescue" the patient, and the unwritten code of surgeons "demands that no patient if salvageable be allowed to die if an operation can save the patient."[3] I once knew a terribly frail and disabled nursing home emphysema patient, who developed some kind of abdominal problem that the doctors felt necessitated surgery. She agreed to the surgery, but after the operation was unable to leave the hospital because she could never be weaned off of the respirator. Instead of returning to the nursing facility, which had been her home for several years and where she received extremely nurturing care, she had to remain in the hospital intensive care unit where she died several weeks after the surgery. I always felt that this surgery was pointless and wondered whether the patient was informed of all of the possible risks. Doctors do not own patients. It is the patient who should have autonomy over his own body and who is the one to make life and death decisions.

---

3. Sherwin Nuland, *The Way We Die*, (New York: Alfred A. Knopf, 1994), page 253.

Even a competent patient who is very sick can use an advocate to help secure all of the necessary information in order for him or her to make the most informed and appropriate decision. The advocate can be a family member or close friend, a clergyman or clergywoman, or even a nurse or social worker on the health provider's staff. Try to choose your advocate well in advance in case there is an emergency.

Advances in medicine have made it difficult often to tell when death is imminent. Most people today decline slowly from chronic diseases of the heart, lungs and kidneys with unpredictable courses, whereas earlier people were more apt to die quickly from infections, accidents and heart problems. And unlike thirty years ago people are more apt to die in hospitals surrounded by medical technology rather than at home. Patients need to discuss with their doctors about "end of life planning" in advance rather than relying just on the written advance directive, but with managed care it is difficult to find the time to do this until a crisis has set in. Both patients and physicians need to be educated more.

Oftentimes patients' wishes are not followed only because they are not specific enough in their directives, or because the written directives have been misplaced or lost, or because relatives disagree about an interpretation of the patients' wishes. Often, doctors may overrule the family and refuse to stop treatment because they feel the course of the disease has already been too unpredictable, or they are afraid of lawsuits if they turn off life support. Therefore, the American Medical Association has developed a two and a half day course for doctors on how to deal with families and on the psychological and medical details of taking care of people whose systems are shutting down, including the use of effective pain control. Doctors taking the course are urged to initiate discussions with patients while they are still well on what they want when they are terminally ill, and make periodic reviews.

The attending physician should tactfully inform the patient that he or she is terminally ill. Many patients sense they are dying anyway before it becomes imminent, but unless death is openly discussed, games can be played and then issues are not dealt with. The patient can enter into a kind of unspoken conspiracy with the doctor to protect the doctor and the family. Sometimes, it is most helpful, if the patient opens the subject. This disclosure is understandably difficult for a doctor, but it is something that must be made openly to all so that the patient can do the things that he or she must do before the end. These are what are called the "unfinished business" of expressing our love to and sharing memories with those who are closest to us, healing rifts, and expressing what has meant the most to us during our lives. There are always some issues that cannot be resolved, but if we make the effort and are offered some help in doing so, we will be considerably freed. With all of this, the person's death will be as peaceful and comfortable as possible.

Hospice

A hospice is a service given by an interdisciplinary team of health care professionals to a terminally ill patient in a hospital, nursing home or in a private home. By definition, the patient is expected to die within six months, and no treatment is given other than palliative care to make the patient as comfortable as possible. Above all else, emphasis is placed on pain relief. The hospice also emphasizes helping the patient deal with the psychological and spiritual aspects of dying so that maximum peace is achieved. Assistance is also given to the family and to friends to deal with emotional issues around the patient's dying.

Gwen used a hospice when her husband was dying in 1996. Forty years before that he had had x-ray treatment in the abdomen for intestinal lymphoma and part of the intestine was removed. In 1994, another lymphoma was found and he was placed under the care of an oncologist, and in 1995 received a six month course of chemotherapy, which made him very irritable, depressed and difficult to live with. At the end of the six months, she felt they "found each other again," and there was a period of great closeness over the next seven or eight months before the first signs of a carcinoma were found. She described lymphoma as "like wallpaper shredding and carcinoma like the studs of a house giving way." His doctors found the cancer everywhere. Further surgery was done on his intestine and also on his bile duct, which was constricted. Through it all, he continued to chop wood and to drive to his workshop in a nearby town where he made very fine jewelry. In the summer of 1996 he was hospitalized but kept begging to go home, where the local hospice service would follow him. He was brought home the day before he died accompanied in the ambulance by the hospice nurse who stayed until two in the morning. Before she left she gave him a tranquilizer as he was convulsing and also because he kept trying to get out of bed. She left pain medication and instructed the family on how to give it. The hospice nurse returned at 7 a.m., and was unobtrusive while the family said their farewells, and then helped Gwen wash her husband after he died. Gwen spoke with great appreciation and respect of hospice, saying that they helped prepare the family for all of the steps to expect in the dying process and that they were always respectful of everyone.

I recently heard of a 67 year old woman who was dismissed from a hospice because she outlived the specific time limit of six months. She had multiple cancers, a colostomy and an ileostomy, but chose not to take chemotherapy, and was able to drive herself and to take walks. At times the will to live is phenomenal.

One important need mentioned repeatedly in books and articles is life review for the dying patient. I happen to think that a life review is psychologically helpful for all elderly people, and of course that is precisely what we all are doing when we reminisce so much. I was particularly conscious of this when I visited nursing homes as a regulator and would briefly interview patients about their care. Just the slightest observation on my part would prompt patients to spontaneously give me a five-minute social history that would be wrapped up in the end with what they saw as their greatest contribution in life. Invariably for the men what was important was their work, and for the women their families. They seemed to crave the chance to take stock of their lives. Subsequently, when I did work in nursing homes, I took many social histories, and whenever possible I tried to secure information even from the patients who were not entirely alert. I felt that it was terribly important for them to realize that they had had a special and unique place in this world. Some physicians, such as Dr. Robert Butler, suggest that memory in the process of a life review might be a trigger for biochemical and neurological changes in the brain that might lead to end of life ecstatic and mystical experiences. Many writers about death also mention an almost palpable sense of tremendous love that emanates from the dying patient just before the end.

The Role of Friends

One often feels very helpless as the friend of a dying person. I felt so at one point when a friend with advanced cancer gave me information that made me think that she was dying. The feeling of frustration was exacerbated by the fact that I lived more than a hundred miles away from her and could not visit spontaneously or even easily. I wanted so much to do something for and with her, and anticipated the enormous sense of loss I would feel when my old friend would finally leave us. I consulted my minister for some help with my own feelings and was then able to proceed with the relationship, and though we saw each other only infrequently I kept in regular telephone contact, and occasionally wrote. The calls had to be timed to the small window between her chemotherapy and other treatments when she had enough energy to talk on the telephone.

Visiting is a complex problem for friends, for the following questions run through one's mind. Should I visit? How often should I visit? When and what should I say? What should I not say? What can I do to help? Should I offer to help? Is it all right to hug and to touch?

Above all else be natural, be yourself, chat about things you always have talked about, but at the same time be sensitive that she or he may prefer to choose the topic. Your friend may want to talk about his or her illness. Let that happen. Often, just listening is enough to make him or her feel better. You should not be uncomfortable if there are silences, for there is comfort in companionable silence, and he or she may not have the energy for much talking. Take along photos of past occasions for people always enjoy reminiscing. Listen very carefully to your friend; if you are relaxed, you will be able to. Don't anticipate what he or she is going to say, just wait, look at that person and listen and accept whatever is said, even if anger or sadness or fear is expressed. He or she needs to be able to express honestly whatever he or she is feeling, and you, if you are a good friend may be the one to whom those feelings can best be expressed. Expect to see changes in mood from day to day and do not be surprised if the same topics are covered more than once. Repetition is often how issues are resolved.

Do not say you know how she or he feels, for no one knows how another person who is dying feels. People usually say that sort of thing when they are uncomfortable in what they consider a stressful situation and they do not know what to say. To say that you know how your friend feels is a kind of arrogance that might only make him or her angry and close off communication. Don't tell the person he or she looks great when he or she doesn't. It is very difficult, but try not to say "How're you doing?" If they are dying, they are really doing very badly. It may be better to say, "How are you feeling today?" for there will be days when he or she will feel badly and others that are better days. You will make mistakes, but your friend will forgive you. Above all else, at this point especially, honesty is important to the relationship.

Listen to your friend's account of her illness, be empathetic, but do not compare her illness with someone else's for that only diminishes him or her as a person. Also do not compare his or her treatment with someone else's, and do not talk about some new treatment you have read about, for that might shake his or her confidence in the treatment he or she is receiving.

Rather than leaving it up to your friend to think of some way you might help, just <u>do</u> something. Bring a book or magazine, bring in the mail and sort it, interpret and fill out medical insurance forms, offer to help with laundry or grocery shopping; offer to relieve the caregiver or give them some help with meal preparation, transportation, baby sitting etc. There are a multitude of concrete everyday tasks that you might do to help.

As your friend nears the end, he or she will want to see only a few people, so don't be hurt if that person withdraws.

You will sense when is the last visit. Make sure you tell your friend then how much your friendship has meant to you and how you will miss him or her, but that he or she will continue to make a difference in your life.

A group of friends can be of enormous help to the dying person. I know of at least two churches that have organized a group of people to care for the sick and dying in the congregation. One church named this group the 'Moon Sisters," and since the congregation is an aging one in their 60'and 70's, there have been a number of deaths in the last few years, many of them women with breast cancer. The church keeps a list of the "Moon Sisters" who will be used for transporting the patient to medical appointments, for shopping and other household tasks, and for sitting with the patient and giving whatever care is needed. About fifteen years ago, this group was started by the minister and several of the women in the congregation. In those years, the women have learned to accept many difficult situations and strong feelings but have certainly offered a real ministry, especially to those people who did not have family nearby. The minister herself joined in the care. Every patient dealt differently with their last days, some with rage, some determined to beat their cancer, some to live life to the hilt as they already had. One decided that she wished to be aware and yet as pain free as she could be and just a few days before her death described the balancing act she had to undergo to achieve this so that she could continue to attend concerts, museums and do her art work. Another woman, who had been an active member of the congregation had a family that closed ranks during illness, so that it was hard for the church to visit her. She was the type of person who all of her life gave to others, and then found it hard to accept help when she needed it the most.

When I heard all these accounts of loving, compassionate help, I could think of no better way to express one's religion.

In addition to helping the terminally ill patient, friends can also be of enormous help to the family. Again, concrete help such as cooking and shopping or providing respite care are welcomed, as well as calls of concern. However, unless you have a close relationship with the family, do not keep calling at times of medical crisis, especially if it is obvious that the family is under stress. You can detect whether the call is helpful or only an intrusion by the relative's tone of voice, unresponsiveness or an urgency to end the call. Their needs are more important than yours at this time.

The Role of the Clergy

The same church with the Moon Sisters group has had a hospice administrator come to the church to give a Sunday morning program. Another church under the minister's leadership held an eight week workshop for twelve people around issues raised by death such as cemeteries, burials, funerals and caring for the dying in the most compassionate way, and all of the many feelings around these issues. There was very specific information given about terminology, about laws governing disposal of the body, and about the cost of funerals, cremations and burials. There were discussions about the meaning of life and death and biblical and other readings, and then the minister followed up with a Sunday sermon on that church's position on the meaning of death and an afterlife.

A third congregation I am familiar with has perhaps twenty percent of its members who are retired or who are approaching retirement. Some people in that group had either already made major moves or were considering making them and felt they needed help in making other decisions about their last years. They requested that the minister set up a series of meetings to discuss issues of particular concern to them, which included housing, county services for the aged, nursing homes and adult homes in the county, and how to prepare financially for such care. There were also discussions about memorial societies, the costs of funeral and burial, and organ and body donation and how to arrange for them. More and more churches that I know of are providing sermons, informational meetings, exploratory workshops and individual counseling on issues of dying.

The role of the clergy with the sick and the dying is of paramount importance. Clergy can be enormously helpful in acting as an advocate for the patient when he or she is too sick or confused. This may mean interpreting medical conditions and treatment to the patient and in turn conveying to medical personnel the patient's wishes on the Living Will if the medical power of attorney is not present. I know of one minister who keeps copies of congregants' advance directives and Medical Powers of Attorney in the church files. Gwen's priest acted as her support and intermediary with the funeral director. Before her husband came home from the hospital, her priest gave him a last anointment to provide him with strength and peace, gave communion to the family in the hospital, and very actively helped the family prepare for the funeral service. Some clergy are chaplains attached to hospitals, institutions and hospices.

I interviewed one such chaplain who is employed by a hospice that covers a wide geographical area. She was trained in a special clinical pastoral program for older students at Union Theological Seminary in New York, and since the federal guidelines for hospices require chaplains on staff, this is where many chaplains are being employed.

According to regulations, she must do a spiritual assessment within a week of the patient entering the hospice program. As part of her assessment she notes whether the patient is connected to any particular church, whether he or she wants a sacramental ministry, and whether he or she has spiritual strengths or weaknesses. Among strengths, she includes whether the patient is cooperative and is able to communicate, whether he or she has spiritual discipline, gets strength from prayer, is facing completion of life issues, and is facing the reality of his or her condition. She will find out whether the patient wants his or her own clergy called, and decides how she can be of help, and whether to put that person on a visiting schedule. By regulations, she must also do an assessment of the family. One way she tries to reach hospice patients is to ask them to tell a story, and through their fantasies she is able to understand the patient's underlying emotions. If the patient wishes her to pray with him or her, she uses these emotions in the prayers and thus patients feel doubly heard by the chaplain and by God. She also does some spiritual comforting of staff at weekly staff meetings and conducts funerals for hospice patients.

Some denominations require hospital chaplaincy training of candidates for parish ministry. One Protestant minister served his chaplaincy training during his second year of seminary at a general hospital in a large mid-west city. One night when he was on call he was asked to see the family of a Roman Catholic woman who was dying of cancer; the family had already been waiting several hours for their parish priest. The student informed the family that although he had an Irish name he was not Catholic but was a member of a liberal denomination. They were pretty insistent, as they could see that their mother did not have much longer. Fortunately, that day he had learned the anointing procedure from his clinical pastoral education supervisor and had with him an anointing card, and was given some mineral oil from the nurse. As he was speaking some of the words and dabbing on the oil, the patient opened her eyes and looked right at him, convincing him that this was a holy moment, which the family also witnessed. When I read about this experience, I agreed that yes, this was a holy, ecumenical moment for all involved.

If the clergyman or clergywoman is particularly sensitive and has dealt with his or her own feelings about death, he or she can do all kinds of things to help the patient and family at the time of death. If the patient is still alive the minister will try to help them achieve closure, and may reach this point by asking questions of the patient, particularly asking if there is anything that the patient regrets. With the family, clergy give support and grief and crisis counseling, may act as intermediary with medical personnel and funeral directors, and help the family plan for the funeral service.

If they are flexible, clergy can often provide imaginative and sensitive help such as the following example. A widow friend of mine died at age 62 from a sudden attack of angina while hiking in California. She had not shared her medical condition with anyone, not even her children even though her physician in the East had urged angioplasty, which she had chosen not to have done. Just a few months before her death she had moved to California to be near her son and daughter, both in their mid-twenties, but had retained membership in her New York church and remained in close touch with its minister. When Julie died, her daughter, not knowing the minister, contacted a member of the church who called the minister, who within 24 hours was on the plane flying to California, where she spent the weekend with Julie's children. The first thing the minister did was clean Julie's house and discard the backpack that Julie had on when she died, which the children could not bear to look at or touch. She collected money that was in Julie's house for the children, counseled them, arranged for immediate cremation, and on Sunday conducted a memorial service in Julie's church in California. Before leaving on Sunday night, she planned with the children the memorial service that would be held in the church in the east and carried Julie's and her husband's ashes back on the plane. She subsequently kept in close telephone contact with Julie's children before they returned to New York for the large memorial service held two months later. I would hazard a guess that what she did that weekend was not written in any job description or talked about in any seminary course, but what she did was what was so desperately needed.

ASSISTED SUICIDE

A brief history of assisted suicide shows that it was common in ancient Greece and Rome. Socrates opposed suicide as moral weakness whereas the Stoics supported "chosen death" as one of the greatest benefits of being human. Atticus, a First century B.C. Roman, had cancer of the colon and committed suicide. Seneca, born in 3 A.D., slashed his wrists, and had already written, "the best thing which eternal law ever ordained was that it allowed to us one entrance to life, but many exits." According to Pliny, Titius Aristo gathered friends around him ordering them to question his physician as to the gravity of his illness, and saying that he would exit life with the doctor's poison. Before the Hippocratic Oath, Greek physician assisted suicides were so common that the prohibition against it in the oath became a source of protest.

The British Euthanasia Society was founded in 1935, the United States society in 1938. The practive among the Inuit of killing their sick and elderly was almost always voluntary and had to be done by a relative in order to reinforce kinship bonds. Before the killing a feast would be held at which the person to be killed would pass on his or her wisdom, and after the death, there would be imposed a period of confinement and dietary restrictions as a penance for the person who helped with the death. There now would be a better climate in which to discuss the controversial issue of assisted suicide if Nazi euthanasia during the 1930's and 1940's had not occurred, for the greatest fear around the issue of assisted suicide is that there might be widespread individual and societal abuse.

The Oregon Death With Dignity Act was the first law in the world that offered people the option of assisted suicide. It took effect after a great deal of opposition from the Roman Catholic Church and right to life groups, and court hearings. It first appeared as a proposition on the Oregon ballot in 1994, at which time Oregon voters approved of the proposal by a vote of 51%. The United States Ninth Circuit Court of Appeals turned down an appeal to reverse the vote made by the National Right to Life Committee, the National Legal Center for the Medically Dependent and Disabled, and the Catholic Church. The Oregon legislators sent it back to the voters in November 1997 for a revote, which made it law.

In the meantime, on January 8, 1997 the United States Supreme Court heard two assisted suicide cases from the states of New York and Washington. On June 6, 1997, the court handed down a unanimous decision that assisted suicide was not a constitutional right and that laws making it a criminal act in both states did not violate Americans' liberties or the equal protection clause. In the New York case, the court upheld distinctions between letting a patient die and assisting in a suicide, but returned the issue to the state, at the same time leaving the door open for assisted suicide cases to come again before the Supreme Court.

At this point, there is certainly a fine line between "making die" and "letting die." In 1990, the American Hospital Association estimated that 70% of the daily six thousand deaths in this country are "somehow timed or negotiated with all parties privately concurring on withdrawal of some death-delaying technology or not even starting it in the first place."[4] A 1997 California study put this number at around 90%. So, according to these two studies, most Americans die by withholding, withdrawing or refusing treatment. This is considered dying naturally, but is also referred to as "passive euthanasia."[5]

What is called "modern managed death" with dying patients who have no chance of recovering may involve stopping the use of antibiotics, stopping heart medications, stopping chemotherapy or unplugging machines. However, the most alarming practice is that medications are sometimes given to dying patients who are designated to donate organs in order to hasten death so that the organs are kept healthy for the donee.

In Holland, before physician assisted suicide was legalized in 2000, the practice was tolerated if very strict guidelines were followed by the attending physician. In 1984, the Dutch Medical Association stated that as a medical body it agreed that under certain circumstances euthanasia could be justified. The Free University's medical faculty has set up a training program for medical students in euthanasia, death and grief. Because Holland has a state supported health care system, doctors knew their patients and their

---

[4] *Marilyn Webb, The Good Death, (New York, Doubleday, 1997, page 395*
[5] *Webb, page 377*

families for many years and made house calls, particularly if there was a terminal illness in a family member. There were also many hospices in Holland, which offered a number of choices. The physician received no fee for the euthanasia. The following guidelines were used by 65% of Dutch hospitals:

1. The patient has made a persistent, voluntary, and competent request for assisted suicide.
2. The patient's suffering is thorough and unrelenting with no prospect of improvement.
3. The patient has full information of his or her condition.
4. Alternative treatments are known and are not wanted.
5. The case is documented in writing and no certification of natural death is issued.

After the event, the physician made a report to the coroner, who passed information on to the prosecutor. In 1996, an article in the New England Journal of Medicine reported on a study done in Holland, which showed that between 3 and 5% of all deaths were as a result of euthanasia. The number of cases had remained essentially the same since an earlier study done in 1990. The percentage spread was because the researchers could not decide whether an increase in narcotics that caused death could be included as euthanasia. Dutch studies also show that 25% of assisted suicides fail, and physicians then have to use a lethal injection.

There were safeguards against abuse in the Dutch guidelines. The patient had to do the asking for assisted suicide, a second physician had to see the patient and the patient had to repeat his request to that doctor. A date was set, and again the patient had to make the request of the physician four days in advance. On the scheduled day, the doctor explained the procedures and got a reaffirmation from the patient. The patient himself then took the mixture of drugs. Even if the family objected, the patient's wishes were paramount. In Amsterdam, physicians met frequently to discuss the ethics of certain cases where euthanasia had been requested. In 2001, assisted suicide was entirely legalized in Holland.

Doctors often become adversaries rather than advocates at the end of life. Most U.S. physicians were trained to keep patients alive as long as possible using as many measures as possible. The worst kind of death is in a hospital with all of its attendant medical technologies, which are used only to prolong dying. Most physicians are afraid of losing their licenses if they help a person to die, even though several surveys in different states have shown that most doctors are increasingly in favor of legislation that would allow physician-assisted suicide. Without such legislation doctors have to answer to medical societies, ethics committees, the press, religious groups, and the existing laws.

If you feel compelled to discuss the issue of physician-assisted suicide with your doctor, it should be easier if you have a long relationship with him or her. You should present your wishes to your doctor, then find out what he thinks about this. You can use a very direct approach, such as "You should know that I'm a member of the Hemlock Society," or an indirect one such as "I've had some experience with a difficult death. If I'm in a position of not being able to recover from a terminal illness I do not want that kind of experience." Most doctors will understandably hedge or will even throw you out of their office. If you still feel strongly, then look for another doctor.

Those who are eligible for physician-assisted suicide under the Oregon Death With Dignity Law are residents who:

> 1. Were told by their doctor that they had an incurable and irreversible disease that would, within reasonable medical judgment, produce death within six months;
> 2. Had this prognosis confirmed by another doctor;
> 3. Appeared to have no evidence of clinical depression or untreated pain or other symptoms;
> 4. Made an oral request for help in dying;
> 5. Made a written request that must be witnessed by two other people to ensure that the request was a voluntary one. There must be a fifteen-day waiting period.

The opposition to assisted suicide is almost as strong as it is to abortion and is spearheaded by the same right-to-life groups: the Catholic Church and the religious right. Oregon has been the only state to pass a physician's assisted suicide law, although some twenty other states have attempted initiatives on the ballot. A great deal of money has gone into defeating these efforts.

I personally feel that there is a difference between abortion and assisted suicide. First, the person who is to die must be competent and must over a period of time request the assistance and demonstrate that he has not been pressured into making the decision. A fetus cannot make a decision. Second, as good as hospice care is, at least 5% of patients experience such intense pain and emotional distress that they cannot be relieved by palliative care. Third, as most assisted suicide laws are written, it is the patient who commits the act of suicide; the physician does the assessment and prescribes the drugs. This presents a problem for the patient who is physically unable to take the drugs himself or herself, such as Sue Rodriguez in British Columbia, Canada who made a court appeal. Fourth, the Dutch guidelines and the Oregon law are written with safeguards to protect against abuses. Fifth, in both Holland and in Oregon the percentage of people who have chosen assisted suicide is very small. In Holland only 3 to 5% did so, while in Oregon during the first year that the Death With Dignity law was in effect there were only fifteen patients who took advantage of it. Sixth, many people have stated that if they knew there was a law in effect allowing assisted suicide they would feel great security and control and would probably never need to take advantage of it. This paradox has happened in Holland.

There is a crisis in end of life care in the United States. Oregon's death with dignity law is humane. Surely the issue is one of fundamental rights of choice and control over how we die so that we may avoid unnecessary and severe suffering.

SUMMARY

Dying is certainly a natural process, which is easier if it is faced squarely ahead of time. The "good death" is achieved through conscious decisions that the patient and his health provider make about his medical treatment and terminal care. Part of this is planning ahead of time through the use of a Living Will and a Medical Proxy about what you want for terminal care and who you wish to make decisions in case you are unable to do so.

There are certain elements in common with every good death:

1. The physician should always tactfully inform the patient and his family that he is terminally ill. No games should be played about this.
2. Excessive treatment is not given that only extends the process of dying.
3. As much pain medication is given as is needed to keep the patient comfortable.

4. The dying patient is given respect and is involved as much as possible in decisions.
5. Emotional issues are addressed.
6. The family is given as much spiritual, emotional and physical help as they need.

Hospice follows all of these principles.

—Family members, friends and clergy can be very comforting if they are truly helpful, responding to signals from the patient and family without being intrusive.

—Life Review, which is psychologically important to the patient, may be done quite naturally during the dying process or earlier. This review gives the patient a clear picture of what his life has meant to him and to others, and can be one of the last acts in achieving peace.

There are a small percentage of patients whose pain at the end cannot be managed by medication, and who may choose assisted suicide if it is legal. There is much controversy over this issue, for religious reasons but also out of a fear that there might be societal or individual abuse of such a practice. Safeguards have been built into the law in Oregon, and to a lesser degree in Holland, and so far in both countries it has been only a small number of people who have chosen this route. Many people feel that assisted suicide should be an option open to them.

Chapter VIII

In Memoriam

> Brother, I have come through many lands
> And over many seas, to bring you
> The last service death demands.
>
> > I speak, but your ashes do not answer.
> > You cannot hear me where you are.
>
> Here are the offerings, food for the dead (I keep
> The custom that our fathers handed down.)
> They are wet with tears.
>
> > Take them from my hands, brother, and with them
> > Greeting and a long good-bye.
>
> —*Catullus, #101. Translated from the Latin by Brooks Wright and read at his brother's memorial service, 1995*

The above elegy was written by the Roman poet, Catullus, who was thought to have lived between 87 and 57 B.C. The poem was entirely appropriate almost 2000 years later in capturing the grief felt at the loss of a brother. I could have chosen a love lyric written by John Donne to his dead wife in the 17th century or by Thomas Hardy to his in the 19th century, or one written in 1998 by one of my favorite contemporary poets, Donald Hall, a year after his wife had died from cancer. Grief is both a universal and a timeless emotion. It must be comforting to be able to express one's grief as have these poets, but I cannot believe that poets feel any more intensely than do other people. They just have the ability to express their grief more eloquently.

BEREAVEMENT

As well as grieving after the death of a person who has been close to us, we sometimes experience anticipatory grief when we know someone is going to die. All of the same feelings we have after the death can precede it: panic, great emptiness, guilt, numbness, anger and a conviction that this is unjustified punishment on the part of God or fate. After the death the survivor will experience these same feelings but also may not be able to put out of his or her mind the loved one's death and the unusual things that sometimes happen at that time. A friend of many years whose husband died 20 years ago at the age of 51 of his second heart attack recently told me of her husband's last night in the hospital. His doctors called her to the hospital after they had revived him during the night with electric paddles. When she arrived at her husband's bedside, he, who had always been a skeptic, described to her a dream he had had the night before, in which he walked down the hallway toward a door that closed. This door closing took place at the time he was revived, and he then died within hours of relating his dream. She recounted this near-death experience as if it had taken place yesterday. Anyone's death belongs to the dying person, but also to those who survive to grieve. Sometimes the grief can last for years.

Recently I tried to think of what the worst kinds of deaths are for survivors. Would the list include a young child's loss of a parent; a parent's loss of a young child, a loved one's violent death by murder or accident; the loss of grown children by elderly parents; the death of a parent or child from whom one has always been alienated; the death of an ex-spouse from whom one is divorced or separated, or the death of a beloved spouse to whom one is bound as if one? It might even be a friend for whom one feels a kinship that is closer than one feels toward any family member.

Some of these losses are especially hard because they are unnatural and unexpected, such as the loss of a grown child, or the loss of a child's parent, or loss from murder or accident. The death of the alienated or divorced spouse is difficult because the survivor grieves as much for what was lacking in the relationship as for the loss itself. Perhaps after the death of an ex-spouse, the survivor grieves deeply for the good days in the marriage and also for what the couple did not have. Whatever the relationship, it is natural to grieve for people who have meant a great deal to us, for if we are alive and caring we will grieve, and how long this lasts is an individual matter, as is how we learn to deal with the grief. It is the person who doesn't grieve that we should worry about.

A close friend who is now eighty lost his grandfather when he was six years old. The death, which was unexpected, took place in the outhouse of the family farm. The child witnessed his grandmother breaking open the outhouse door, heard her scream that his grandfather was gone, watched as his mother and grandmother carried his dead grandfather across the yard, his pants hanging around his knees, his buttocks dragging on the ground when the two women lost hold. He watched while his grandmother frantically tried to get help on the crank telephone, and afterwards the neighbors circled around the body. The recollection was vivid, but the child was never comforted nor was he given an explanation that would help ease his pain. Instead, he was pushed away and was told that such matters were only for grownups. The memory of the scene burned in him until he finally wrote the following poem when he was almost eighty. The act of describing so vividly that scene from more than seventy years earlier freed him so that he was then able to finally grieve for his grandfather and other members of his family in a way he had been unable to do until then.

Easter 1925

Bursting with six year old life
I rocked the dead hay rack
long since off its wheels.
Over there the outhouse
and Grandma, anxious,
yells at the stinking door.

"John! John!"
No answer from inside.
One pry with a bar, and the door
swings open like a great stone rolled away.
"Grace! Grace!
He's gone! He's gone!"
I saw it all; I heard it all.

How, Mother grasping his arm pits
and Grandma at his knees,
they carried him toward the house.
How his head lolled,
how his arms dangled,
and with his trousers indecently down!

Grandma's grasp slips and
he falls, bare buttocks to the dirt.
"Oh Grace! I've bruised him!
I've bruised him! I've bruised him!"

In the house Grandma
cranks wildly at the phone.
"I can't help it if the line is occupied!

(continued next page)

John Chambers is dead!
The neighbours in a circle
around Grandpa on the floor.
But he wouldn't keep his mouth closed —
a rude, red-black, moustache fringed yawn,
till someone pressed the big family Bible
under his chin
the way you'd prop up a thing.
I saw it all; I heard it all.

Easter. Oh seek him not
in the shit house sepulchre,
for lo two weeping women
have carried him into the house
and laid him on the floor.

In the springtime of my years, death,
scatological death,
entered my life.

—Gordon McLean, 1995

Perhaps if that six-year old child had been taken aside, and for as many times as he needed, was held and given an explanation, he would not have been so haunted by this scene for almost his entire life. But when he wrote the poem he was able to finally resolve this old, old issue as much as is humanly possible, as we all can do.

Some people can come to terms with the death of a close one without outside help. Others, most especially children, need the help of friends, family or professionals. Many young children have experienced the death of a family pet, or without their families knowing it have gathered together friends to provide a funeral service for dead animals or insects they have found. However, I do not think we should ever expect children to be able to handle alone the prospect of or the reality of a death in the family of some loved one or of some other person who means a great deal. Neither do I think that a child should be shielded, for, that alone, gives a message that death is not natural or that it is to be feared and avoided. Consequently, these attitudes will be deeply ingrained for many, many years. Just as we adults need to say goodbye to the dying or departed person, so a child needs the help of those closest to him and understandable answers to his questions. Do not explain the death as sleep or as a trip; these false explanations will only create many more problems. Give a child the choice of whether he wishes to view the body, and encourage him to attend and, if possible, participate in the religious ceremony.

Often the child will act out his feelings of confusion and anger with nightmares, sleeplessness, violence, moodiness and isolation. Do be patient, and give as much physical affection as you can. Inform the school and other people who have responsibility for him about the death, his behavior and the probable feelings behind it, and do not hesitate to get professional help for the child if the behavior continues too long or is too destructive to him and to others. Your local mental health association or mental health clinic should be a good resource for help or for referral to professionals who can help the child and his parents. In addition, your clergyman should be able to give you counsel. Of all of the professions, the clergy deal most frequently with death, and are a source of solace, especially to those who believe in an afterlife.

Even for an adult who has already had in the course of things many losses of various kinds, the loss of a loved one can be traumatic and the grieving can be a lengthy process, sometimes never ending. Some therapists who work with the bereaved feel that there are five normal stages of grieving. The first stage is one of numbness and denial in which the death is still too new for the person to fully feel the impact. The second stage is a yearning for and preoccupation with the lost person, followed by a third stage of openly expressed anger and protest. The fourth stage may be one of great disorganization, anxiety and guilt. The person may openly say "if only I had done this or that it would not or might not have happened." This phase culminates in the emotional realization of the loss, and then in the fifth stage of grieving reorganization takes place and a gradual letting go of the lost person. It is helpful to keep in mind these possible steps in the grieving process, both for ourselves, but for others who are grieving, so that we will be more observant and sensitive and patient when family and friends are undergoing bereavement.

As human beings, we are connected to each other, some people more so than others. Thus, the presence and support of other people at the time of grieving, however long it takes, is immeasurably helpful to most people. Perhaps, close friends are the ones who we will find are the most comforting, but generally it is the ties of family that we turn to first. Whatever your relationship is with the grieving person, do not avoid contact even if it can be nothing more than a letter. Most especially, do not avoid the subject of death. Cry and grieve with the person, reminisce about the lost one, help in whatever way you can to allow the bereaved person to mourn, and expect to be there for the "long haul." Sometimes the death can be so unexpected, so painful, so devastating that one cannot find the right thing to say. In such instances, say just that or just say with feeling that you are sorry or give the bereaved person a hug or a touch on the shoulder or the arm. In this way, you will convey empathy without being dishonest. Do not, emphatically do not say you understand how the bereaved one feels, because you don't, for every grief is different from every other. Instead, get the bereaved to tell you what their loss means to them!

The survivor, if possible, should not grieve alone, but should make the effort to be with other people as much as possible and should not make any major life changes for at least a year. A grief support group can be very helpful and most communities offer this service through churches or social agencies.

For many adults, prayer and religious ritual can help. For others, it may be the actual preparation for a funeral or memorial service, and for many people it can help to participate directly in a service where the essence of the departed one's personality and character can be captured and a life review done. Gwen's family and close friends took part in preparing for her husband's funeral (see Chapter VII.). There was to be a wake in the home, so Gwen helped the hospice nurse to wash her husband's body and prepare it for the viewing. During the three-day wake the sense that Henry's spirit was present was overwhelming, especially as he was a jolly person, and around the bed where his body lay there was a good deal of bantering, which Gwen felt sprang from him. At one point a butterfly flew into the room and hovered there as if Henry's soul was there in that lovely butterfly. Gwen's son-in law, who is a carpenter, made a casket out of lumber which her husband had cut. The children placed flowers in the casket and accompanied Gwen and the priest to the funeral parlor to make funeral arrangements. Friends who were potters made the urn into which Henry's ashes were to be placed. Even now, frequently Gwen feels the presence of her husband, and at times the feeling is so strong that she is tempted to read to him as they always did. Next to the chair where she sits and reads is a picture of her husband and new grandson taken a few months before Henry's death, an affectionate portrait of two people two generations apart, who look almost identical. It is apparent that all of the emotional support and concrete help given by family and friends was the most meaningful way for them to express the love they felt for this man. It was also very helpful to the family in coming to terms with his death.

Religious rituals become a focal point for expressing one's grief. At that point and elsewhere, do not be afraid or embarrassed to cry. For both men and women this is an appropriate and honest expression of grief and often is very beneficial. Do not hesitate to turn to family and close friends for comfort and reminiscing. The comforter's role should be primarily one of listener; his or her love and concern will be felt and will be a consolation. In addition, many people find bereavement support groups of enormous help, for the bereaved person often feels that only someone who has undergone the same sort of experience can understand and suggest ways of dealing with the grief. These groups can be found through local social agencies and mental health clinics or perhaps in churches or synagogues. If the adult survivor's depression lasts too long or interferes too much with normal functioning, he should not hesitate to seek professional help.

PRACTICAL CONSIDERATIONS

There are always many practical considerations at the time of a death, which must be attended to immediately.

If possible before death takes place, get to the safe deposit box and remove the contents, as the bank must by law seal it as soon as they know of the death. Notify all bank accounts, pension accounts and social security. The survivor's own social security and pension checks should already be going into a separate account in the survivor's name so that there is income coming in until the death benefits are settled.

The doctor who makes the death pronouncement makes out the death certificate. The mortuary that you use will get the death certificate from the doctor and will give it to you. Make at least six copies, as death certificates must be presented in several business transactions. The mortuary places the obituary in the newspaper. Be sure to give the mortician any extra information that you wish to be included. Some people have their obituaries prepared in advance so that important information will not be forgotten, which can easily happen during the initial grief period when there is so much pressure.

Get in touch with your life insurance agent or the insurance companies directly to notify them of the death. Also contact insurance companies regarding other policies including car, house and any other kind of insurance so that name changes can be made. Do not forget your health insurance, especially if it is not in your name. There is usually a grace period allowed for sometimes as long as forty-five days before you must take out individual insurance.

In arranging plans with a mortuary, it is advisable to have someone else accompany you to act as advocate or at least to see that you are not pressured into ordering items that you have no intention of buying. Someone else can take the role of the level-headed outsider in an emotionally charged situation (see later section in the chapter entitled "The American Way of Death").

If you have an attorney, I would suggest that you consult him on the insurance, the deceased's will and living trust, if there is one and other legal and business questions you may have.

Funerals and Mourning Practices

Over several generations, my family did not have a tradition of funerals, memorial services or burials, and the death of relatives was never discussed. I do not know why this was so. I had a fraternal twin whose death at the age of three months was never discussed with me, and consequently I never dared ask about him until I was an adult, despite a sense of having been very close to him and therefore feeling a great void with his death. After all, we grew together for nine months in the same womb. I'm sure that the baby's death must have been very upsetting to my parents, so perhaps this is why they avoided talking about their loss. (It is a family that does not generally deal directly with vital issues.) I would have understood if they had explained that they did nothing about a funeral service or burial because they were so hard up during those years, but never at any time was there an explanation. There was no funeral or memorial service and it never occurred to them later that I needed to be given a reason for his death and to be consoled for I, too, had been grieving. His ashes were distributed by the funeral parlor, and so there was also no burial place on which to focus grief in later years. With this kind of denial of a death, there is also a kind of denial of the life itself.

Funeral rites have a very important psychological value to the survivors. They provide a formal ceremony that acts as a point of transition from this life to the next and a focus on which survivors can concentrate their grief and remember the deceased. Rituals may be formal and traditional, or simple and personal. The body may or may not be present, the casket may or may not be open, ashes may or may not be on display, and a clergyman may or may not lead the service. The family may choose for the service not to be held in a house of worship, but instead in the family home or even outdoors in some favorite spot of the deceased's. Whatever the service is like, or wherever it is held, it is usually the occasion for the extended family to gather. Often the deceased will have written out general or very specific directions for the funeral service. I'm sure that most people try to carry out such wishes, but in the end a funeral service is really for the benefit of the survivors.

Certain religions more than others place stress on ritual at the time of death, both in the home and in the house of worship through various phases of mourning. For generations, Jewish families have followed certain customs. For Orthodox Jews, burial must take place within twenty-four hours of the death unless a Sabbath or other holy day intervenes. For Conservative and Reform Jews, this rule is not adhered to so strictly. Jewish law forbids elaborate adornments, so a plain wood casket and a simple linen shroud are used. There are no flowers; instead, people are encouraged to make contributions to a charity. Although Reformed Judaism does permit cremation, urging that the ashes be buried in a Jewish cemetery, the practice is considered alien to traditional Judaism. Cremation is considered the deliberate destruction of human beings, which have been made in the image of God, and therefore is frowned upon by the Orthodox and Conservative. Funeral services at which the deceased is eulogized are short and are followed by a graveside ritual.

Shiva, the first period of mourning for Jews, begins right after the funeral service and continues for seven days, actually often fewer days as mourning is prohibited on the Sabbath or religious holidays and Shiva is not resumed after these days. Many Reform Jews "sit Shiva" only for the first three days. The obligation to "sit Shiva" is limited to the immediate family, which does not leave the home for the whole period except for worship on the Sabbath. A large candle is kept burning for the full seven days, during which time daily worship is held in the home so that the mourner's prayer, the Kaddish, may be said. During the seven days friends and neighbors come to pay their respects and express their condolences. They come bearing food and offer whatever practical help they can. After the first seven days, a second period of mourning takes place for eleven months during which the Kaddish is repeated daily. The first thirty days have particular solemnity and sometimes a special service is held on the thirtieth day. Sometime before the first anniversary a memorial stone is unveiled at the graveside. On the anniversary of the death, known as Yahrtzeit, the family again recites the Kaddish and lights a candle in memory of the deceased. After the first year of mourning, on Yom Kippur, the Day of Atonement, and on the last days of Passover, Sukkot, and Shavuot, anyone who has been a mourner recites Yizkor, a special memorial prayer. In short, the Jewish mourning period is long and is celebrated both publicly in the synagogue and at the graveside, and privately in one's home with family and close friends.

Changes have taken place in the Roman Catholic Funeral Mass and funerary and mourning practices. All of the rites for the dead are performed for baptized members of the church and for candidates and catechumans in the Rite of Christian Initiation of Adults, the process by which people become members of the Roman Catholic Church. What used to be called the Last Rites are now called the Sacrament of the Sick and can be given at any time for a person who is very ill, but not necessarily terminally ill. The priest performs an anointing, rubbing the holy oil on the forehead and the hands of the sick person. If the person wishes, the Sacrament of Reconciliation may be celebrated. Before the funeral service, a wake or viewing of the body is not obligatory but can take place either in the mortuary or in the church. A ritual for the deceased may be held either before or after the Mass of the Resurrection. The casket may be open before the Mass, but it is closed during Mass.[1]

The following information was taken from guidelines developed by the Diocese of Tucson. Traditionally the Catholic Church has followed the practice of burial or entombment in the manner of Christ's own burial in the tomb. However, cremation is now allowed by the Roman Catholic Church if guidelines that are developed by each diocese are honored, and if the request for cremation is not motivated by a "denial of Christian Dogmas or because of a sectarian spirit, or through hatred of the Catholic religion or Church."[2] If there is any doubt about motives for cremation, the parish priest is to refer the request to the chancery office or cemetery office of the Diocese before denying the Church's burial rites of the deceased. The cremated remains are allowed in the church. If there was no Funeral Mass before the cremation, a memorial Mass may be held. The Church does not allow strewing of the remains. Instead, "the cremated remains should be buried or entombed to provide a recognized place for memorialization."[3] The Diocese requests that no publicity mention cremation and that the cremated remains be interred privately in a Catholic cemetery with a priest or deacon in attendance.

There are a growing number of Moslems in the United States but there is little information that I could find on their funerary practices. However, on February 8, 1999, the funeral was held for King Hussein of Jordan, who had just returned to his country to die after unsuccessful cancer treatment in the United States, and there were media glimmerings then of Moslem funeral and mourning practices. Of course, as a head of state and a significant

---

1 Telephone interview with Sr. Joyce Rowland, Our Lady of the Valley Roman Catholic Church, Green Valley, Arizona.
2. Our Lady of the Valley Church, Cremation Guidelines.
3. Ibid.

leader in the Middle East peace process, there were thousands from many countries who came to pay their respects. Although King Hussein's fourth and present wife had been an American, according to Muslim tradition she was not allowed to be present at his funeral. The rite was a male affair. She stayed at home to accept condolences from other women, including Hillary Clinton. The only exceptions were female heads of state, but even they did not appear at the gravesite in deference to the tradition that burials in particular are such important occasions that they should be attended only by males. The tradition arises out of the Moslem teachings that unrelated men and women should not mix. Once the man is buried, the women are allowed to visit the grave, beginning on the day after the burial.

There are prescribed Moslem rituals in preparing the body for burial. First the body is scented with musk and is wrapped in a white linen shroud. In the resting position, the head must point toward Mecca, the Muslim holy city. The viewing takes place before the funeral. With King Hussein's funeral, as the dignitaries and family processed past him, each Muslim stood before the casket with both hands opened upwards, quietly saying a prayer or the first passage in the Koran as a sign of obeisance to Allah. Then, with head bowed, the mourner would wipe his face with his two hands, as a sign of sorrow. The funeral service consists of a few prayers and a short sermon but no eulogies or songs. At the end of King Hussein's funeral his body was taken to the gravesite and according to Muslim tradition was removed from the casket and was buried directly in the ground. The total mourning period is forty days.

For those people who are unaffiliated with any religion, but who wish to have a very personal ceremony, I recommend Ernest Morgan's *A Manual of Death Education and Simple Burial*. At the back of the book are samples of simple death ceremonies with suggestions for prayers, music and readings. Friends of mine who have used this section of the book have found it very helpful.

Protestant services are usually held in the church to which the deceased belonged with its minister in attendance. Usually the funeral service follows a prescribed ritual with appropriate prayers and hymns and a short eulogy said by the minister. If cremation has been done, a memorial service is held with or without the ashes present.

The following memorial service is an example of a non-traditional and very personal rite.

Priscilla, who at the age of 42 was told that she had breast cancer, which was so advanced that no treatment was effective, planned her funeral during the last few weeks of her life with her parents, her partner, and her minister. The service was totally personal and unusual but very moving. Priscilla was a lesbian, a feminist and a neo-pagan member of a liberal denomination. A very forthright and honest person, but at the same time a very warm one, she had many, many friends so that the church where the service was held was filled. The service began with her partner lighting candles to the gods of the north, the east, the south and the west. There were readings by lesbian and non-lesbian feminists, a eulogy by the minister and recollections by close friends who shared their love for her and experiences with her. There were chants and drumming and shaking of gourds. Then, at the end of the service to help send her off, the ten women who had cared for Priscilla during her last days sang a lullaby. It was a most touching and appropriate service for her.

"The American Way of Death"

In 1963, Jessica Mitford published *The American Way of Death*, which exposed abuses of the funeral industry. It had such an effect on American life that the Federal Trade Commission subsequently introduced regulations to protect funeral patrons, cremation became much more common, and memorial societies and their continental association were considerably strengthened.

The book was a thorough job of investigative reporting of the funeral industry, presented in a witty, at times hilarious manner. Jessica Mitford found a whole new vocabulary used in the funeral industry: "grief therapy" for all the work done by the funeral director; "funeral director" rather than undertaker; "caskets" instead of coffins; "coaches" instead of hearses; "floral tribute" in place of flowers; "loved ones" rather than corpses; "cremains" instead of ashes, and "slumber room" for the room where the body lies awaiting the funeral. She looked into the cost of caskets, funerals, embalming, burial plots, cremation and all of the auxiliary expenses such as flowers, music, limousines, etc. Because of the family's emotional vulnerability at the time of death, because of their ignorance of funeral industry's practices, and because of undertaker's sales pressures, she found that costs vary according to what the traffic will bear. In 1963 the funeral expense was the third largest for a family after expenditures for a car and a house.

Embalming, for instance, is not required in any state except when the body is to be transported by common carrier or when there are other unusual circumstances. Yet people have the impression that embalming is required for public health reasons, and so without the family directly stating that they do not wish embalming, there is implied permission for the undertaker to go ahead with it. This happened to my family when my mother died in 1976.

When we met with the funeral director, we carefully explained that we wished the body to be cremated, never expecting that embalming would be done. When the bill arrived there was a sizable charge for embalming, which the funeral director explained was required by law. Because we did not know the funeral laws of New York State, and because we did not have the emotional reserve to make a stand, we paid. In 1984 the Federal Trade Commission's rules that were adopted included a stipulation that it is a fraudulent and deceptive act for a funeral director to represent that state law requires embalming when it does not, except in specified situations.

In 1963, pathologists told Jessica Mitford that the body of a person who has died of a non-communicable disease presents no public health hazard. In the past where there have been large epidemics, they have been caused by seepage from graves into the water system, so the solution to preventing epidemics lies in improved sanitation, as the organisms cannot be totally eliminated by embalming. Even with embalming and the use of sealed metal caskets, there is no assurance that a body will remain intact, as anaerobic bacteria that thrive in an airless atmosphere will take over.

From the standpoint of the funeral director, embalming is desirable to preserve the body through the funeral and committal, as most funerals are conducted with open caskets. Along with the embalming a great deal of cosmetic work is done, as well as hairdressing and attention to the attire. Because there is to be a viewing, or in funeral speakease a "memory picture," the salesman will urge the family to choose the most expensive casket. Besides the casket, there are other artifacts, as Jessica Mitford calls them: clothing, shoes, mattresses for caskets, the hardware and lining for the casket, burial vaults, chapels, fancy architecture for the funeral home, and various rooms used before and during the funeral. All of these add to the cost. It does help if you can afford it to pre-arrange your funeral plans with a funeral director. You will be making the plans at a time when you and your family are not emotionally distraught and therefore more vulnerable.

Clergymen have become much more active in accompanying families to funeral homes to help them plan a funeral that they can afford and to direct them to the less expensive caskets. For this reason, funeral directors are not happy with the presence of clergymen.

In 1975, the Federal Trade Commission tried to institute some consumer protection regulations that would include the following requirements.

> 1. The Consumer's Right to Choose. The FTC would require an itemization on a quotation so that the family could choose only what services it would want.
> 2. Prices would have to be quoted over the telephone
> 3. Undertakers would be prohibited from misstating the law in regard to embalming.
> 4. The cheapest casket would have to be displayed with the others.
> 5. Undertakers would be prohibited from telling customers that the "eternal sealer" casket would preserve the embalmed corpse for a long or indefinite length of time.

There was considerable lobbying and pressure from the funeral industry so that gradually the regulations were eroded and weakened. By 1978, two of the items had been dropped: the requirement to display the cheapest caskets along with more expensive ones and the prohibition against trying to influence a buyer in his choice of funeral. By 1996, both the National Funeral Director's Association and the

FTC announced that funeral homes would no longer be fined for violations of the regulations; offenders would be placed in the "Funeral Rules Offenders Program," under which offenders could make a voluntary contribution to the U.S. Treasury Department that could be lower than an imposed fine. Offenders' names would not be publicized. However, the Funeral and Memorial Societies of America have still been able to get the names of offending funeral directors, and then have been able to post those names.

One positive change arose from an amendment to FTC rules that prohibited handling fees. This change brought about the rise of the retail coffin industry, by which the ordinary citizen can buy his coffin in a retail store at a price seventy-five percent lower than those offered through the funeral director. Lisa Carlson, the executive director of the Funeral and Memorial Societies of America, says that generally funeral directors mark up coffin prices about three hundred and fifty percent as against retail coffin stores which mark up by one hundred percent. In order to compete, some funeral directors are reducing the cost of caskets but raising their service costs to make up the difference. Another change made in the funeral industry in recent years has been the growth of multi-national monopolies, which of course operate in such a way as to push up the costs even more.

I don't know whether the success of what is now called the "death care" industry is a reflection of an increasingly materialistic American society that is largely concerned with conspicuous consumption and keeping up with one's neighbors. The extravagant ostentation of the modern American funeral and American cemeteries suggests this. The depth of one's grief is not measured by how much one pays for a funeral or burial plot. In the 1963 edition of *The American Way of Death,* Jessica Mitford said that English and other European funeral practices were still very different from American funerals. Theirs were simple affairs, which the family and perhaps a few friends attended. The coffin was wood and never open at the funeral, often cremation was chosen and then the ashes were strewn, and the cost of everything was affordable. In the 1998 edition, Ms. Mitford said that the big American monopolies are moving into England and the style of things is beginning to change.

MEMORIAL SOCIETIES

Memorial Societies are cooperative, non-profit organizations that enable their membership to secure simple, but dignified, economical funeral arrangements. There are over one million members in societies in the United States and Canada. Often the local society will arrange contracts or agreements with one or more funeral directors for economical services, and will provide information that is helpful to members in planning funerals and in disposing of the body, such as organ and body donation, cremation and burial. Most of the societies are manned with dedicated volunteers. There is a one-time fee of between ten and twenty-five dollars for membership, and some societies collect a small "records charge" when forms are processed at the time of death. At the time a person joins a memorial society he is asked to fill out a pre-arrangement form which allows him or her to indicate detailed funeral planning. There are no absolute rules that must be followed; however the literature makes it clear that most members do not agree with embalming, which usually is not required by law. Also, they do not agree with the use of cosmetics or open casket viewing. Instead, the literature urges that members choose a simple, low-cost coffin and simple services. They choose whether they wish burial, cremation or body donation. I found that filling out the form helped in formulating what I specifically wanted for a funeral. If you look in your telephone book under "funeral services," you should be able to find the telephone number for your local memorial society. Membership is transferrable for little or no charge if you should move.

The local memorial societies belong to the Continental Association of Funeral and Memorial Societies, Inc., which serves as a clearinghouse for consumer complaints in regard to funeral transactions and which can assist people in filing a complaint with the appropriate state or federal agency. Through publicity and educational materials, the Association acts to increase consumer awareness about funeral practices. They also inform members about organ or body donation.

ANATOMICAL DONATIONS

When a person joins a memorial society, he or she is given a form to fill out for organ or body donation should this be something he or she wishes to consider. A Universal Donor Card for carrying in a wallet can be secured by sending a stamped self-addressed envelop to the Continental Association of Funeral and Memorial Societies, Inc. (see chapter notes for the address.) In some states, there is a place on your driving license where you can indicate that you wish to make an organ donation. There is still an enormous shortage of organs for transplant, and medical schools need bodies for use in anatomy labs. I am fairly certain that if a person has a history of cancer, organs will not be used for transplant, but medical schools can use such a body, unless it is so deteriorated by cancer that it is of little educational value. This also applies to degenerative diseases also, but check with your nearest medical school.

SUMMARY

It is natural to grieve publicly and privately for the loss of a loved family member or friend or even a national leader, as this country did with the untimely death of President Kennedy, or for a beloved public figure such as the worldwide grief shown at the time of Princess Diane's death. For the psychological health of the survivor, whether adult or child, grieving must take place particularly after the death of a close loved one. Each religion has its own special funeral rituals, or if a family wishes, a very personal service can be designed that is more to the liking of the family and more appropriate for the deceased. There is psychological advantage to some kind of a service since the rite provides a focus for the survivor's grief. If the grief is not given a chance to be expressed, it just burrows itself in the psyche and sits there, only to emerge in expected ways or not at all. Without some way of expressing the grief, it is extremely difficult for people to come to terms with the death and in turn to later be able to face subsequent losses.

If possible, the family should prepare ahead an obituary and even arrange in advance funeral plans with a mortician so that they do not have undue pressure after the death, which is a time of great emotional distress. If these have not been done, do not hesitate to ask your clergyman or some other person who is knowledgeable and whom you trust to act as an advocate with the funeral home. Memorial Societies provide a good way of planning ahead for a simple and inexpensive funeral. It is also advisable to write down ahead of time the steps that must be taken to settle business affairs when a death takes place.

Chapter ix

The Managed and The Managers:
How to Survive The Systems

These days everyone has a sad story to tell about health maintenance organizations. In fact, it seems as though everyone except the insurance companies and their executives is unhappy with the HMOs, but feels helpless to fight the monster. Recently, I tried to remember when they first came into general use, but couldn't. I believe the first health maintenance organization in the West was Kaiser-Permanente in California, which had a reputation for good care and is now the largest non-profit health maintenance organization in the country. In the eighties Kaiser bought out another group in White Plains, New York, twenty miles north of New York, but I've never heard of any other Kaiser operations around New York. Although in the eighties there was a good deal of talk about the high cost of medical care, things seemed to continue in much the same way at least in the East, until the early nineties. At that time, there was a sudden surge of HMOs and the managed care concept permeated the whole medical care system so that everyone, even those who didn't belong to an HMO, was affected by rules that didn't always make sense.

Now, there are so many problems with HMOs and managed care that a day doesn't go by without there being several articles in the paper about a system that still has a lot of wrinkles and is very unsatisfactory to many people. It has reached the point where HMO jokes are regularly told by health care workers, and health maintenance organizations have become the butt of television medical dramas. "The shows reflect the widespread image of HMOs as faceless, heartless monoliths that would rather save a penny than save a life. ... The dramas give voice to the audience's common complaints about HMOs: not enough individual attention or choice of doctors, a maddening lack of logic in the rules of coverage, the Kafkaesque nightmare of dealing with a slow-moving bureaucracy about an issue as personal and urgent as health."[1]

HEALTH MAINTENANCE ORGANIZATIONS AND MEDICARE HMOS

A Health Maintenance Organization is both a provider and insurer of health care. It is a network of physicians, hospitals and other health care providers. The services that are offered vary with the HMO, but all offer preventive care. Some offer prescription drugs, dental care, hearing aids and eyeglasses; others offer less. Some models of HMOs have their own medical centers where you receive your medical care, laboratory, x-ray, and perhaps pharmacy services all in one place. Other types such as Individual Practice Associations (IPA's) offer medical services through private practice physicians who provide care in their own offices. Point of Service (POS) HMOs allow you to receive some health services outside the plan at an added cost and with the approval of the primary physician. With these plans, in order to see a specialist, written approval must be secured from the primary or "gatekeeper" physician. Other

---

[1] Caryn James, "On the Doctor Shows, Public Enemy No. 1," N.Y. Times, 9/8/98.

plans which have become particularly popular are the preferred provider organizations, the PPO's, which allow their members to go to any doctor without securing permission, although it costs them more to go to physicians and hospitals outside the organization's network. The PPO'S now have forty percent more members than HMOs. As more people reject the more restrictive HMOs in favor of the more flexible PPO'S, questions are arising as to whether quality health care can be delivered at a reasonable cost.

If you are considering joining an HMO, do read the description of the plan very carefully. What are its Point Of Service (POS) benefit options, if any? What is the breadth of its services? What are its limitations? If a prescription plan is included be sure to read the particulars. What is the maximum annual amount allowed on drugs, where can you get prescriptions filled, and are you limited to generic drugs? Check on how easily it will be to get emergency care and where you go for emergencies after hours and how and when you must notify the HMO about emergency and urgently needed care. (If you are travelling outside the United States, you will have to purchase special insurance. If you are going to be living in another part of the United States for several months, and you know that you will need to receive regular medical services, you will have to purchase insurance, as membership in an HMO is not portable.) With most HMO's, you will be required to use only doctors and other providers who belong to the network, except for emergency or urgently needed care, or if your primary care physician refers you to someone outside the network for some special reason. You must choose a primary physician who is affiliated or under contract with the HMO that you are considering. That doctor will coordinate your care.

If you belong to a Medicare HMO you continue to pay your Medicare Part B premium that is withheld from your social security check, and in turn the HMO provides you with all Medicare hospital and medical benefits. You will also pay a co-payment for service. As a Medicare recipient, you will only be allowed to join special Medicare HMO plans.

How Managed Care Now Affects Everyone

I have found that even those people who do not belong to an HMO are the victims of some of their very questionable practices. My husband and I do not belong to an HMO, but hold Medicare supplemental insurance. Over the years, occasionally we have been caught in the web of managed care practices that in urgent situations at times have not made sense and at many other times have only served as annoyances. With managed care there always seems to be an initial telephone barrier or a delay in providing timely and appropriate treatment, presumably to try to save dollars, but of course eventually those dollars have to be paid anyway. For instance, after hip surgery that I had several years ago, I developed blood clots in both of my legs and was very sick. When I tried to reach my orthopedic surgeon on a Friday, I was unable to get past a clerk who urged me to call my primary physician, and over the weekend when I also developed a fever, I could not get a covering doctor to do anything. Then, on Monday I could only get an appointment with the surgeon by forcefully demanding to see him that very day. When he did see me, he immediately put me in the hospital. Over several days time, there had been barriers set up to prevent me from getting the care that I needed very badly.

I have heard about one hospital and read about others where a patient who stayed several days never had bed linen changed or the room cleaned. One of these was a maternity unit where even the baby's diaper pail was not emptied. These hospitals may have saved money on housekeeping costs but they certainly did not maintain aseptic standards to prevent infections.

Just a year ago, my husband became very ill indeed with what eventually was diagnosed as an acute drug reaction that caused a number of very dramatic events including near kidney failure. He was taken to the emergency room, but after being stabilized was allowed to go home. Nevertheless, he continued to get increasingly sick over several days time, during which I had to drive him more than twenty miles every day for laboratory tests. As his kidney function worsened, he became increasingly weaker. I finally had to insist that his internist put him in the hospital where he remained for five days on IV, and kidney specialists were brought in daily to assess what the cause might be. By the time he was discharged, the doctors still did not know what he had and prescribed that a number of CAT scans and other tests be done. Yet, according to the strictures of managed care under which the hospital operated, the scans could not be done while he was still a patient in the hospital because the tests were not directly related to the diagnosis with which he was admitted. So, as sick as he still was, we again had to make the twenty-mile trip to Tucson for daily CAT scans and blood tests. Such rigid rules are never in the best interests of the patient, but only serve budgetary interests. Several applicable jokes are, "You go in with a headache; they do a credit scan before they do a CAT scan," and "HMO's, you know what HMO's stand for? Have money or die."[2]

The University of Rochester did a study on the amount of time a physician can give to a patient, whether that patient

---

2. *Ibid.*

belongs to an HMO or not. The average patient has twenty-three seconds before his doctor interrupts him, so that the patient has a one in four chance to finish his presentation to the doctor. Managed care gives the doctor eight to ten minutes for each patient. With the pressure of time in mind, the doctor assumes that the first item that the patient brings up is the most important one, whereas the patient may only be using it as an "icebreaker," so he may walk out dissatisfied. Be sure to prepare ahead for your visit to your doctor; make a list of things to be discussed in order of importance and a list of your medications, and when you start the interview, tell your doctor how many items you have to discuss with him. Even though my husband and I are not members of a managed care plan, almost invariably after a few minutes our doctors are looking at their watches, no matter how serious the medical problem is that we are presenting.

SOME OF THE ECONOMICS

Today, managed care plans are entrenched in the economy. Since the early nineties, the health care system has been left in "the tides of the marketplace." Most workers do not really have a decision in their health care plans. What is offered to them has been worked out by management, and an HMO is a more economical plan for the company. According to the American Association of Health Plans, sixty-one percent of the population is enrolled in managed care plans. "Managed care so far is largely an insurance phenomenon...so far, we've had not much impact on the quality of care,"[3] stated the chief executive of Kaiser Permanente of Oakland, California, the nation's largest nonprofit health maintenance organization. Forty states have developed new regulations for health maintenance organizations, but none of them have adopted the same ones and there is no agreement on a comprehensive plan.

---

[3] Peter Kilborn, "Reality of H.M.O. System Doesn't Live Up to the Dream," N.Y. Times, 10/5/98.

It is large corporations with thousands of employees which determine the cost of and the kinds of services provided by the managed care groups. It is purely a matter of clout and supply and demand economics. The large companies can also use their power to obtain a satisfactory balance between good care and low prices, in addition to a number of health care options offered to employees. On the other hand, small businesses are seeing the costs for employee health benefits rising at phenomenal rates, perhaps as much as five or ten times that of the big companies. Analysts of managed care are saying that good management can curb the cost of errors and excess of care. Carelessness only adds to the cost of care, so analysts are looking at what is called "evidence-based medicine"[4] to help doctors make better decisions about treatment. For instance, Kaiser Permanente is beginning to make a computer record of patients' charts, in order to learn what treatments work best.

The majority of HMOs lost money in 1997; several of them, including Oxford Health Plans and United Health group, a sizable amount. When this happens, a vicious cycle then sets in, for companies that show such poor profits then attract fewer investors. Yet, ironically, even the companies that are losing so badly continue to give their executives mammoth salaries and stock options. In 1997, the chief executive of United Health Care made ten million dollars including the value of stock options, and the founder of Oxford Health Plans got a nine million dollar severance package when he resigned in 1998. The most astonishing figures of all were for the former C.E.O. of Columbia/HCA who drew a $900,000 salary and a $720,000 bonus in 1996, followed by a five million dollar severance pay and a $950,000 annual "consulting fee" for five years.

4.Ibid

The two ways that are now used to save money, raising the cost of premiums and cutting back on services will only work for so long, for if this is done very much, customers will object strenuously and will change to another plan if they can. In addition, most Medicare HMOs just cannot make it financially, as the federal government only gives them a set amount for each patient.

In 1998, when the government decided to sharply limit Medicare payments to managed care plans beginning in 1999, dozens of HMOs either abandoned their services or reduced them and 400,000 patients were to be dropped by 1999. Even when they are financially solvent, the Medicare HMOs have little incentive to provide the sickest with quality care, for if they do they would only attract a lot more of the sickest. Because they are not paid more for their sicker patients, they can only thrive by serving the healthiest population. Therefore they are trying to lure healthy senior patients with extras such as prescription plans and vision care.

Of course, in addition to greed there are other reasons for the high cost of medical care. According to David Rothman, technology bears the greatest responsibility for the high cost of United States medical care. Expenditures on medical instruments and supplies are eight times what they were in 1960, and patients have come to expect that they will be the beneficiaries of the latest and most complex equipment.

I have never heard much discussion about states putting a cap on the money awarded in medical malpractice lawsuits. It would seem as though doctors over-prescribe tests and procedures mainly from fear of being sued for medical negligence, and they certainly pay large sums of money for malpractice insurance. Why are law associations so much more effective than medical associations in lobbying against controlling the high awards of medical malpractice suits? Surely, a cap on amounts of awards given in medical malpractice suits could save much money in tests and insurance premiums as well as in the awards themselves. The public is certainly very conscious of the outrageous amounts of money that are often awarded in malpractice and other lawsuits involving insurance companies. Three years ago, I was part of a panel being called for jury duty in an accident case that was obviously going to involve a great deal of money because of the nature of the injuries. There was so much strong feeling among a number of the prospective jurors about what they referred to as "deep pocket" that the panel had to be dismissed and another one called. The lawyers obviously felt that those jurors who had already been selected were probably tainted by the discussion, so even they were dismissed.

Patients Rights and Managed Care

According to a ruling of the United States Court of Appeals for the Ninth Circuit, Medicare patients enrolled in HMOs have a constitutional right to due process when they are denied service. This ruling affirmed an earlier one made by a federal district court in Arizona which declared that patients must be given prompt notification when a benefit has been denied, a full explanation for the denial, and an explanation of the appeal mechanism.

Currently, Medicare patients can easily switch back to regular Medicare from Medicare HMOs as long as they make the change within a designated period of time. The "Switch rates" vary from four percent in the most popular Medicare HMOs to fifty-four percent in the least, and therefore are a good measure of satisfaction with the HMO. *Newsweek*, in its annual ranking of health plans, has used "disenrollment" rates as one of the factors in rating an HMO.

Lobbyists in Washington such as the American Association of Health Plans declare that if patients are given the right to sue insurers that refuse to approve medical treatment, rates would increase and businesses would drop employee health care coverage, which would mean the end of managed care. On the other hand, supporters of a right to litigate say that whatever medical decision is made, even if it is a refusal to approve specific treatment, responsibility must be taken for such a decision. Since September 1, 1997, Texas has allowed lawsuits as well as a separate process to appeal insurance decisions. Quite contrary to the claim that there would be a landslide of suits, the experience in Texas is that as of September 1998 there had not been a single one filed. However, it is expected that there will be lawsuits, and already lawyers have ads in papers seeking patients as clients, and conferences are being held around the state to educate lawyers on the new law. There also have been fewer appeals of insurance decisions than were expected, yet half of those appeals have gone against the insurers. In addition, Texas doctors are reporting that HMOs are now more willing to go along with their treatment plans.

One of the complications to a law such as Texas' is the federal law passed in 1974, ERISA, the Employee Retirement Income Security Act, which bars malpractice suits against employer-sponsored health plans. Government employee plans, government programs such as Medicare, policies bought by individuals and some small-employer plans are not subject to ERISA, the original goal of which was to keep multi-state corporations from having to deal with a mass of different state regulations. Probably one reason why there have been no lawsuits as of September 1998 is uncertainty as to how open for litigation the field is because of ERISA. The chief concern is whether the Texas law can override the Federal protections against lawsuits under ERISA without congressional action or court action to resolve the issue. Now, there is a wait-and-see attitude. However, there have been more complaints to the state Insurance Department, which regulates insurance companies.

Part of the new Texas law is to set up an organization and a process for making appeals. The Texas Medical Foundation, which is the organization that has been designated to do the reviews, has a doctor in the appropriate medical specialty review the medical record and then make a decision. He may consult other specialists but he neither sees the patient nor the doctor involved. The insurer pays the cost of the review.

Litigation is a major issue in the chasm between the Republicans and Democrats in trying to work out a federal bill on patient's rights. Another issue is the accessibility of emergency care for HMO members without their having to get prior authorization, and without an extra charge for an out-of-plan hospital. A plan to define patients' rights and to regulate HMOs was passed by the House of Representatives in July 1998 but could not even get to the senate floor for debate because of such profound disagreements between the two parties.

One reason that Texas was able to pass its law allowing litigation against HMOs was that many patients complained to their state legislators about unsatisfactory care. One of the lawmakers was so persuaded by some of the more extreme stories that he was impelled to push the bill through the legislature. This same thing happened in Nevada after Louis DeGeorge, a retiree, was left with spinal and hip injuries and splintered teeth after an automobile accident. He was taken to an emergency room where a physician examined him and ordered an M.R.I. test. However, when he got the physician's report there was no mention of his back, hip and jaw injuries, no reference to the M.R.I., and no referral was made to a dentist covered by his HMO. Still in severe pain four months after the accident, he finally got a copy of the report on the M.R.I., which showed he had two herniated discs. He unsuccessfully made twenty calls to the HMO for a referral to a dentist approved by them, and finally, in frustration, chose a dentist from a newspaper ad, who charged him $26,000. A referral to a back specialist took seventy-five days, and that doctor referred him to another specialist, who saw him after an additional twenty days. He finally filed a complaint with Family Health Plan (F. H. P.), his HMO, then took it to the Health Care Financing Administration, then through several other layers, and finally was seen by an administrative-law judge in Tucson, who finally heard the case in Las Vegas. However, because he had gone outside of his plan to see the dentist he lost his case. He then insisted on testifying before the legislature and was so angry that he wouldn't shut up until he was allowed to speak. In addition to him, there were many others, all very articulate and moving, who testified and contributed their own horror stories.

As a result of this testimony, Nevada now has HMO patient rights regulations, which may be an example for other states. Under the Nevada law, health maintenance organizations may not offer incentives to doctors for the denial of care. They may not include in contracts with physicians what is called "gag clauses," which prevent them from disclosing to patients that they have medical options outside of the plan. They may not retaliate against a doctor who takes the side of a patient or who assists a patient in an appeal. They must permit female patients direct access to obstetricians and gynecologists without having to go through a primary physician. HMOs must allow doctors to help decide which prescription medications are covered or necessary. They must permit medical personnel to help determine the length of hospital stays.

Because the public didn't want national health insurance as conceived by the Clintons in the early nineties, the health care system was allowed to run wild and the free market took over. Many people thought that the private sector could provide health care more efficiently and less expensively. This has proved not to be true. Look at the enormous and obscene salaries and perks that HMO and insurance company executives get. Look at the number of denials or delays of service that are made in the interest of saving money. Look at the increasing cost of premiums and the decreasing quality of service. Consider how often health care professionals, particularly doctors, must practice a kind of professional dishonesty, because they are not able to inform patients of all options, or because they may be compensated for the number of patients who are kept out of the hospital, or because they are not allowed the freedom to prescribe drugs of their choice that may cost more. "The most imposing fact about the market-medicine HMO system, now spreading at enormous speed across the land, is that nobody voted for it, nobody was consulted about it, and nobody elected it. Yet, it holds the power of life and death over patients, and arbitrates the professional role of doctors and nurses, and is accountable only to itself and to unforeseeable fluctuations in the stock market."[5]

Medicare, which is national health insurance for the elderly, is a public program that is functioning better than the private sector programs. Why does the public view national

---

5. Christopher Hutchens, "Bitter Medicine," Vanity Fair, August 1998

health care with such loathing, calling it "socialistic," which to many Americans is the most pejorative term that they can think of? If "socialistic" partly means that the federal government assures that all citizens will receive a certain standard of health care, then certainly universal health care is socialistic. Also, by that definition so is Medicare, and I don't know anyone receiving Medicare coverage who is willing to give it up.

National Health Care and Universal Health Care

The United States and South Africa are the two remaining major nations of the world that still do not have universal and portable health care. One fifth of our citizens do not have health insurance. Many of these are children. These uninsured families and single people are the working poor who earn too much money to qualify for Medicaid and who are uncovered through their jobs. In some states such as New York, special programs have been instituted to provide health care for the children of working families whose earnings are below a certain level. However, this still means that the parents do not get medical coverage, and so rather than paying a full private fee for a doctor or medicine they more often than not go without the care they need.

The Clinton Health Plan

In 1993, just after President Clinton came into office, he appointed Hillary Clinton and Ira Magaziner to head a committee to develop a universal health plan that would be presented to Congress. Their first political error was that meetings were held in secret, which infuriated a great many people, including congressmen and interested segments of the health care community whose support they needed. The second error was that the plan that they did come up with was even more "rococco and Kafka-like"[6] than what people already knew.

---

6. Ibid.

The most positive thing about the Clinton plan was that it assured that every American would be covered for health care. But to guarantee that everyone would be insured and would also have bargaining power, the plan would have grouped Americans into alliances. In each state, there would have been one or more of these groups that would have such responsibilities as revenue collecting, data collecting, dispersal of information and legal tasks. In addition to individuals who had not before had insurance coverage, an alliance would include both big and small employers. The alliances would solicit competitive contract bids from hospitals, doctors and other health care providers. It was thought that this kind of competition would be the factor that would primarily control costs. In addition, a National Health Board was to set budgets that the alliances could not exceed. It was not clear how the setting of budgets was going to affect the breadth of services, or how standards of service were to be regulated, nor how much federal money would be needed for the administration of the alliance and to cover the already uninsured workers.

A great many of the large managed care companies such as Aetna and Cigna were threatened by the idea of competition and government regulation, and therefore instituted a campaign against the Clinton plan. Many people did not feel that the plan was clearly presented, and they saw it as cumbersome and bureaucratic. The middle class also could not see what advantage such a plan held for them, nor did the politicians.

THE CANADA HEALTH ACT

In 1946, the citizens of Swift Current, Saskatchewan, Canada, established the first public health insurance program in North American, making health services available to all residents, and in 1947 the same province introduced the first hospital insurance program. In 1965 a royal commission called for universal and comprehensive national health insurance with minimum standards for the whole of Canada. The next year Canada's Medicare program was initiated with the federal government paying fifty percent of the cost to the provinces, which were to develop and administer their own programs. In 1977, the fifty-fifty cost sharing was replaced with 5 year block grants so that the provinces would have more control over their own health spending. Finally in 1984 the Canada Health Act was passed unanimously in the House of Commons. The Act encompassed five principles: plans had to be public and non-profit, comprehensive, universal, portable, and accessible, and should allow the federal government to withhold funds if the provinces did not comply with these. Between 1985 and now there have been various cuts in federal funds going to the provincial programs. Despite federal cuts over the last fourteen or fifteen years, Canadian citizens continue to be generally satisfied with·the system.

The Health Plan for Ontario

Each province submits an annual report of its health services under the Canada Health Act. For instance, the report sent in by the province of Ontario for April 1, 1996 through March 31, 1997 states its plan under the five principles of the Health Act: public administration, comprehensiveness, universality; portability; and accessibility. It is a non-profit plan under the Health Insurance Act, administered by the Ministry of Health of the province to provide insurance for the cost of services in hospitals and health facilities by physicians and other health care practitioners. Step by step, the 1996 Ontario Health Plan defines its services.

In-hospital services include accommodations and meals at a ward level, nursing services, laboratory, radiological and other diagnostic procedures, necessary drugs and other preparations, the use of operating rooms, obstetrical delivery room and anesthesia facilities.

Outpatient services include day surgery, rehabilitation therapy, laboratory, radiological and other diagnostic procedures. Services also include the use of home renal dialysis and mechanical feeding equipment and drugs, supplies and medication for hemophiliac patients. Specific drugs are provided for home use such as Cyclosporin for transplant patients, AZT for AIDS patients, as well as drugs and equipment for a variety of other conditions.

Ontario also provides mental health services, including psychiatric hospitals, ambulance services with a co-payment component, and dental treatments for patients with cleft lips and cleft palates. Visual assessments and a drug benefit program are provided for people in certain categories such as those 65 years old or older, for residents of long-term care facilities (nursing homes) or homes for special care (adult homes), for people receiving services under a home care program, and people receiving public assistance. There is also what is called the Trillium Drug Program for people who are so incapacitated that they must spend large sums of money on prescription drugs; and also an assistive device program that provides oxygen and various equipment and another program that gives an annual grant to seniors for diabetic equipment.

With certain exceptions, all residents of Ontario, eligible for the program after a three- month waiting period, must register for the plan. Each resident must live in Ontario 183 days out of any twelve-month period to be covered. It is possible for a resident who must go out of the province for a temporary period for work or study to maintain continuous coverage as long as he notifies the Ministry of Health in advance.

The same rule applies to residents who go out of the country temporarily; they must notify the authorities in advance. However, for continuous coverage, there are restrictions that apply to the nature and duration of the out-of-country absences. Payment in other provinces of Canada will be made at the standard rate charged in the province where the hospitalization has occurred. Out- of country emergency hospital costs are reimbursed at Ontario rates. Payments for physicians or other health practitioners will also be paid at the standard Ontario rate, or the billed rate if that is lower.

Insured services provided by physicians and dentists in the province of Ontario are paid primarily on a fee-for-service basis, and physicians either "opt in" and bill the Plan for all service or "opt out" and bill their patients for all services. Non-participating physicians can bill the Plan directly for certain specified groups of patients and through an associated medical group for services rendered in public hospitals, nursing homes and other institutions. The Government of Ontario negotiates with the Ontario Medical Association to determine payments for physician services.

In Ontario, as in other provinces, there is a good deal of discussion of the reform of long term care services, emphasizing home care services as an alternative to residential care.

Some of the Practicalities

Canadians from British Columbia whom I know are very pleased with their system. They also help pay for Medicare out of their pension check, as we pay for ours from our Social Security check. Their Medicare plan, unlike ours, does not require large amounts of paperwork of recipients. However, it includes a drug plan for which patients must pay a dispensing fee of 5 or 6 dollars for all but the most expensive medicine. Our friends do have to purchase extra insurance to cover them during the months they are away from Canada, only because they are away for so long. They have also told us about the long waits for elective surgery, and the numbers of people who have been referred to the United States for surgery, because there are not enough hospital beds across Canada.

An article in the March 1, 1999 *McLean's*, a Canadian magazine similar to our *Time* magazine, discussed the problem of the hospital crisis which is occurring all across Canada. Because of a growing population of elderly people who are frailer and need more medical care there are not enough nursing home beds. Therefore, badly needed acute care hospital beds are being used by chronic care patients who cannot be treated elsewhere. Also, nurses have been leaving the system because of the devilishly hard work, and also because they can come across the border to the United States for better pay. In 1997, 4 thousand nurses in Quebec took advantage of the offer of early retirement packages. Five years ago, the federal government slashed its health care funding to the provinces which administer their own health care plans, so that there has not been the money with which to increase the supply of beds. As a result, patients are being turned away from hospitals, surgeries are being cancelled, cancer patients are being flown across the country or to the United States for care, ambulances are being turned away from emergency rooms, and patients are lined up in hallways and emergency rooms for days. There was an account of a cystic fibrosis patient who had a donor and a date set for replacement lung surgery, but whose surgery had to be cancelled because there was no bed to be found and no available nursing team. The donated lungs were just disposed of.

At the time of the printing of the *McLean's* article, it was announced that the federal government was budgeting an extra $11.5 billion (Canadian dollars) for health care over the next five years. This represented a surplus as a result of the slash made in 1995. The aim of the new money was to hire more nurses, to reduce the waiting lists for cancer treatment and increase the number of long-term care beds in order to free acute care beds. In Ontario alone, it is hoped that there will be an increase of 20,000 nursing home beds by early in the next century.

The Swedish System of Social and Health Programs for the Elderly

The Swedish population is taken care of "from the cradle to the grave," and in turn pays high and complicated taxes. There are direct income taxes paid to the national and the local governments, national taxes on income from investments and capital, national inheritance taxes, national real estate taxes and also indirect taxes such as sales taxes. Employers also contribute toward social and health programs for employees; in 1997, these charges totaled almost 33% of wage and salary payments, and were charged as business costs. For individuals, the national income tax was 25% of all income earned above a certain point. On the local level, the average income tax rate is about 31% of the taxable income, making a total of 66% taken out of income for taxes.

In Sweden, people normally retire at 65, although one may choose to do so at the age of 60 at a lower pension. The national pension scheme includes a basic pension that is based on residence in Sweden and a supplemental pension (ATP) based on income from gainful employment. To receive a full basic pension, a person must have lived in Sweden at least 40 years after the age of 16 or have earned ATP points for at least 30 years. Adjustments are made for people who do not meet the basic requirements for the two kind of pensions. Those who retire at the age of 60 may receive a partial pension and continue to work part-time until the age of 65.

The elderly in Sweden are provided with an array of health and welfare services. The main thrust of the care of the elderly is to enable them to remain in their own homes as long as possible. Ninety-two percent of the Swedish population does continue to live in ordinary homes. There are enormous human and financial benefits to keeping people out of institutions, therefore municipalities adapt homes to the needs of the elderly at little or no charge. Home care services consisting of assistance with shopping, cleaning, cooking, laundry and personal hygiene are also provided by the municipality at fees that vary with each municipality and are based on the person's income and the number of hours of help needed. Most elderly people who still live at home see the district nurse and doctor at a district health center. If a person finds it too difficult to get to the district health center, a district nurse makes a home visit. If an elderly person needs hospitalization, the aim is to return the person to his own home, if possible; geriatric wards can also be used for respite care to give the family looking after him some relief. In 1995, 10% of the elderly over 65 and 20% over the age of 80 needed some kind of home care. If a relative is taking care of the elderly person at home, he or she may be paid for his services by the municipality. If relatives must take time off from work for care of the elderly person they may be compensated from the social insurance system for a total of up to 60 days a year for care to each relative or close friend.

According to the Social Services Act, alternative housing shall be available for those who can no longer manage independently in their own homes. Since 1992, it has been the municipalities that have been responsible for all of the special types of housing, which include "service homes" which are comparable to our assisted living facilities, old age homes, nursing homes, and special group homes for patients with senile dementia. People living in special housing pay rent and service charges, the fee for each of these being based on a person's care needs and income, excluding capital

As elsewhere in the world, because of growing numbers of elderly people and the resultant shortage of institutional beds, private profit-making alternatives and cooperative owned and administered housing have become more attractive. In 1995, private interests accounted for 5% of all care for the elderly, yet even where private care organizations provide the care they are still financed and monitored by the municipality.

Sweden had a weaker economy than ours during the 90's, which means that it will be difficult for the national government to keep up with the increasing demand for services. The enormous and increasing needs of the elderly are challenging the moral imperative that Sweden has felt in caring for its elderly population. To date, it has felt that the public sector had the primary responsibility for the care of this age group by trained and qualified staff. Because of escalating needs, "the principle of free or heavily subsidized health care and social services for all citizens on equal terms will be difficult to maintain."[7] In the future, emphasis will probably have to be placed on the needs of the most dependent elderly in order to make the most efficient use of scarce resources such as medical personnel and

---

7. The Health Care System in Sweden, 11/97 publication of the Swedish Information Service.

institutional beds. Those who can afford to will probably turn to private resources. More emphasis will be placed on informal care such as families and voluntary associations. Such changes will be a response to increasing needs, not a change in ideals. There is and will be still a consensus on the principle that the state is universally responsible for the care of its elderly, although in practice services may be more narrowly defined.

What I find so impressive about Sweden's health and welfare system is that it is expected that the public sector will assure that there will be a basic standard of health and well being for all people. That is the return its citizens get for the high taxes they pay. In such a system, there should be no person who cannot get the care he or she needs because of no insurance or insufficient private funds, as happens in this country. Also, in such a system, there should not be the huge chasm between the rich and the poor that you find in the United States.

Summary

You may ask what all of the above information means to us? I hope it gives a picture of some of the problems of a health care system such as ours that is based on profit, of the numbers of adults and children who are not covered, and the numbers of services and treatments that are denied to us. I have also tried to show how other countries view their responsibility for their aged citizens. The Canadian, English and Swedish systems impose high taxes to provide from cradle-to-grave extensive health and in Sweden social services too. There is no one who is uncovered. Yet there are problems with these systems too. Because of increasing numbers of aged residents with serious health problems, there is a shortage of hospital and nursing home beds, and non-emergency surgeries have to be delayed, which has driven Canadians to seek such surgeries in the United

States. Sweden, as a partial solution, is emphasizing more home health care as an alternative to nursing home care. Nevertheless, to repeat, despite the problems in these other systems, no one is without basic care, as happens in the United States.

Chapter X

Take Hold and Seize the Day

As we speak
Envious time has passed.

Seize the moment,
Count on tomorrow
As little as you can.

—Horace: Odes I, xi, 8

All of us at any age, but especially in our older years, are both the managed and the managers. But taking hold and managing our lives means many things, depending on our physical and mental capacities and our living circumstances. We must decide that, whatever our condition, we still can make decisions about ourselves and the larger world, set new goals and work toward them. Sometimes these goals must be very limited if we have serious physical or mental problems, but a willingness to be flexible is absolutely essential, as abilities and circumstances can change so fast for the elderly.

The following are some of the areas where we can act as managers. There are larger social issues on local, national and international levels that elders can be involved with. There are also personal issues such as our health, our finances, our relationships with others, that we should manage ourselves. We also have our roles as "elders" who believe they have a right and even an obligation at times to pass on what they have learned. Above all else, almost every researcher and professional working with the older population agrees that there are certain tasks of the last years that should be part of seizing today.

TAKING HOLD POLITICALLY

At times most of us feel helpless about exerting our influence to make changes, especially in a society as complex as ours with an economic system over which none of us have much control and with huge lobbying interests that wield a great deal of power. Yet in a democracy individuals can still make a difference. Supporting the party of our choice with money and votes, signing petitions, and writing letters to public officials are still effective ways of making changes. Consider what happened to regulations on HMOs in Nevada and Texas as a result of complaints to legislators (see Chapter IX). Legislators are powerful, but they need our votes, and so have to be responsive. Even in our seventies and our eighties, we must still realize that we have a voice and that there are ways that we can make our selves heard. It is not fair to complain if we are unwilling to put in whatever small effort we can to effect changes. Even if that effort is just a letter to the newspaper, or a telephone call, an E-Mail or a fax to a representative's office, or helping to stamp and address envelopes, it is worthwhile.

Just in the last few years, our small town in upstate New York was faced with the possibility of a merger of three hospitals in two adjoining counties that would greatly reduce the Ob-Gyn services in the area. One of the hospitals was Catholic and as a result of the agreement its policies on sterilization, abortion and birth control would be followed in all three hospitals. The decision for the merger was justified for financial reasons but had been made without community consultation or public meetings. When the merger plan was publicized, protest committees were organized very quickly in the two counties. They were active and vocal and worked hard over almost a year's time to educate the communities to the grave consequences of the merger decision. Frequent public meetings were held, many newspaper articles were written and protest signs appeared on the lawns of many homeowners. Because there was so much community opposition, within a year the hospital boards reversed the decision. In turn, the protest committees decided that they would not abandon the ship, but would work with the local hospital in any way they could to resolve the financial problems that had prompted the original decision to merge. There were people of all ages and social groups who participated in the protest and their work proved that community action is still effective in bringing change.

I have heard so many people of retirement age say they have put in their stint on political causes, that they are tired and it is now time for them to rest. Yet these same people gripe incessantly about things in their community without doing anything positive.

Even nursing home patients who are competent should be encouraged to educate themselves on issues, to express themselves and to vote, but unfortunately too little is done to stimulate such interests. If they were encouraged to discuss current issues and to vote, they would have a greater feeling that they and their ideas still count.

Issues that are of foremost interest to the elderly are the future of Social Security and Medicare, which are due to give out in 2013 because of dwindling funds. A seventeen member federal advisory commission looking for ways to save Medicare, after meeting for two years, disbanded on March 1999 so divided that it could not even come up with a report. I have heard of mighty few community forums or the kind of town hall meetings that President Clinton led in the early nineties on the problem of the future of Social Security and Medicare. Would it not help for legislators to know how the public stands on the various proposals that have already been made? As the recipients of Social Security and Medicare we should speak up responsibly about the medical and social needs of the aging population.

My husband and I participate in a small monthly discussion group in Green Valley that two or three years ago discussed the future of Social Security. The group unanimously concluded that it would favor people with incomes above a certain level paying more taxes on their Social Security pensions and more for their Medicare premiums. Unfortunately we never did publicize our views through a newspaper letter or to our legislators, so we were guilty of just what I have been criticizing in people our age: a passivity and willingness to let things ride, and have someone else take the responsibility.

Of course, there are many other issues of concern besides Medicare and Social Security. Such examples might be the environment, education, welfare rights, the plight of the homeless, separation of church and state, the death penalty, First Amendment rights, or how much our country is to involve itself in the problems in other countries. Of course, these are just a few that come into my mind, and, naturally, one cannot alone solve the problems of the world. But if you choose one problem and decide that you want to make a contribution to its cause, that is a beginning. You can then go to the internet or the yellow pages to find organizations that are trying to deal with that particular concern, send for information, make a financial contribution, or offer your services. If you are housebound, there might be something that you can do from your home for that cause.

Politics Aside ...

Politics aside, it is essential for elderly people to take responsibility for their health care and many other personal concerns. There is a great deal of medical information available on television as well as in newspapers and magazines, and of course on the internet. If people wish to know if new drugs or procedures are appropriate for them, they should speak up and ask their physicians. If they feel they are not getting enough information from their doctor they should ask questions, ask for copies of tests, or ask for referrals. If the answers or service are not satisfactory, again they should assert themselves, and if there is no change, then they have a right to look for a new doctor or group. If they feel that there has been a very serious deficiency in the quality of service they have received, they should not hesitate to complain to the proper authorities, through the complaint mechanism in their HMO or to the local medical association or regulatory agency, which is usually the state or local health department. People need to be more assertive and they have the right to be. Just because we are over sixty-five does not mean that we must simply accept things as they are.

Many women of our generation have not been responsible for financial matters in the family and have told me that they are really quite ignorant about the stock market, insurance, pensions and the myriad of other money considerations that have occupied their husbands. On the other hand, those women who had careers, even if they did not pay the bills, were more knowledgeable about such matters since they were earning money, perhaps setting up pensions, and certainly seeing their earnings going into separate or joint banking accounts. Whichever category one falls into, it is essential, especially in pre-retirement days, to share actively in the planning and distribution of earnings so that one is prepared for assuming financial responsibility should one's husband become incapacitated or die suddenly.

In order to be wholly responsible for ourselves we must be flexible at all times. In our elder years, physical changes take place very quickly, which may mean our needs suddenly become very different. If we are mentally competent, we are the ones to determine what we need to alter and then take an active role in making different arrangements. As an example, many people wait too long to make different housing plans, and it becomes evident to everyone close to them that they are no longer well enough to live alone. Or even if they live with a partner, whatever the present housing situation is, it suddenly becomes too burdensome to manage. Stubbornness, ambivalence or denial may freeze a person into not making a timely decision about a more appropriate living situation. Underneath all of this, of course, is the ultimate inability to face our own mortality.

I was interested to read that New York Senator Daniel Patrick Moynihan and his wife Elizabeth, who have lived on a five hundred acre farm in upstate New York since 1964 decided in June 2000 to sell the farm that had meant so much to both of them. At 73, he had decided to retire, and she, who also was over 70, recognized how much work the farm was for them at their age, even though this was where they had spent their summers and raised their children. She explained that those days were over, that there are stages in life and it was time to simplify, like everyone else. After their decision was made, Mrs. Moynihan promptly put the property on the market and was looking forward to moving. Of course, very few of us are in such financial circumstances with such large properties. Still, we can learn from this example that once we face our own frailties and our own mortality it is best to move on to more appropriate circumstances so that life is easier and we can be more productive during our remaining years.

Another example of flexibility with changed needs is an acquaintance in Green Valley, a divorced man in his late eighties who had lived there more than twenty years in good health and active in the community. In 1999 when he had his annual physical at his HMO, the physician's assistant sent him for blood tests because of the yellowish color of his skin. I was at the lab when he came in to have tests and we sat and chatted for a few minutes. He said he was never ill, but that lately he had felt very tired. He was obviously anxious. The tests indicated possible problems with the liver. When further tests showed that he had an advanced case of cancer of the liver, he was given a few months to live. Within a week he had packed up most of his belongings and moved back to the large mid-west city where he came from and where his daughter lived. On his insistence, for the sake of his daughter who had cared for her terminally ill mother two years before, he moved into an assisted living facility, and shortly thereafter married a travelling companion of many years. Before he died three months later, he had settled his affairs and had said goodbye to all of his many friends. Without forethought and readiness he could not possibly have made all of the changes he did within such a short period of time.

In order to free ourselves and to prepare our families for what we wish, we need to think about and share with those closest to us what we wish for our last years and how we wish to die long before we have arrived at that point. Doing this frees us, our families and significant others.

THE HEALING TASKS

I was going to name this section *The Last Tasks* and then realized that these tasks are not ones that should wait until the very end of our life, but still are essential responsibilities to be undertaken before we die.

There are of course those clerical tasks mentioned elsewhere in the book: the preparation of our wills, trusts, living wills, medical power of attorneys, decisions about possessions not covered by the will and all of those other things that tie up loose ends. Among these, are our written preferences about how and where we want to be taken care of in our last days, what we want for a funeral or a memorial service and where we want to be buried or our ashes strewn.

In our role of elders, we may wish to write letters to those who mean the most to us, for example our grandchildren, to convey to them what in life has meant the most to us, what we have learned and wish to share with them. Of course, we must keep in mind that those people will have to find for themselves the things and the ways that will mean the most to <u>them</u>.

Being human means that we are imperfect and vulnerable. As such, we may have hurt those who are closest, or those who too may be fragile. We in turn may have been badly hurt by others and have never been able to forgive them. Forgiveness and mercy are important to all of the major religions, but putting aside religion, the practice of forgiving is psychologically healing to both the forgiven and the one who does the forgiving. If the relationship means anything to us, we feel uneasy and there continues to be a barrier until we have been able to make amends if we are the offender, or are able to forgive if we are the injured. Perhaps, we need to forgive ourselves first before we can make amends. Whatever they are, these acts are what most people call the unfinished business that must be done near the end. If they are done near rather than at the end, there is still time to enjoy a different relationship that will be remembered.

The Successful Elders

As I have worked on this book I have met some remarkable people, some of whom I have interviewed, others I have read about or heard stories of or have just observed. I would like to share with you the stories of some of these people, who range from sixty-five or seventy to one hundred and five.

President Carter's defeat in his bid for reelection in 1980 was devastating to him and to his wife, Rosalyn. He was only fifty-six, had not visualized himself returning to Plains, Georgia, where his family had lived for one hundred years, at least not at that point. The family business was not doing well, leaving him with a debt of more than a million dollars, and he did not know what he was going to do with the twenty-five or thirty years left to him. He quickly put behind him his disappointment about the election defeat, and to pay off his business debts sold his peanut warehouse and made arrangements for the publication of his memoirs. Successful with his first book, he then turned to a writing career, publishing more than a dozen books after his retirement. This led to his starting to write poetry, and even a novel that is set in the south. Both he and Rosalyn are professors at Emory University; he has set up the Carter Center in Atlanta, and has become involved in international mediation, sometimes initiating contacts himself and at other times being asked by several administrations to act as a mediator. He and Rosalyn have continued to be physically active, setting aside time each day for exercising, tennis, fishing, running and even climbing mountains, including Mount Kilimanjaro. Both of them volunteer in different areas of interest and both build houses for and publicize the work of Habitat for

Humanity. One of his favorite hobbies is carpentry, which gives him a great deal of satisfaction and is also relaxing and absorbing.

President Carter stresses the importance of having the time to spend with friends and family. Having been married over fifty years, he says his relationship with Rosalyn is closer and more intimate than ever, and they do almost everything together. Now that they have the time, with accumulated frequent flyer mileage and money from savings, they take some kind of trip with their children and grandchildren each year to a different destination. It gives the family a chance to be together and there is enough flexibility for each generation to enjoy themselves.

What impresses me most about President Carter, even in his late 70's, is his vitality, his enthusiasm and positive outlook, the variety of productive work he continues to do, his sensible balance between work and recreation and the cherishing and maintenance of his close relationships with family, friends and neighbors. All of this is a good recipe for successful living at any age, but to continue to be involved in such a vibrant way and in so many activities is remarkable at his age.

I talked over the telephone with a hundred and five year old woman in a village in upstate New York. Widowed, she still lives in her own home, with meals-on-wheels providing her with the big meal of the day. She attends church every week, is a member of the local historical society, reads and maintains membership in the county needlework guild. When I asked her what she felt had contributed most to her good health and long life, she said it ran in her family but that she had also always enjoyed life, and had been happy and active, which she felt were contributing factors.

I am an inveterate reader of obituaries, and was even when I was much younger. I find they are very interesting and that many times they reflect what qualities and activities are most valued in our society. Recently, in Green Valley, I read an obituary for an 86 year old woman who continued to work until the day before she died. Dr. Paul Scharf, at the Fellowship Community (see Chapter V) felt strongly that meaningful work was a key factor in successful aging.

While I was waiting in my doctor's waiting room one day, I started chatting with a woman who writes a weekly gossip and activities column for our local newspaper. When I talked with her she had lived in the village about a year, having moved up from the Bronx. She told me that she was in her seventies and had known no-one when she moved to the village, but felt then that writing the column would be a good way to meet a lot of people. Shortly after the move, she approached the newspaper with her idea for the column and within the year everyone knew who she was. On September 10, 1998, I clipped one of her columns just after she had returned from a trip to Ireland with almost 90 people from one of the local Roman Catholic churches. In that column, in a witty, lively, chatty way she described her trip and the people she met all over Ireland, but she also picked up on the usual local activities and birthday greetings and jokes. The day she was in the doctor's office she had brought a blind neighbor for his appointment.

Recently, at a Green Valley party, I was told about a 90 year old resident of Green Valley who was currently traveling to various parts of the country promoting a book of his, *Survived to Tell An Autobiography*. Edward Keonjian was born of a large Armenian family in 1909 in Tiflis, Georgia, and even as a small child was interested in electronics. At age seventeen he left his family to attend the Leningrad Electrotechnical Institute, where later he earned his doctorate. In the winter of 1941 when the temperature was minus 45 degrees, the Germans advanced on Leningrad and surrounded it, leaving 3,500,000 people blockaded and without electricity, power, food or heat. People were starving and had to resort to desperate ways of staying alive. Many died. Keonjian himself collapsed and, taken for dead, was removed to a mass grave. A woman walking by noticed some movement in a hand that was sticking up, and by moving bodies found Keonjian, who was still alive. After being nursed by his rescuer, he was reunited with his wife and child and went on to become a distinguished professor of electronics here in the United States. Recently, he was honored at the University of Arizona with a conference room named after him. But frankly what interested me most about this man is that he still had enough vitality at the age of 90 to promote his book in various parts of the country.

THE FINAL RESPONSIBILITY

As well as being assertive about our own needs and those of our peer group, perhaps the most important responsibility means continuing to be involved with other people, our family, our friends, reaching out to new people to offer friendship and also to other people who may need our help. There is loneliness and need in every sector of society.

Whether one is religious or not the following biblical passage serves us well.

> *Whatsoever ye would that men should do to you, do you even so to them.*
> —Matthew 7:12

SEIZE TODAY

So, no matter who we are, no matter where we live, or what our physical condition is, we can still be our own masters, significantly involved in what happens to us. We can even affect what happens in the greater society. In order to do all of this, we must squarely face our age and our limitations and adapt to them. However, chronic disease or disability do not mean that we are useless and should passively wait for death even if we are in an institutional setting. Instead, we should cherish every minute left to us, and engage ourselves, at times passionately, with other people and with the world around us. Above all else, with flexibility we can still grow and explore our capabilities in order to stretch our minds and our hearts.

REFERENCES

AGING

Friedan, Betty, *The Fountain of Age*, (N.Y., Simon & Schuster, 1993).

Carter, Jimmy, *The Virtues of Aging*, (N.Y., Ballantine Publishing Group, 1998).

Rowe, John W. &Kahn, Robert L., *Successful Aging*, (N.Y., Pantheon Books, 1998).

"UA prof survived being buried alive in Leningrad Siege," *The Arizona Daily Sun*, 7/28/97 and Dave Ricker, "GV resident is honored by UA for his pioneering work in microelectronics," *Green Valley News*, 4/14.99.

ALZHEIMER'S DISEASE

"Everybody Needs A FRIENDD," A Caregiver's Resource Manual, *Alzheimer's Association, Southern Arizona Chapter* (Tucson), 1996-1997.

Marion Roach, "In an N.Y.U. Lab, Premonitions of Alzheimer's, *N.Y. Times*, 12/1/98.

"Brain scan detects Alzheimer's long before symptoms show up." *Arizona Daily Star*, 1/1/99.

Dave Ricker, "Missing Green Valley man located," *Green Valley News*, 12/2/98.

Regina Ford, "'Safe Return' program helps Alzheimer's who wander and become lost," *Green Valley News*, 10/2/98.

ASSISTED SUICIDE

Humphrey, Derek, *Jean's Way*, (N.Y., Dell, 1978).

Humphrey, Derek, *Final Exit*, (Eugene, Oregon, Hemlock Society, 1991).

Mullens, Anne , *Timely Death*, (Vintage Canada 1996).

Neils, Rob, *Death With Dignity FAQS*, (Dubuque, Kendall-Hunt Publishing Co., 1997).

"An Appointment with Death," TV Ontario, shown by WGBH Boston in 1993.

Sam Howe Verhovek, "Oregon Reporting 15 Deaths in Year Under Suicide Law," *N.Y. Times*, 2/18/99.

CANCER

Lawrence K. Altman, M.D., "Good News From The Front In The War Against Cancer," *N.Y. Times*, 1/26/99.

Jane Brody, "Diet Is Not A Panacea, But It Cuts Risk Of Cancer," *N.Y. Times*, 12/1/98.

Jane Brody, "Living Proof: Mammograms Are Not Always Enough," *N.Y. Times*, 3/9/99.

Glenn Fleishman, "Turning To The Net To Lift The Shadows of Cancer's Dark Days," N.Y. Times, 7/9/98.

Denise Grady, "In Breast Cancer Data, Hope, Fear and Confusion," *N.Y.Times*, 1/26/99.

Denise Grady, "Software to Compute Women's Cancer Risk," *N.Y. Times*, 1/26/99.

Alice Lesch Kelly, "It's No Fun, but It May Save Your Life," *N.Y.Times*, 2/17/99.

Sam Howe Verhovek, "A Former General Fights For Seattle's Schools While Fighting for His Life," *N.Y. Times*, 9/3/98.

"Mammograms Cause Anxiety In the Elderly," N.Y.Times, 9/16/98.

"Vaccine can stem colon cancer recurrence, study finds," Arizona Daily Star, 1/29/99.

"Study Says Tomatoes Cut Risk of Cancer," *N.Y. Times*, 2/17/99.

"Internet health scares to be ignored," editorial in *Green Valley News*, 3/10/99.

DEATH & DYING

Denise Grady, "At Life's End, Many Patients Are Denied Peaceful Passing," *N.Y. Times*, 5/29/00.

Denise Grady, "Charting a Course of Comfort & Treatment at the End of Life," *N.Y. Times,* 5/30/00.

Stephen Levine, *Meetings At The Edge*, (New York: Doubleday, 1984).

Levine, Stephen & Ondea, *A Year to Live*, (N.Y. Anchor Books, 1984).

Andrew H. Malcolm, "A. M. A. Rule: Step Toward a Social Policy on Dying," N.Y. Times, 3/17/86.

Memorial Committee of the Unitarian-Universalist Church of Canton, N.Y., *Visiting A Dying Friend*, (Canton, N.Y., Unitarian Universalist Church of Canton N.Y., 3 ½ Main St., Canton, N.Y. 13617).

Sherwin Nuland, *The Way We Die*, (New York: Alfred A. Knopf, 1994).

Marilyn Webb, *The Good Death*, (New York: Doubleday, 1997.) This is the most comprehensive book I found on the subject of death.

Mark A. Uhlig, "Plan to Treat the Dying Passes After Lobbying," *N.Y. Times*, 7/9/87.

FINANCIAL PLANNING

Ernst & Young, *Retirement Planning Guide*, (John Wiley & Sons, Inc., 1998).

Don Moreau, "Can You Afford Your Future?" *Modern Maturity*, July, August 1998.

Abby Schultz, "A U.S. Warning of Sorts, About Fees and 401(k)'s" *N.Y. Times*, August 2, 1998.

Fred Brock, "New Pension Plans Are Cash & Carry," *N.Y. Times*, 3/21/99.

Planning Your Retirement, (Washington, D.C., AARP Fulfillment, 1995).

Jay M. Rosen, "Building a Nest Egg: An Exercise in Constant Guesswork," *N.Y. Times*, 3/21/99.

Consumer Booklet- *Affordable Financing for Long Term Care*, publication of NYS Partnership for Long Term Care (long term care insurance).

Mark Wexler, "To Buy Or Not to Buy," Modern Maturity, May-June 2000 (long term care insurance).

Benefits for Older New Yorkers, 1995, N.Y. State Bar Association, Elder Law Section.

FUNERAL PRACTICES

Rabbi Morris N. Kertzer, Revised by Rabbi Lawrence A. Hoffman, *What Is A Jew?* (New York, Simon & Schuster, 1993).

Telephone interview with Sr. Joyce Rowland, Our Lady of the Valley Roman Catholic Church, Green Valley, AZ.

Douglas Jehl, "Following Tradition, An Affair For Men," *N.Y. Times*, 2/9/99 (account of King Hussein"s funeral).

Douglas Jehl, "Allies and Enemies United in Grief," *N.Y. Times*, 2/9/99.

Caesar E. Farah, PhD., *Islam, Beliefs & Observances*, (Hauppauge, N.Y., Barron's Educational Service, Inc., 1987).

Ernest Morgan, *A Manual of Death Education and Simple Burial*, (Burnsville, N.C. 28714, Celo Press, 1984).

Mitford, Jessica, *The American Way of Death*, (N.Y. Simon & Schuster, 1963).

Mitford, Jessica, *The American Way of Death Revisited*, (N.Y. Alfred A. Knopf, 1998).

GERIATRIC CARE MANAGERS

Sara Rimer, "The Growing Business of Helping Elders," *N.Y. Times*, 3/4/99.

GRIEF

Viorst, Judith, *Necessary Losses,* (Simon & Schuster, 1986). A profound discussion of the many losses that we all experience.

Wortman, June ACSW, *Grief,* a talk given on March 5, 2000 to the Unitarian-Universalist Congregation of Green Valley, AZ.

HEART ATTACKS & STROKES

"Bouncing Back from Heart Attacks," *N.Y. Times,* Cause to Cure Supplement, 9/27/98.

"The Language of the Heart," *N.Y. Times,* Cause to Cure Supplement, 9/27/98.

"Hypertension: Be Aware of Your Risk," *N.Y. Times,* Cause to Cure Supplement, 9/27/98.

"Heart Disease and Women," *N.Y. Times,* Cause to Cure Supplement, 9/27/98.

"Adding Estrogen for Clearer Vessels," *N.Y. Times,* 2/2/99.

Gina Kolata, "A Promoter of Programs To Foster Heart Health," *N.Y. Times,* 12/29/98.

Joannie M. Schrof, "Stroke Busters," *U.S. News and World Report,* 3/15/99.

Regina Ford, "Professor tells Rotary about the importance of preventing strokes," *Green Valley News,* 12/23/98.

Sandra Blakeslee, "New Therapy Helps Some Stroke Patients," *N.Y. Times,* 2/2/99.

"New drug found effective in reversing strokes," *Arizona Daily Star*, 2/5/99.

Robert McCrum, *My Year Off: Recovering Life After A Stroke*, (New York, W. W. Norton, 1998.)

HOUSING

Catherine Collins, "Some Communities Span Cradle to Grave," *N.Y. Times*, 3/21/99. On NORCS (natural occurring retirement communities).

Dennis Hevesi, "The Elderly Face Housing Choices," *N.Y. Times*, 5/14/00.

Joy Alter Huber, "Like It Here. The House Is Paid For. I Think I'll Stay!" *N.Y. Times*, 3/21/99.

Ed Severson, "Live-At-Home Longer," *Arizona Daily Star*, 12/3/99.

Information from Nina Lynch, Dutchess County New York Office of the Aging.

Information from the manager of Wells Manor HUD Housing, Rhinebeck, N.Y.

Sara Rimer, "Leftist Causes Keep An Old Age Home Active," *N.Y. Times*, April 6, 1998. On Sunset Hall, 2830 Francis Ave., Los Angeles, California 90005.

Eleanor Charles, "For Affluent Elderly, An Array of Housing Choices," *N.Y. Times*, September 13, 1998.

Alan Oser, "New York Area Retirees Get More Housing Choices," N.Y. Times, May 10, 1998.

CO-HOUSING

Jennifer Peck, "Co-Housing Gains Ground, But Some Eye Shared Housing With Suspicion," *Boston Globe*, 11/30/97.

William A. Davis, "Instant Community. In The East Coast's First Urban Co-Housing Project, 85 Cambridge Residents Will Share Space and Ideals." *Boston Globe*, 3/26/98.

Kathryn McCarmart & Charles Durrett, *Co-Housing*, (Ten Speed Press, 1988).

CONTINUING CARE

Richard Levitan, "From The Cradle To The Grave," *Yoga Journal,* July-August 1993, reprinted in pamphlet published by The Fellowship Community, 241 Hungry Hollow Rd., Chestnut Ridge, N.Y. 10977.

Admissions packet, Duncaster, 40 Loeffler Rd., Bloomfield, Conn. 06002.

Admissions packet, Pennswood Village, 1382 Newtown-Langhorne Rd., Newtown Pa. 18940-2401.

Admissions packet, Kendal at Hanover, 80 Lyme Rd. Hanover, New Hampshire 03755-1218.

RETIREMENT COMMUNITIES

Catherine Reagor, "Arizona Builders Wooing Baby Boom Retirees," *Arizona Republic*, 10/3/98.

Brochures and film, Sun City, Arizona Visitors' Center.

John Howells, "The Best Places to Retire in America," *Consumer's Digest*, Summer 1998.

Packet from Leisure World, 23522 Paseo de Valencia, Laguna Hills, CA. 92653, tel. 1-800-711-9273, http://www.leisureworld.com.

Don Terry, "In This Brand New City, No Shortage of Elders," *N.Y. Times*, 3/4/99.

Rick Bragg, "Fearing Isolation in Old Age, Gay Generation Seeks Haven," *N.Y. Times,* 10/12/99.

MANAGED CARE

Caryn James, "On the Doctor Shows, Public Health Enemy No. 1," *N.Y. Times*, 9/8/98.

Milt Freudenheim, "(Loosely) Managed Care Is In Demand," *N.Y. Times*, 9/2/98.

Peter Kilborn, "Reality of H.M.O. System Doesn't Live Up to the Dream," *N.Y. Times*, 10/5/98.

Reed Abelson, "For Managed Care, Free Market Stock," *N.Y. Times*, 1/3/99.

Christopher Hitchens, "Bitter Medicine," *Vanity Fair*, August 1998. Among other considerations, a penetrating expose of CEO salaries in insurance companies that operate HMOs.

"Does Managed Care Work?" Newsweek, 9/28/98.

David J. Rothman, "Beginnings Count: The Technological, Imperative in American Health Care," *Oxford University Press*, n.d., reviewed by Andrew Hacker in the *New York Review*, 6/12/97.

"Ranking the Health Plans," *Newsweek*, 9/28/98.

PATIENTS' RIGHTS

"Due Process For Medicare Patients," *N.Y. Times*, 8/22/98.

Carol Marie Cropper, "In Texas, a Laboratory Test on the Effects of Suing HMOs," *N.Y. Times*, 9/13/98.

Robert Pear, "Common Ground on Patient Rights Hides a Chasm," *N.Y. Times*, 8/4/98.

Robert Perar, "Senators Reject Bill to Regulate Care by HMOs," *N.Y. Times*, 10/10/98.

MORTICIANS

Jessica Mitford, *The American Way of Death*, (New York, Simon & Schuster, 1963), updated version, *The American Way of Death Revisited*, (New York, Alfred A. Knopf Inc.,1998).

Jim Yardley, "Selling Coffins From a Storefront," *N.Y. Times*, 5/29/98.

Beat the High Cost of Dying, Continental Association of Funeral and Memorial Societies, 33 University Square, Suite 333, Madison, Wisconsin, 53715. Information on Memorial Societies.

NATIONAL HEALTH PLANS

Andrew Hacker, The Medicine in Our Future," *N.Y. Review*, 6/12/97. Information on the Clinton Health Plan.

Mark Nichols, "Turning Patients Away," *Maclean's*, 3/1/99.

Information on Sweden was taken from the following publications of the Swedish Information Service, 1 Dag Hammarskold Place, N.Y., N.Y. 10017-2201:
  a. "Taxes in Sweden," 9/97.
  b. "The Care of the Elderly in Sweden," 8/96.
  c. "The Health Care System in Sweden," 11/97.

PHYSICIANS

Sharon R. Kaufman, *The Healer's Tale*, (Madison, Wisconsin, University of Wisconsin Press, n.d.).

Robert Lipsyte, *In The Country of Illness*, (New York, Alfred A. Knopf, 1997).

Norman Cousins, *Anatomy of An Illness as Perceived by The Patient*, (New York, W.W. Norton & Company, 1979).

Anatole Broyard, *Intoxicated By My Illness*, (New York, Clarkson N. Potter Inc., 1992).

Jerome Groopman, M.D., *The Measure of Our Days*, (New York, Viking, 1997).

Atul Gawande, "When Doctors Make Mistakes," *New Yorker*, 2/1/99.

PHYSICIANS' TRAINING

Sara Rimer, "New Frontier For Medicine: Treating The Elderly," *N.Y. Times*, 9/24/98.

Jennifer Steinhauer, "Once Again, There is a doctor in the house," *N.Y. Times*, 12/27/98.

Sandeep Jauhar, M.D., "When Rules for Better Care Exact Their Own Cost," *N.Y. Times*, 1/5/99.

PSYCHOLOGY OF ILLNESS

Robert Lypsite, *In the Country of Illness*, (New York, Alfred A. Knopf, 1997).

Susan Sontag, *Illness As Metaphor*, (New York, Vintage Books, 1979). A tiny gem.

Susan Sontag, *Illness As Metaphor And Aids And Its Metaphors*, (N.Y., Anchor, 1990).

Sandra Blakeslee, "Placebos Prove so Powerful Even Experts Are Surprised," *N.Y. Times*, 10/13/98.

Robert Lipsyte, "Don't Take Your Medicine Like a Man," *N.Y. Times*, 2/17/99.

Natalie Angier, "Why Men Don't Last: Self Destruction as a Way of Life," *N.Y. Times*, 2/17/99.

Groopman, Jerome, *The Measure of Our Days*, (N.Y. Viking, 1997).

Winower, Sidney J. Dr., *Healing Lessons*, (N.Y., Little Brown & Co., 1998).

RECREATIONAL VENICLE TRAVEL & RESORTS

Robert W. Stack, "Riding Off Into the Sunrise to Keep the Sunset at Bay," *N Y. Times*, 7/9/98.

Peter T. Kilborn, "Deluxe Motor Homes Reflect Nation's Booming Economy," *N.Y. Times*, 7/4/99.

Beth Baker, "Home Away From Home," *AARP Bulletin*, September 1998.

Chiori Santiago, "House Trailers," *Smithsonian Magazine*, June '98.

SEX & MARRIAGE

Warren E. Leary, "Older People Enjoy Sex, Survey Says," *N.Y. Times*, 9/29/98.

Gina Kolata, "Women and Sex: On This Topic, Science Blushes," *N.Y. Times*, 6/21/98.

Jennifer Steinhauer, "Viagra's Other Side Effects: Upsets in Many a Marriage," *N.Y. Times*, 6/23/98.

Jane E. Brody, "Facing Viagra's Emotional Ripples," *N.Y. Times*, 3/26/98.

Paula B. Doress-Waters & Diane Laskin Siegal, *Ourselves Growing Older*, (New York, Touchstone, 1994).

Sara Rimer, "For Aged, Dating Game Is Numbers Game," *N.Y. Times*, 12/23/98.

Davida Rosenblum, "The Old in One Another's Arms," *N.Y. Times*, 4/9/98.

Philip Smith, "Love Boat Miracle," *National Enquirer*, 1/5/99.

Denise Couture, "For Better, For Worse," *Modern Maturity*, July-August 1998.

TRAVEL

Stephanie Faul, "Volunteering for Vacation," *Car & Travel* (AAA Automobile Club of N.Y.). "On-Line Planning," *N.Y. Times*, 8/16/98.

"Where to Look for the Best Travel Bargains," *Modern Maturity*, Sept./Oct. 1998.

AAA Benefits-Write to Car & Travel at Box 371158, Omaha, Nebraska for information on services.

Elderhostel, 75 Federal St., Boston Mass. 02110, www.elderhostel.org.

SAGA Holidays, 222 Berkeley St., Boston MA. 02116, 1-800-952-9590.

Grand Circle Travel, 347 Congress St., Boston, MA. 02210, 1-800-321-2835.

RESOURCES

GENERAL INFORMATION

American Association of Retired Persons
601 E. Street N.W. Suite 500
Washington, DC 20049
Phone: 202-434-2300
Fax: 202-434-2320
(Membership fee; low cost publications on many subjects of concern for aging.)

Gray Panthers
2025 Pennsylvania Avenue N.W., Suite 821
Washington, DC 20006
Phone: 202-466-3132
Fax: 202-466-3133

National Association of Area Agencies on Aging
1112 16th Street N.W., Suite 100
Washington, DC 20036
Phone: 202-296-8130
Fax: 202-296-8134
(List of aging resources in local areas)

National Caucus and Center on Black Aged, Inc.
1424 K Street N. W., Suite 725
Washington, DC 2005
Phone: 202-637-8400
Fax: 202-347-0895

National Council on the Aging, Inc.
409 3rd Street S.W., 2nd Floor
Washington, DC 20024
Phone: 202-479-1200
Fax: 202-479-0735
(Information on services for aging)

National Hispanic Council on Aging
2713 Ontario Road N.W., Suite 200
Washington, DC 20009
Phone: 202-745-2521
Fax: 202-745-2522

Older Women's League
666 11th Street N. W., Suite 700
Washington, DC 20001
Phone 202-783-6686
Fax 202-638- 2356
(Seeks to improve the image and status of older women)

HEALTH

Alzheimer's Association
919 North Michigan Avenue, Suite 1000
Chicago, IL 60611
Phone: 800-272-3900
(24 hour hotline for resources and local support groups)

American Cancer Society
1599 Clifton Rd. NE
Atlanta, Georgia 30329
Phone: 800-227-2345
(Information, local chapters may loan equipment, transportation services and support groups)

American Diabetes Association
1660 Duke Street
Alexandria, Virginia 22314
Phone: 800-232-3472
(Information on disease and local associations)

American Geriatrics Society
770 Lexington Avenue, Suite 300
New York, N. Y. 10021
Phone: 212-308-1414
(List of Geriatric Physicians)

Hearing Aid Helpline
20361 Middlebelt Road
Livonia, MI 48152
Phone: 800-521-5247
(Product information, referral to local support groups, directory of hearing specialists)

American Heart Association
7272 Greenville Avenue
Dallas, TX 75231
Phone: 800-242-8721
(Education, referral to local associations)

American Parkinson's Disease Association
1250 Hyland Boulevard, Suite 4B
Staten Island, NY 10305
Phone: 800-223-2732
(Referrals to local chapters providing information on local services and physicians)

Arthritis Foundation
1314 Spring Street NW
Atlanta, GA 30309
Phone: 800-283-7800
(Information, referral to support groups)

Medic Alert Foundaztion
P.O. Box 381009
Turlock, CA 95381
Phone: (800-344-3226)

(Information on emergency medical identification, provides ID bracelet, necklace or wallet card)

National Association for the Visually Handicapped
22 West 21st Street
New York, NY 10010
Phone: 212-889-3141
(Visual aids catalog, large print lending library)

National Council on Alcoholism and Drug Dependence
12 West 21st Street, 7th floor
New York, NY 10010
Phone: 800-622-2255
(Information, referral to chapters)

National Institute of Neurological Disorders and Stroke
Information Office
31 Center Drive, MSC 2540
Building 31, Room 8A06
Bethesda, MD 20892
Phone: 800-352-9424
(Information about strokes and rehab centers)

Families, USA
1334 G Street NW
Washington, DC 20005
Phone: 202-628-3030
Fax: 202-347-2417
(Organization of health care consumers)

DEATH

Choice in Dying
200 Varick Street
New York, NY 10014
Phone: 800-989-9455

(Publications on pain management, medical treatments & living wills).

Continental Association of Funeral and Memorial Societies
200 I Street NW Suite 530
Washington, DC 20009
Phone: 202-745-0634
(Information about alternatives for funeral planning & referrals to Memorial Societies)

The Living Bank
Phone: 800-528-2971
(Information on organ donations)

National Hemlock Association
P.O. Box 11830
Eugene, Oregon 97440
Phone: 503-342-5748
(Information and publications on assisted suicide)

National Hospice Organization
1901 N. Moore Street, Suite 901
Arlington, VA 22209
Phone: 800-658-8898
(Information on local hospice groups)

Nursing Homes and Caregiving
Aging Network Services
4400 East-West Highway, Suite 907
Bethesda, MD 20814
Phone: 301-657-4329
(National referral service for geriatric care managers)

American Association of Homes and Services for the Aging
901 E Street NW. Suite 500
Washington, DC 20004

Phone: 202-783-2242
(Free brochure on caregiving)

American Health Care Association
1200 15th Street NW
Washington, DC 20005
Phone: 202-833-2050
(Publications on nursing homes)

National Association of Professional Geriatric Care Managers
1604 N. Country Club Road
Tucson, AZ 85716
Phone: 520-881-8008
(Referral to care managers in local areas)

U. S. Department of Health and Human Services
Health Care Financing Administration
7500 Security Boulevard
Baltimore, Maryland 21244
Phone: 800-638-6933
(Booklet & audiocassette, *The Guide to Choosing a Nursing Home.*)

HOUSING

Assisted Living Facilities Association of America
10300 Eaton Place, Suite 400
Fairfax, VA 22031
Phone: 703-691-8106
(Consumer information)

Continuing Care Accreditation Commission
901 E Street NW, Suite 500
Washington, DC 20004
Phone: 202-783-7286
(Lists accredited housing by area)

Federal Housing Administration
Phone: 800-245-2691
(Has names of local lenders in FHA insured reverse mortgage program)

Shared Housing Resource Center
6344 Green Street
Philadelphia, PA 19144
Phone: 215-848-1220
(Information and referrals to local organizations)

Co- Housing Network
1705 14th Street #160
Boulder, Colorado 80302

Co-Housing (Journal of Co-Housing Network)
P.O. Box 2584
Berkeley, California 94712

Sonora Co-Housing,
531 E. Roger Rd.
Tucson, AZ. (520) 570-6052
Website: http://www.igc.org/tndc

LEGAL

American Bar Association
Commission on Legal Problems of the Elderly
740 15th Street NW, 8th floor
Washington, DC 20005
Phone: 202-662-8690
(Literature on Medigap insurance, advanced medical directives & housing rights)

National Academy of Elder Law Attorneys
1604 N. Country Club Road
Tucson, AZ 85716

Phone: 520-881-4005 or 520-325-7925
(National Registry of Elder law attorneys, pamphlet)

TRAVEL & EDUCATION

Elderhostel
75 Federal Street
Boston, MA 02110
Phone: 617: 426-7788
(Catalog of educational trips in U.S. & abroad for people over 50)

Institute of Lifetime Learning AARP
1909 K Street
Washington, DC 20049
Phone: 202-434-2277
(Resource center, publications)

Interhostel
University of New Hampshire
6 Garrison Avenue
Durham, NH 03824
Phone: 603-862-1147
(International travel-study for people over 50)

Senior Net
1 Kearney Street
San Francisco, CA 94108
Phone: 415-352-1210
(Newsletter, publications for people over 55 using this nationwide network)

U. S. National Senior Olympics
14323 S. Outer Forty Road, Suite N300
Chesterfield, MO 63017
Phone: 314-878-4900
(Information on Senior Olympics)

Index

Symbols

401K 19, 24, 25, 27

A

Adult homes 6, 122, 123, 125, 127, 129, 130, 140, 211, 263
Advanced Practice Nurses 163
Alexander, Ross 168
Alzheimer's
    7, 31, 69, 105, 121, 123, 137, 183, 184, 185, 186, 187, 188, 285, 300
Anatomical Donations 8, 244
Assisted suicide 7, 214, 215, 216, 217, 218, 219, 220, 221, 286, 303

B

Bereavement 7, 11, 224, 229, 231
Bofoellesskabers 94

C

Canada Health Act 261, 262
Cancer 7, 14-15, 32, 105, 136, 154, 155, 156, 157, 164,
    165, 166, 168, 169, 170, 171, 172, 173, 174, 175, 176, 184,
    189, 190, 191, 197, 198, 199, 200, 201, 206, 207, 210
    213, 215, 224, 237, 239, 245, 266, 267, 278, 288, 289, 302
Cantine Island Co-Housing 6, 96
Carter, President Jimmy 279, 280, 285
Chalice of Reposes 201
Clergy 7, 34, 203, 210, 211, 212, 213, 221, 228, 233, 241, 245
Clinton Health Plan 8, 260, 294
Co-Housing 6, 93, 98, 99, 100, 102, 104, 117, 152, 299, 300, 310
Colonoscopies 173, 174
Continuing Care Retirement Communities 7, 130
Cooperative Santa Elena 109
Cousins, Norman 155, 156, 295

D

Dating 6, 76, 124, 297
Dean, Dr Ornish 179

Diet 103, 126, 128, 166, 173, 175, 176, 177, 179, 182, 183, 190, 215, 286
Doctors 7, 49, 58, 74, 81, 128, 134, 157, 158, 159, 160, 161, 162, 163, 165, 166, 167, 168, 172, 177, 178, 179, 180 185, 186, 197, 198, 203, 207, 208, 209, 210, 224, 225 226, 230, 253, 255, 257, 258, 260, 262, 264, 265, 266, 310
Duncaster 7, 132, 133, 134, 136, 292
Dutchess County 88, 89, 90, 91, 114, 125, 291

E

Embalming 239, 240, 241, 243
EPIC 33, 117
ERISA 256, 257
Ernst & Young 288
Estrogen 171, 179, 186, 290

F

Fellowship Community 93, 144, 163, 164, 165, 167, 310
Financial Planning 5, 23, 288
Food Stamps 116, 117
Funerals 7, 11, 210, 212, 233, 239, 240, 243

G

Gambling 64
Gays and Retirement Communities 6, 108
Geriatic Care Managers 35
Green Valley, Arizona 101, 103, 104, 106
Green Valley R.V. Resort 39
Groopman, Dr. Jerome 156, 295

H

Health Care Proxy 5, 34, 197
Health Plan for Ontario 8, 262
Heart attack 79, 168, 171, 177, 178, 179, 180, 182, 183, 224, 290
Heart disease 7, 67, 79, 168, 171, 173, 176, 179, 180, 182, 183, 184, 189, 290
High blood pressure 67, 173, 176, 178, 182
HMOs 152, 162, 247, 248, 249, 253, 254, 255, 256, 257, 259, 272, 293, 294
Holland 216, 217, 218, 220, 221
Home Energy Assistance 116

Home Maintenance & Repair 114
Hospice 7, 21, 128, 200, 201, 204, 205, 210, 211, 212,
    217, 219, 221, 230, 303
HUD 6, 41, 88, 90, 91, 92, 96, 100, 176, 291

I

Internet 23, 25, 26, 51, 76, 174, 175, 176, 274, 275, 287

J

Jewish Funerary and mourning practices 42, 82, 125, 234, 235

K

Kendal at Hanover 135, 136, 137, 292

L

Legal Packet 5, 34
Legal services 88, 118
Leisure World 6, 76, 102, 107, 108, 293
Lesbian 6, 65, 79, 80, 108, 238
Life review 206, 221, 230
Lifeline Telephone Service 117
Lipsyte, Robert 154, 163, 295, 296
Living trust 5, 29, 30, 232
Living Wills 5, 33, 36, 195, 278, 303
Long term care insurance 31, 32, 288, 289

M

MacArthur Foundation Study on Aging 13
Malpractice insurance 254
Mammograms 172, 173, 286, 287
Marital Breakups 6, 69
Meals On Wheels 86, 116
Medical malpractice 160, 254, 255
Medicare 8, 18, 31, 58, 116, 119, 139, 143, 161, 162,
    174, 248, 250, 254, 255, 256, 259, 260, 262,
    264, 273, 274, 294
Memorial Societies 8, 211, 239, 242, 243, 244, 245, 294, 303
Mitford, Jessica 239, 240, 242, 294
Mobile Home Communities 6, 108, 109, 110
Moslem Funerary practices 236, 237

N

Nan's Hacienda 4, 6, 127
National Institute of Neurological Disorders 180, 302
National parks 49, 50, 53, 59
N.Y. University's Silberstein's Aging and Dementia Research
       Center 185
N.O.R.C.S. 82
Nursing homes 7, 12, 14, 18, 31, 73, 88, 91, 122, 123, 125, 129,
       131, 138, 139, 141, 143, 144, 145, 149, 158, 186
       187, 188, 201, 206, 211, 263, 264, 268, 303, 304
Nutrition Sites 116

O

Office of the Aging 4, 60, 64, 83, 87, 88, 90, 91, 113, 114, 115,
       116, 117, 118, 119, 123, 291
Oregon Death With Dignity Act 215
Oxford Health Plans 253

P

Partnership Long Term Care Insurance 32
Pennswood Village 135, 292
Pensions 18, 23, 25, 26, 27, 118, 267, 274, 275
Power of attorney 5, 34, 36, 123, 197, 211, 278
Prescription plans 33, 254
Psychology of Illness 7, 163, 296

Q

Quartzsite 4, 5, 46, 47

R

Rainbow's End 44
Reverse Mortgages 83
Rhinebeck, New York 4, 125, 200
Rodriguez, Sue of British Columbia 219
Roman Catholic Funeral 235

S

Scott, Willard 14
Sex 6, 13, 22, 65, 66, 67, 68, 69, 73, 74, 76,
       77, 78, 79, 80, 108, 167, 297
Simeon Center 6, 95, 96

Sloan-Kettering Institute 200
Social Security 17, 18, 24, 26, 35, 77, 103, 116, 117, 231, 250,
    264, 273, 274
Sonora Co-Housing 6, 98, 305
Sontag, Susan 164, 165, 296
Steiner, Rudolf 96
Stroke 7, 17, 168, 171, 176, 177, 178, 179, 180, 181, 182,
    183, 189, 290, 291, 302
Sun City 105, 292
Sunset Hall 6, 125, 126, 291
Swedish System of Social and Health 8, 266

T

Tour Groups 5, 52, 54
TPAs 181
Trailer Estates 110
Transportation 26, 59, 82, 87, 92, 118, 146, 147, 208, 300
Tucson, Arizona 88

U

United Health Care 253

V

Viagra 6, 66, 68, 69, 297
Volunteering 5, 48, 49, 50, 60, 136, 298
Voyager R.V Resort 41

W

Wells Manor 6, 91, 92, 291
Widowhood 74, 75
Wills 5, 27, 28, 29, 35, 36, 278, 303
Withdrawal of Treatment 7, 195